# Workplace Clinics and Employer Managed Healthcare

## A Catalyst for Cost Savings and Improved Productivity

D1293686

# Advance Praise for *Workplace Clinics and Employer Managed Healthcare*

"This book provides a thoughtful and pragmatic perspective of the evolving role and importance of employer-sponsored worksite primary care clinics. Employers are beginning to shift their focus away from strictly a cost-based approach to employee health, and are increasingly seeking to maximize the value of their healthcare investments. For many employers, worksite clinics represent a means to not only provide medical care, but also optimize the use of other employer health benefits, improving employee health and generating organizational value. While the concept may be straightforward, the implementation is complex. Through his systematic approach, the author has provided an excellent primer for individuals who want to gain a clearer understanding of worksite clinic strategy and operations."

**Bruce Sherman, MD, FCCP, FACOEM**
**Consulting Medical Director, Global Services**
**The Goodyear Tire & Rubber Company**

"Are you paying more for your company's health-care year-over-year, but feel that your workforce is no better off for it? You are not alone. Many companies—the majority in fact—find themselves in similar straits. In this book, Mike LaPenna has thoughtfully accumulated the key insights from his career supporting worksite wellness solutions for employers. There is no health-care topic timelier nor more important than the shift to value-based purchasing of on-site services. CEOs, CFOs and HR professionals will all benefit from a careful reading of Mike's book."

**Dr. Raymond Zastrow**
**President**
**QuadMed, LLC**

"Every employer, large and small, needs to read this book. The fundamental issues regarding health benefits are dissected in a thoughtful way and new approaches and perspectives offered. Mike LaPenna has a lifetime of experience in healthcare and his analysis of the many alternatives every employer needs to consider is refreshing. Every benefit manager can find something of interest in this book."

**Robert P. Harrison, PhD.**
**President, Lake Michigan College**

"Mike LaPenna is one of the nation's leading experts on how onsite clinics can contribute to the health and productivity of employee workforces."

**Larry S. Boress**
**President & CEO**
**Midwest Business Group on Health**

"Michael LaPenna gives us a "HOW TO" book that can impact on one of the most complicated and controversial issues we face; health care delivery. In today's healthcare environment it is critical to find solutions which increase the value delivered by the healthcare system. New approaches must be implemented to simultaneously improve quality and access and at the same time reduce costs. Mr. LaPenna shares his insight and experience in a way that can aid company's and providers interested in implementing workplace health care programs. On site delivery systems offer great promise to improve both quality and value."

**Alan Lieber**
**CEO, Overlook Hospital**
**Atlantic Health Systems**

"I have had the opportunity to know and work with Mike La Penna for the past five years. The services that he has been able to provide to us as a healthcare system working with our local business partners, is invaluable. Mike and his organization truly set a standard on being proactive when it comes to helping employers look at how to save money in health care costs while improving overall health of their work group. The responsiveness of the La Penna Group is outstanding and we are grateful to them in allowing us a means to cementing our business relationships."

**Judy Gavigan**
**Director of Sales**
**Wheaton Franciscan Healthcare**

# Workplace Clinics and Employer Managed Healthcare

## A Catalyst for Cost Savings and Improved Productivity

# A. Michael LaPenna

*Foreword by Ford Brewer, MD, Medical Director,*
*Toyota Manufacturing of North America, Inc.*

CRC Press
Taylor & Francis Group
Boca Raton   London   New York

CRC Press is an imprint of the
Taylor & Francis Group, an **informa** business

A PRODUCTIVITY PRESS BOOK

Cover image: RVK Architects, San Antonio, Texas; www.rvk-architects.com

Productivity Press
Taylor & Francis Group
270 Madison Avenue
New York, NY 10016

© 2010 by Taylor and Francis Group, LLC
Productivity Press is an imprint of Taylor & Francis Group, an Informa business

International Standard Book Number: 978-1-4200-9244-8 (Paperback)

---

**Library of Congress Cataloging-in-Publication Data**

---

LaPenna, A. Michael.
  Workplace clinics and employer managed healthcare : a catalyst for cost savings and improved productivity / author, A. Michael LaPenna.
       p. ; cm.
  Includes bibliographical references and index.
  ISBN 978-1-4200-9244-8 (pbk. : alk. paper)
  1. Occupational health services. 2. Employee health promotion. 3. Clinics. I. Title.
  [DNLM: 1. Delivery of Health Care--economics--United States. 2. Employer Health Costs--United States.
3. Workplace--United States. W 84 AA1 L24w 2010]

RC968.L37 2010
658.3'82--dc22                                                                                      2009042471

---

**Visit the Taylor & Francis Web site at**
**http://www.taylorandfrancis.com**

**and the Productivity Press Web site at**
**http://www.productivitypress.com**

# Dedication

This book is dedicated to the memory of Harry V. (Larry) Quadracci (1936–2002), who, if he did not invent on-site healthcare, certainly perfected it. He grasped the concept of a healthcare benefit not just being about sick people but about the wellness and well-being of the entire work force and their dependents. He expanded an on-site safety and first aid program to a fully staffed primary and specialty physician office in order to better serve employees and their families. In doing so, he ignored the advice of lawyers, financial counselors, health providers, and health plan designers. I was one of the people that he routinely ignored.

**Harry V. Quadracci (1933–2002)**

In one memorable encounter, he commented that his company paid for healthcare services so that employees could actually use them—and he wanted to make sure that they were available and of the highest and most dependable quality. He felt that if the company paid for healthcare that went unused, everyone lost. His orientation to value went to the core of the issue in every aspect of every product and purchase made by his firm. He would either find a supplier that could deliver value, or he would have the team at Quad/Graphics make it on-site. He once remarked that Quad/Graphics made its own printing presses, ink, and paper . . . Why not medical care?

His vision defined employer managed healthcare and redefined the concept of workplace medicine. His commitment to quality and value led Quad/Graphics to a redeployment of the healthcare resources in a fashion that would balance short- and long-term goals of not only the company but of the employees as well. Many of the firms providing care on site today are "discovering" ideas that Harry Quadracci had almost 20 years ago.

# Contents

# Foreword

In early 2003, I was asked by Toyota to review the way that we deliver healthcare to our employees and to look at all possible ways to improve upon that process. As people may be aware, the Toyota philosophy embraces the analysis of process change and redesign to ensure that the outcome of any effort we make results in high quality and high value. I determined that the twin principles of quality and value would guide my research.

For background, I knew that we would be soon developing a plant in San Antonio that would be the largest and most technically advanced automotive production facility in the world. Other teams of Toyota engineers and designers were already at work improving upon their parts of the production and delivery process to ensure the investment the company had programmed for Texas would rank among the finest Toyota could develop and to model features that other plants, present and future, could look to as a model. Healthcare and the benefit design process could not be designed based on conventional wisdom and accepted dogma. My efforts would have to result in a "best in class" solution.

I visited a number of other installations and did extensive background research with a team of dedicated Toyota staff and, through the hospitality of many of the organizations referenced in this book, I began to develop a sense that there were a few other firms doing things differently. They were challenging convention and providing a very high level of healthcare right at the plant site. Beyond that, they were designing wellness and prevention and occupational medicine within the healthcare delivery process and including beneficiaries within the health delivery scheme. These ideas were not entirely new, but the basic thought process and result seemed to be a new approach, and I was determined to find the very best examples of this type of programming before we committed to a design of the Toyota facility and health delivery system.

Through this process, I met Mike La Penna, Jeff Beird, and Dorothea Taylor of The La Penna Group, a consulting firm in Michigan, at a conference they sponsored for firms that were delivering care in a format that was focused around employer-sponsored on-site healthcare. This was in 2004, and I learned that many of the attendees had well-developed programs and evidence-based results that confirmed my thinking that the on-site program would be the design of choice for San Antonio. I learned that many of the conference attendees were long-term clients with whom Mike La Penna and his team had worked for years.

As I designed our San Antonio program, I came to rely heavily on my staff at Toyota and the team at The La Penna Group for strategy, analysis, and implementation. Together, we believe, we have taken the best elements of on-site programming and made them available to our associates and their dependents in our San Antonio assembly plant. Like every process at Toyota, we have benchmarked this process and we continue to learn from our Texas Team Members and from our own process development and re-engineering. I am pleased to say that we are building upon a successful program design and a base set of projections that produced very dependable standards for comparison. For Toyota, that is saying a lot.

We could not have accomplished what we did without the input and support of The La Penna Group. I am happy to see that many of the ideas and background information that they shared with us over the many months of program planning and implementation are now available for others to access. I learned the value of many of these ideas by traveling around the country, talking to other medical directors, and observing first hand the programs that they designed. For the first time, this material is available in book form.

At Toyota, we continue to learn about all of our production methods and support systems. We pride ourselves on our flexibility and commitment to change for the sake of product improvement and in support of customer satisfaction. My product and the product of my team is healthcare. Our customers are our fellow Team Members at Toyota and their families. Our product is the highest quality of healthcare. What Mike La Penna has refined in book form is a template or a design for these customers and for the healthcare product. Any employer who wishes to take the journey from being a healthcare payer to the realm of action and implementation will need this book as a start. Mike's knowledge of the healthcare industry and of the way things work (versus the way they should work) is expansive, and his presentation of the material associated with how benefit plans and delivery systems interact is simple and straightforward.

If there is one key idea to take from this book, it is that the "on-site clinic" is a catalyst that allows all other programming to "work better" and to be more coordinated and internally complementary. Studying the employer site to embark upon some kind of healthcare service will only serve to highlight all of those other aspects of the benefit program that relate to primary care and benefit design. Once this step is taken, the other factors will tumble into view and the picture will get at once more complex, but, at the same time, the vision will become simpler.

We are buying healthcare without any clear understanding of how to value healthcare. We need to take a step back and ask ourselves, as we have with many other production inputs, whether we can simply make it better than we can buy it. Once we have formulated the question, we will realize that there is no single or simple answer. We will, I believe, come to realize we have to rethink our entire healthcare purchasing scenario and collaborate with all of the elements of the healthcare system to ensure short-term efficiencies and near-term effectiveness. I believe an on-site clinic is a key element of that process, but it is only one element.

Mike La Penna's book outlines the many aspects of how to think about an on-site program and how to implement one once the decision is made. These features alone recommend the book as a valuable reference, but there are other parts of the book that address important tangents and support programs that complement the employer-sponsored on-site clinic. The underlying premise is that the employer must first start, as Toyota did, with planning and design. Hopefully, this book will give those who are embarking on this process a much needed road map.

Ford Brewer, MD
Medical Director
Toyota Motor Manufacturing of North America, Inc.

# Preface

*Employer managed health* \ imp•loi•yer ma•nijd helth \ (1) A condition that results when the firm that employs a worker actively manages that worker's healthcare benefit. (2) An approach undertaken by self-funded firms when they finally tire of failed cost-control measures and exorbitant third-party intermediary fees. (3) The natural response of employers to the current market conditions that promote increasing healthcare costs without any relation to performance or value.

# Acknowledgments

I would like to thank all of those who contributed to this book by sharing their knowledge and background in ambulatory care processes, medical systems delivery, benefit design, and how all of these factors can be developed on the work site. I am especially indebted to Jeff Beird, who originated many of the feasibility studies on which this material is based and whose analyses have benefited many firms who have used them in their planning processes. The book draws from many monographs prepared by Dorothea Taylor, who views employer on-site programming from the consumer and provider perspective. Any operational wisdom or practical observations offered in this book have been borrowed from work originally done by Jeff and Dorothea. Where possible, I have credited their work.

I want to credit and thank my son, Anthony, who took many of the photographs in the book (unless otherwise credited) and, lest someone think of this as nepotism, I would point out that he is an award-winning professional photographer and photojournalist whose work has graced the pages of many national advertising campaigns, newsmagazines, and journals.

Most of all, I am also indebted to the many firms that have allowed us to work with them and that have selflessly shared not only their program philosophy and background, but also have allowed full access to their statistics and performance history. The book could not have been written without the material and experience made available through the kind support of Quad/Graphics and its subsidiary, QuadMed. Len Quadracci, MD, Ray Zastrow, MD, and John Neuberger have always given me guidance and support in our efforts to define this trend, and any one of them could have written this book themselves. I must also thank Ford Brewer, MD, and all of the Team Members at Toyota Motor Manufacturing North America for providing us access to a "boot camp" training session in project implementation and in process design. Scott Roach, Patrick Johnson, Carol Sampson, and John Runge allowed me a laboratory in which to confirm ideas that represented the very best of thinking on benefit design and healthcare delivery in the employee work site.

I was also privileged to visit with on-site service providers from many of the firms listed in the Appendices, and each of these organizations generously gave of their time not only to answer a variety of queries about their firm and its internal workings, but also to provide background information critical to the formation of the underpinnings of this book. In addition to those already listed, I want to especially thank Jim Hummer who founded Whole Health Management, Mel Hall and the staff of Comprehensive Health Services, Roger Merrill, MD, of Perdue Farms, Brent Pawlecki, MD, of Pitney Bowes, and Trace Devanny and his support team at Cerner Corporation. I am also indebted to Jeff Mahloch of Briggs and Stratton, who helped me to better understand the role of organized labor in a program of this nature. Ray Fabius, MD, also generously gave of his time and expertise to help me better understand how the processes at CHD Meridian have been developed and moved from concept to service delivery.

The book would not have substance if it were not for the many firms and consultants who have been quietly developing the field of on-site workplace health programming and the fine tuning that is now underway at sites that have been providing care in this manner for decades. Many of these firms assisted by responding to various requests, and numerous program administrators assisted us with survey material.

The most important lesson learned is that this is a field that is undergoing dramatic change, and it will provide a fertile source for innovation and ideas for many other areas of healthcare delivery as these service sites continue to demonstrate and quantify the value of on-site programming. The other important observation is that these firms are eager to share their experiences and to assist other firms new to the game with their insight and experience. It is my hope that this book will channel some of that wisdom.

# Chapter 1

# Introduction: Workplace On-Site Healthcare as a Catalyst for Cost Savings and Improved Productivity

An on-site clinic is simply one tool among many in the arsenal of benefit design and healthcare delivery. However, it is the one tool that acts as a catalyst to improve the performance of the rest of the arsenal.

The real focus of the programming for a self-funded firm should be the realization that they are developing an entire healthcare program, the purpose of which will be to manage all aspects of the healthcare dollar, not just the care that occurs "on-site."

This is all about the management of the health status of a specific and distinct population—the workforce of the firm and their dependents.

## The Traditional Focus of the Healthcare Purchase Negotiation Has Been, and Will Be, "Cost"

The concept of an employer attempting to manage healthcare cost is not new. There are numerous national and regional statistics that relate to the cost of healthcare and the challenges that employers face in providing it for their workforce.* Healthcare has become, and will continue to be, a challenge that transcends cost and that pushes employers into competitive advantage (or disadvantage) among their peers. With globalization, the fee-for-service structure of healthcare in the United States will be a continuing factor in localized workforce design as well as regional and international competition. No matter what form of cost control is attempted in healthcare, it is generally accepted that recent inflationary trends in energy, malpractice coverage, and healthcare personnel shortages will return healthcare to double-digit inflation for the near term. Businesses are beginning to realize that these new challenges can no longer be met with traditional tools—or with conventional thinking.

Firms are looking for new ideas and approaches at the same time that the country is in the midst of a recession and at a political crossroads. There is no new program on the horizon for consumers or businesses to anticipate except the concept of "consumer-managed health," which will depend largely upon "consumer-available information," which is still under construction. Firms, municipalities, and governmental agencies are limiting healthcare benefits and shifting responsibility to the consumer on an individual basis or, in some cases such as the auto industry, to aggregate consumers in the form of the transfer of risk to a union surrogate. No one can really describe how all of this will work except to say that things are going to be different, and "different" will mean more pressures on healthcare providers, patients, and payers (business and government). As many pundits have observed, this is the "perfect storm" of rising prices and consumer cost-shifting in an environment where conventional programs are failing to deliver consistent value and where information is imperfect and difficult to obtain. There are many reports of change, but few reports of breakaway success stories.

This introductory chapter is not intended to be a report on medical inflation or a lament over the challenges of benefit design. I resisted quoting exact statistics so that the reader could reflect on their own experiences and impressions. The balance of this section assumes that there is general agreement on the trends and shared frustration for finding any real solution. This book will report upon the handful of forward-thinking firms that began to implement various programs to individually take on the challenge

---

* An excellent treatment of healthcare cost history and trends is offered by Michael E. Porter and Elizabeth Olmsted Teisberg in their text *Redefining Health Care: Creating Value-Based Competition on Results* (Boston: Harvard Business School Press, 2006, 29–32).

of healthcare cost containment and value design, many of which have been reported on over the years. Initiatives like health promotion, occupational medicine, disease-state management, and the tools popularized (or demonized) by the managed care movement have all been well represented in the literature.

## A New Problem That Is Emerging for the Employer Will Be "Access"

Assuming cost is an issue, the other problem consumers (and employers) face is access. Currently, there are shortages around the country of primary care and specialty physician providers. There are also shortages of a variety of ancillary providers like physical therapists, pharmacists, and dentists. The patient with health insurance and reason to use it may not find a provider that is available or, if available, willing to accept their benefit program.

**Figure 1.1    As times get tougher for U.S.-based primary care practitioners, Canadian recruiting intensifies, making access in the United States even more difficult. This is a sign that is targeted at physicians passing through LaGuardia Airport suggesting that there is an easy and simple way to practice in Canada.**

Near-term health manpower studies suggest that the most important component of the healthcare system, the primary care provider (PCP), will continue to be in short supply for decades to come, even if the system is augmented by nurse practitioners, physician assistants, and other mid-level providers.

Employers face the issue of access in almost any community, whether they realize it or not. In some cases, it is limited to the delays their employees face in moving from one component of the healthcare system to the next. In some cases, it may be the inability of an employee to be able to use their healthcare coverage at the prescribed fee schedule because of a lack of an "in-network" or "participating" provider. Employers seldom address this matter except when they plan for the relocation of a plant or a workforce, which will create a surge of jobs (and healthcare consumers) in a region that had previously been rather stable.

## On-Site Health Programming Addresses Cost and Access

This book focuses on one initiative that has yet to be studied and dissected—the "workplace on-site health clinic." This is a term that begs redefinition. Historically, there is little more to be said about on-site clinics that have been placed at the work site for proximity, except that they were probably a good thing for the sake of safety and emergency access. First aid, rapid response teams, and company nursing programs have been supplemented by the occasional health and wellness offerings. These are all healthcare, and they are all positive, but they are not the subject of this book.

These initiatives are simply recognizing employee convenience and addressing incidence-proximity issues. These programs and other patchwork compilations of programs that are described as workplace health access projects do not meet the definition of "workplace on-site health clinic," at least for the purposes of this book.

This book addresses the type of on-site health programming that incorporates the basics of primary care health services similar to those that might be found in a personal physician's office—but made available to employees at their workplace. Beyond occupational health and episodic care, this is a place where the worker's medical record resides and where the worker sees a provider (physician or physician extender) on a regular basis for scheduled appointments and for managed oversight and follow-up. This is the place, or can be the place, where a worker can use his/her benefit program in an environment that is, by the coincidence of planning, at the workplace. The fact that it is provided through the coordination and capitalization of the employer is really irrelevant to the actual services available. However, the employer involvement in capitalization and program planning is integral to the way the primary care service is managed and delivered.

From the employee's perspective, the workplace on-site healthcare programming is an opportunity to become directly involved in the value chain associated with healthcare and, perhaps, to not only understand it better, but to have some direct involvement in it and its provision. This is the step that occurs between being a purchaser and being a provider. It is the difference between being a victim of a system and a participant within it. It is a bold step, and it is one that, until recently, was taken by only a few very forward-thinking firms.

## An Employer Sponsored Program Is More than Just an "On-Site" Facility

The on-site clinic is the most visible part of the movement, but it really reflects only one part of the overall programming. The fact that an employer has developed a physical facility to house primary care medical services means that they have determined that they are now fully engaged in the analysis and the deployment of their healthcare benefit dollars in a unique and direct fashion. The employer has changed not only the rules of the game, but the game itself. The change is one that is fundamental and one that engages the employees and the local providers. For all of the talk of the problems and challenges with the national healthcare system, the employer that embarks upon the development of an on-site health solution has decided to plan and redesign the healthcare delivery system that surrounds its own employees and its own relationship with that part of the healthcare system that it can directly influence.

The most visible part of this movement is the relocation of ambulatory care from a community setting, unmanaged by anything except the forces of fee-for-service healthcare, to an employer managed and monitored site at the workplace. The shortcut name "workplace on-site health," like many shortcuts and acronyms, tells only part of the story. Although one can relocate doctors, nurses, and exam rooms at the employer site of production, it is not done without questioning and challenging the design of the health system. Once this step is taken, it extends the control from the on-site programming to other areas that can be influenced by payer design and contracting.

As employers begin to interact with healthcare providers, they are taking a new approach to the design and delivery of the healthcare product—changing how it is produced, delivered, purchased, and measured. From a firm's first attempt to understand costs, to perform on-site facility feasibility, the management begins to realize the fact that the money spent on the healthcare benefit is not only an increasing component of their production cost, but it is one that is not easily quantified. Often the attempt to understand the role of an on-site program will lead to a realization that the healthcare industry, as it affects the individual employer, is more like a bureaucracy that is designed to report on its product and costs at a social level or on the aggregate although it does send a bill for the services to the individual customer. The payer, in this case the business, is generally not provided with data or reports tailored to the purchases they have sponsored, not to mention the fact they often have no idea of the value of the services that their employees are receiving.

The employer generally begins to realize that the purchases it has paid for have been funneled through a filter defined by what the employees and their dependents feel they need or what they want, instead of what is necessary. This is coupled with what is available locally or in the regional healthcare marketplace. In other words, they might receive different signals and have different access in a community that contains a proportionately higher number of specialty services than they would if they were in a community that has few specialists but an adequate supply of primary care practitioners. The range of choices might also be affected by what is available through hospitals and other healthcare vendors, and the choices may be made more complex (and costly) by having numerous competitive enterprises, each advertising from its own perspective. It has been demonstrated that, with

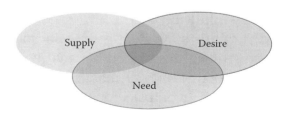

**Figure 1.2   This Venn diagram shows the impossible congruence of need/supply/ desire and what results when these factors overlap in an unplanned fashion. People desire certain services whether they need them or not. The supply of services drives availability. No one really is trying to manage the real need for health services when the payers (employers) are not in charge of the programming.**

respect to medical care, supply is a strong predictor of utilization and cost. It is also well proven that the expenditures are not always for products and services that are actually needed.*

The firm, once it understands that the direction of its healthcare dollars can be more focused through intervention on its part, will begin to make the right decisions. The focus will become the articulation of need, desire, and supply in a manner that produces a more precise and consistent pattern of care. The very existence of data may begin to make the employer a more efficient purchaser if it can find a way to impact consumer choice. All that is needed is a way to define the problem and a forum for delivering the solution. A true revelation occurs when employers realize that they are, in fact, managing a fund that is providing coverage in a form that has been around for many years but that has, in recent years, been somewhat maligned. They are really addressing the health maintenance needs of a specific population— their own employees and dependents. The term "health maintenance organization" (HMO) comes to mind. However, it is really more simply an effort to align the goals of the workforce with those of the firm and the resources provided in the marketplace. The assumption is that the more closely these converge, the better the health status of the overall population and the higher the value of the healthcare purchase (as Figure 1-3 suggests).

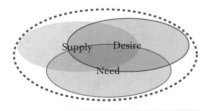

**Figure 1.3   A better solution would be for the employer to actually provide the services (or a major part of them) and help the consumer (employees) better understand what they need versus what they simply desire. The tighter the overlap, the less the cost, and the higher the effectiveness.**

When the care is provided by a specific group of providers that are dedicated to the needs of a target population, it is called a "staff model" HMO (as opposed to a network or open model). Thus, the employer managed on-site healthcare enterprise can really use some of the population management tools that have proven effectiveness from the managed care literature. This becomes especially useful when projecting costs, savings, and projections on the health status of a population.

A staff model HMO is not something that one thinks of as the selling point for an on-site program, and the rest of the book will avoid this analogy, but the reader will make his or

---

* For reference, the reader is directed to the *Dartmouth Atlas of Health Care*, which addresses the relationship between healthcare supply and utilization on a region-by-region basis. The Appendices contain a reference to the Dartmouth information site and other useful background material for the reader who wishes to explore this concept further.

her own connection. Like any generalization, this one works in most circumstances, and it helps to provide a reference for development because HMO literature is very accessible, and the employer can readily apply these standards to the healthcare provided and consumed by their work force. Once the employer begins down the learning curve of healthcare analysis and procurement, it is difficult to limit the scope of their analysis to just what is happening at the plant or on the job site. The employers are managers who can usually recognize an "unmanaged" situation, and few things are more unmanaged than the events surrounding a healthcare program.

## Concern about the Organization of Healthcare Will Be Replaced by Concerns about the Employer Program Organization

One additional clarification about the terminology "employer managed healthcare" addresses the potential confusion with the operational oversight of the clinic. Many of these installations are actually managed by an outside firm that is contracted with for this specific task, but the employer has really arranged for this to occur and has specifically provided for this service with the understanding that there are terms and objectives that must be met. The management of the "mini health system" that is being created can either be direct or occur through a contracting process. Either way, the employer is ultimately the manager.

Internal organizational issues are also presented when the employer considers what place the clinic initiative has within their own organization. Is this a medical function, an independent operation, and/or part of human resources (HR)? Does the clinic incorporate occupational health or do they stand alone and complement each other? Where does the ultimate responsibility lie for oversight and contracting? All of these issues will be raised initially in the development or expansion of on-site services once the planning process is engaged.

Cost control is one of the byproducts of an on-site program, but is not the only positive outcome. These programs are also producing more satisfied healthcare consumers and a higher quality healthcare product overall. Employer direct oversight and involvement requires a higher level of information—more of it and at a higher level of quality. The value construct begins to change for the employer as purchaser as well as for the end consumer. The question of healthcare value is now being addressed by people using a procurement officer in support of the traditional HR staff. This produces a different dynamic that calls effectiveness into question along with indicators that address access and patient satisfaction and all of the feedback loops that are implied as part of contracting and re-contracting process.

## The Purpose of the Book Is to Raise Issues and Offer Solutions

This book is not intended to be another diatribe on the national healthcare system or on cost-shifting, nor on the factors that have contributed to the increase in healthcare cost runs.* Other authors have done it better and the national debate on healthcare reform is again raising each issue to renewed scrutiny. Rather, this is a book on the actual experiences of self-funded employers who are moving the healthcare access on-site and who are directly managing all aspects of their own healthcare delivery system. It is the ultimate "make versus buy" analysis in the supply management chain of medical care. The most visible reference point for this approach is the work-place on-site clinic with a full complement of primary care services, but that is only the external indication of a system designed and preplanned by the employer using a new set of standards and tools to ensure that the health-care purchase is actually one that results in some effective outcome.

The purpose of this book is likewise not to provide a background sum-mary of why firms are considering different approaches but to report on what they are doing and on the challenges and benefits of on-site primary care and all that it implies. This is a how-to manual in the design and implementa-tion of a program to replace the traditional purchasing approach to healthcare benefits with one that is "on time" and "quality-driven." The components are the same, but they have been moved from a community-based environment and a third-party purchase to a location that is at the work site and under the direct contracting perspective of the actual purchaser and end consumer.

This book recognizes that, for the firm that has decided to go this route, there is no instruction manual. This book addresses how to analyze and plan for an on-site healthcare facility, as well how to address the program-matic changes that need to occur to support it. Hopefully, there will also be a few ideas that will be of interest to firms that have already adopted this model and that wish to benchmark their ideas against similar programs.

---

* Ken Terry has analyzed many of the components that contribute to healthcare cost factors in his book *RX for Health Care Reform,* which recounts the failure of healthcare reform in the United States. (Nashville, TN: Vanderbilt University Press, 2007)

# Chapter 2

# Company Planning for Healthcare and Employees' Participation in the Planning and in the "Plan"

Strangely, a "health plan" does not really plan for "health." It is a way for a company to pay for an employee's benefit related to the dollars they spend on sickness and recovery from accidents. There is no overall goal in mind or improvement in the health status contemplated by the company or by the employees. This is a "hoped for" rather than a "planned for" outcome.

The author is indebted to the Medical Director of Perdue Farms, Roger C. Merrill, MD, for his permission to include the vignette that makes up the first part of this chapter. His analogy says it all concerning what can be accomplished in a healthcare system that is "employer managed." He makes important points in a concise and witty manner that allow the reader to compare and contrast several differing concepts. His conclusion begs the question of how far an employer can go to encourage (force?) employees to participate in one program over another (or in none at all).

## A Tale of Two Healthcare Plans

*Roger C. Merrill*

Perdue Farms Incorporated is the 3rd largest integrated poultry processing company in the nation and is the recognized leader

**Figure 2.1    Dr. Roger C. Merrill, Medical Director for Perdue Chicken, strikes a whimsical pose, but the multiple-site program he oversees is anything but casual with over 90% employee compliance in most key areas of measure.**

in innovations regarding ergonomics, safety, production, feed formulations, quality improvement, and quality assurance. As such, it is fitting that the company offers two high quality health plans—one for Perdue Associates (employees) and one for the chickens.

The two plans have many similarities, but also some striking differences; analysis of the plans is illustrative of much that is right—and wrong—with American medicine.

The chicken plan is outcomes-oriented, highly scientific, and cost-effective. Interventions that have proven scientific value are applied without exception to the target populations; no "patient" either opts <u>into</u> inappropriate care or opts <u>out</u> of care deemed valuable by health planners.

By contrast, the plan for Perdue associates has considerable freedom of choice, a characteristic valued by the vast majority of Americans. Associates can—and do—choose <u>not</u> to have screening and primary preventive services felt appropriate by the corporate medical department (even though they are paid at 100% by the company). These include mammography, colonoscopy, PAP smears, childhood immunizations, well baby care, PSA testing, hepatitis B vaccines, and others. In addition, certain medical services are often accessed in spite of recommendations <u>against</u> that care: early surgery for lumbar disc disease, hysterectomy for undiagnosed pelvic pain, self referral to medical and surgical subspecialists in the absence of a diagnosis, and unproven "alternative" medical care.

The chickens' healthcare is the result of lengthy and rigorous outcomes testing which is not allowed to be influenced by researcher bias. All birds receive "childhood" immunizations; additionally, when avian veterinarians and epidemiologists diagnose a viral outbreak in a given population, the healthcare team is immediately mobilized and 100% of the population at risk receives appropriate vaccinations. Feed formulation has been established through controlled trials: under differing weather conditions and at various stages in the chickens' life cycle the feed components and proportions are different. The birds are not "encouraged" to eat properly; company nutritionists <u>insist</u> on it by providing only food that is appropriate. Antibiotics are used sparingly but without hesitation when bacterial infections are diagnosed in a flock (the antibiotics are discontinued several days before the birds are processed to prevent contamination of the meat). As part of the ongoing quality improvement process, when a new treatment is identified, tested, and found suitable it is immediately implemented; when a current treatment, protocol, or feed formulation is found to be inappropriate it is immediately discontinued.

The associates' health plan is extremely generous, has a strong low-cost primary care access component, and includes on-site medical clinics for primary and certain specialty care (women's services, neurology, podiatry, physical therapy). There is an acute and maintenance pharmacy program, a chemical recovery program, and strong emphasis on American Cancer Society and American Academy of Pediatrics recommended tests and services. The plan thus includes many of the characteristics deemed most valuable by U.S. citizens and included in the highest-quality plans around the country. The problem is that there is very little rigorous outcome-based scientific evidence for many of the services covered under the plan: coronary artery bypass grafting, surgical treatment of carpal tunnel syndrome, arthroscopic surgery for knee arthritis, operative treatment of heel spurs, antibiotics for pharyngitis— indeed much of what we physicians do in medical practice in the U.S. has little if any solid foundation in scientific evidence. And services that have proven their value in improving outcomes— often dramatically—such as prenatal care beginning in the first trimester, smoking cessation programs, seat belt use, stepped treatment of hypertension, strict diabetic control, and aerobic exercise—are often ignored or not accessed by the human population. Thus we see that the national healthcare delivery system has served our human population poorly with the "best" in American medicine. Not only do Jim Perdue's chickens *eat* better than we do, their healthcare is also superior!

There are, of course, some disadvantages to the patient-recipient of the chicken health plan: there is no retiree benefit and not even a modicum of freedom of choice. Nonetheless, health planners would exert an enormous positive influence on human populations if they were to apply many of the principles which have proven effective for the chickens: there would be far less preventable disease in humans, and our species would benefit from huge cost savings resulting from elimination of cost—and human—ineffective services.

## Where Does the Employer Draw the Line?

Two other examples come to mind. In one case, widely reported in the news media, Howard Weyers simply challenged employees of his firm to stop smoking by firing anyone who used tobacco products.[1] No one questioned the wisdom of smoking cessation programs, the positive impact on the health status of the employees, or the idea that this would save money for the employees and for the employer. There were wide-ranging discussions about the social engineering that was being designed into the benefit program (and work status) at the company that Mr. Weyers owned. Compliance went up and smoking went down, and the debate continues to rage over the rights of workers balanced against the rights of a company.

In another case in southwest Michigan, from my experience as a consultant, a survey was being conducted among employers regarding health maintenance organization (HMO) penetration and the adoption of specific HMOs in various regions. Surprisingly, one paper plant reported over 90% participation in an HMO product that had a very poor performance record and an extremely limited panel of providers. As a consultant, I felt compelled to find out how this plan was chosen and why employees, given a variety of options, would choose that over others. Simply put, the HMO was the cheapest product available that could be described as a healthcare program, and the employees were offered their options at enrollment with a stack of $100 bills at the "lower cost" and "lower quality" HMO table. The employees could enlist with a plan at a table that had no cash incentives, or they could enroll in the program that allowed an immediate $100 bonus in cash. The employer supplied the cash, not the HMO, and the union endorsed the enrollment process.

Whether one embraces the "quit smoking or be fired" approach or the bald-faced incentive of the "$100 table," the issue is that the employers can guide workers toward choices. The on-site clinic and the related programming that it implies is the one approach that is more elegant and that involves a higher order of informed employee choice. It also is a program that "learns" and can adapt as information on healthcare processes is gained from employee and dependent experiences.

## Employer Plan Design: What Works and What Does Not?

Employers have few options in whether to offer health plans or not. They have many options in how the health plans are structured and funded. There are options regarding co-pays, deductibles, network design, employee financial participation, and plan design. One feature that is increasingly being considered is to move part of the health benefit on-site and under the direct control of the employer. There are many implications associated with this approach, and the results that are being reported are initially very promising.

Subsequent chapters will address benefit design, but this is mentioned here to reflect on the fact that employees are presently very "tuned in" to the structure and capacity of their healthcare plan. If their employer has not changed or altered their benefits, they know of someone who has been through the process. They may have some kind of "health savings plan," and they certainly have been bombarded with consumer-directed healthcare information. The workplace on-site experience may be one that is a new concept, but it will be met with an understanding by the employees that almost everything is changing in this environment and that this includes all of the programs related to their healthcare and their various benefit programs.

What works? The jury is still hearing the evidence. But one thing is certain: the employers (and increasingly, the employees) are on a hunt for credible healthcare interventions that represent true value. Traditional approaches and traditional services are being questioned along with sources of service and types of care. This is a "perfect storm" of healthcare costs, and the failure of cost-saving approaches combines with a "learning moment" for firms, the employees, and their dependents.

## Why Offer Services On-Site?

Simply put, everything works better when an on-site program is part of the healthcare offering. Any number of references will allude to the positive effects of preventive, wellness, and disease-state management programs at the work site. No one argues about whether they are good, but there are several schools of thought on how to measure how good they are.

So what is a business to do? There are probably several programs already on site and more that the employer might consider. Hopefully, the programs could be classified, categorized, or ranked in some manner. One way to do this might be to consider the ranking approach modeled loosely on the Boston Consulting Group market and profit share matrix only using determinants that are defined by cost of the program and the risk or confidence level in their effectiveness.

Certainly, somebody in the firm should be able to guess at cost and effectiveness. Our approach has been to take some of the common programs

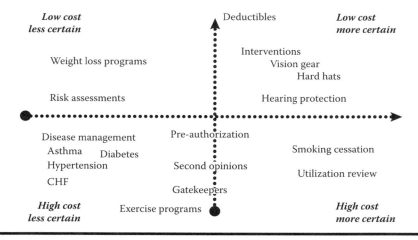

**Figure 2.2   Grid for analysis with no clinic.**
**Low cost programming and higher cost programming are arrayed along with the certainty that there is a payback for the investment in this simple four-quadrant representation.**

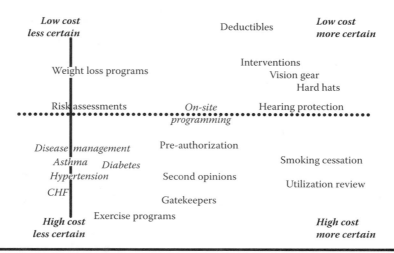

Figure 2.3   Grid for analysis with clinic.
**The on-site clinic ensures a higher certainty for all program initiatives, no matter the cost.**

and just place them on the matrix to allow the reader to consider their own gauge of program value. Did we miss some? Probably. Did we miscategorize a few? Most certainly we did. However, the point is to reflect on those that are in place and their payback and to ask whether there is something that might act as a catalyst to improve the capture or the effectiveness, if not the entire process.

The workplace on-site clinic, for the population it serves, would have a positive effect on all of the programming in the grid. As long as the employer appropriately links the clinic, its staff, and the recordkeeping functions, this is the one catalyst that can improve the impact of almost every other program. If one were to reconsider the *Boston Square* overview, the result would be very different, with most of the programs gaining in value not because of a price advantage but because of additional access to patient information, synergy with medical records, coordination with primary care services, improved professional oversight, collaboration with physician and pharmacy services, etc. The on-site clinic has an impact on all of these programs regardless of the return on investment (ROI) or payback associated with the clinic itself.

Simply stated, the employer that manages the healthcare process and uses an on-site clinic will benefit from a better understanding of all the complementary programming that it employs in the healthcare delivery process. Now, one would ask, if this is true for those who use the clinic, why not try to get more use from this important tool? Generally, the limitation is the scope of the program and the employer's reluctance to include a full application of primary and specialty care and the dependents and their care.

If the reader is not getting my bias by now, they will. This book promotes full involvement at all levels for an on-site clinic staff and for an all-encompassing program. Each chapter, in its own way, will continue to build upon this point.

# Reference

1. Karen Springen, "Light Up And You May Be Let Go," http://www.newsweek.com/id/48633 (October 16, 2007).

*Chapter 3*

# The Myth of the Company Doctor

There is no such thing any more as a traditional "company doctor." The modern firm considers the employees' health to be an asset, not a cost, and the "company doctor" in an on-site health program is really an employees' doctor based in an accessible environment.

## Company Doctors and Company Towns

The term "company doctor" does not have a positive connotation. The idea of a "company town," "company store," or "company script" suggests a worker in bondage and the idea of indentured servitude—economic slavery at all levels. The scene might be one of the introductory vignettes in a movie that wraps itself around the dawn of the labor movement. Another view might be that of the "for hire" on-site medical person who refuses a sick day or who assigns an injured or recovering laborer to a job that is "profiled" to accommodate their special limitations. This is the doctor who represents a "return to work" program rather than a "return to health" process. This image is hardly representative of what the field of workplace on-site health is trying to accomplish.

Historically, many firms simply had to have services of a social nature to maintain a work force. Coal mining and heavy industrial operations required a work force that might be largely immigrant and was relocated by necessity to the plant site or processing area. Few services could be guaranteed through free market response quickly enough to ensure worker relocation and continuing loyalty. Towns and communities needed to be built near the job site. The development of a social infrastructure included housing, entertainment, educational, and medical services. Finding, relocating, and establishing a doctor was simply part of ensuring labor and minimizing down time. Admittedly, one aspect in finding and supplying medical care was to repair and return the injured or sick worker to the production process as quickly as possible and practical.

The companies formed social systems to make sure that the workers and their families became permanent residents. In the early days of the shoe company, Endicott Johnson, over 100 people were employed in their healthcare division, and the company spent almost $1 million per year maintaining healthcare services for their employees and their families.[1] This was in the 1920s, and it was part of what the company called a "square deal for workers" that addressed their various needs in a form of "welfare capitalism." Many examples of company towns and mill towns sprung up as industrialization occurred and companies rushed to the scene of a readily accessible resource that needed to be harnessed, mined, or otherwise exploited. Sometimes the workers were part of the exploitation process.

Whatever the overall purpose, and whether that purpose was practical or altruistic, the employers began to assume a significant portion of the cost of care of the healthcare needs of the work force in an area where they operated. This became part of the industrial and labor fabric of the society. Now, only those employers with a marginal work force and a transitional labor pool can avoid the intrusion of healthcare costs within the financial construct of the product cost. Whenever that cost is recognized, the avoidance of cost or its control becomes a focus of study and effort. As soon as the cost becomes a question, then the question of effectiveness or the product value also becomes relevant. If a firm is a rational economic business enterprise, it will use the same approach to cost control in healthcare that it applies to any other input of production. The problem is that the firms cannot really directly assess quality and the consumptive payback for healthcare services. It has to buy through a broker of some kind and purchase on behalf of an external third-party consumer, yet it is exposed directly to the cost and eventually to the benefit.

# Company Doctors and Company Healthcare Systems

Did Kaiser Aluminum get it right when they formed the first HMO-style system for their employees? Skipping from the traditional "company doc" to attracting workers and keeping them healthy was a big step. The idea changed from providing a doctor to providing a health benefit. These benefits became a component of an overall reward structure that workers came to understand as they began to choose one firm over another and to compare jobs and a work commitment for the long term and for more features than just the hourly pay. Workplace longevity and the sense of some kind of entitlement to a benefit package became a part of the work decision. Rather than having employees relocated to a mill site or a coal mine, the employers began to compete in a labor market where employees had choices.

The Kaiser program, a pre-paid and organized approach to healthcare for a fixed population of employees, was based upon the work of a doctor who needed prepayment from a work force to fund his physician-owned and privately capitalized hospital. Sydney R. Garfield began prepayment for pennies a day at a construction site in the Mojave Desert and was later recruited to establish the Kaiser program to facilitate World War II shipbuilding production. The goal was to create an efficient and effective program that could take care of a huge influx of workers to ensure wartime production. It was a process that was re-engineered to meet the necessity of the time and, like many ideas born of crisis, it worked so well that many of the principles are in use some 70 years later.

Kaiser was building a work force and needed a new way to deliver healthcare that transcended the market capability of the era to meet staggering production quotas. Almost by accident, they designed a modern staff model health maintenance organization (HMO) that was focused on just their own work force and dependent pool. They were not being social engineers, but pragmatists. Looking back on their basic premise, analysts can now compare finite populations with benefit and medical programs of modern design to the medical options available in the free market, fee-for-services, competitive environment. Few firms approach the question from the Kaiser perspective, but any firm that determines that it could benefit from an on-site program is deploying some of the same strategy used by Kaiser in 1942. It is putting together one component of a populations-specific healthcare service that is employer sponsored and employee focused.

# The Redefinition of the Company Doctor

The "company doctor" is not really the "company's doctor" anymore. Employees using benefit programs have choices, and the traditional role of the company doctor is now legislated and licensed in a manner never anticipated by the coal miners and immigrants in the industrialization era. Fifty states have worker compensation standards that not only protect the work force but often impede the integration of care. Accreditation and oversight programs abound, and the organization of medicine into medical staffs and networks assures workers and their families of peer review and commonly agreed-upon quality standards. The medical malpractice environment also serves to protect workers from corporate medical exploitation even as it adds cost and complexity to their care. Privacy is ensured by Healthcare Information Portability and Accountability Act (HIPAA) enforcement, and there are any number of ancillary organizations and disciplines that augment the medical experience—therapists, nurses, pharmacists, etc. Each is integral to a healthcare event and independent, sometimes to a fault, in the care of a single episode of illness or injury.

The worker is in an environment where the traditional or old-style company doctor cannot really exist. The danger now is more from a bad benefit program or an ill-designed healthcare system than from a single practitioner writing back-to-work orders at the behest of management. Rather, a company can hurt a worker now by shifting dental coverage or limiting optical coverage or increasing a co-pay or dropping a covered service.

However, in the competition for a skilled and increasingly technical workforce, companies now recognize the cost of employee turnover, recruitment, and training, and they are able to balance that against benefit plan deficiencies. There are tradeoffs with bad (or uncompetitive) benefit plans, and companies can quantify these costs against what might be saved in a short-term benefit reduction or adjustment. Furthermore, they recognize that healthcare is a product, a process, and that the commodity and its application can be managed for optimum benefit.

Companies now address healthcare on-site, on-campus, and on-the-job. They seldom ignore the fact that they pay for care that is mostly provided off-site and out of the workplace. Long before the term HMO was coined, Kaiser developed a revolutionary concept that can still provide lessons for today's managers.

**Figure 3.1    Two modern-day "company doctors"—Raymond Zastrow, M.D. (Quad/Graphics) and Brent Pawlecki, M.D. (Pitney Bowes)—confer at the QuadMed Clinic about corporate heath status issues.**

## Workplace Health Is More than a Doctor Located On-Site

There are several companies that should be referenced alongside Kaiser as pioneers in this process. Certainly, Gillette and its on-site healthcare pioneered by Dr. William Greer (still in existence today) is one example. Early adapters of employer managed and employee-focused healthcare programs have to include Quad/Graphics, the Wisconsin-based printing giant, and Florida Power and Light. Chapter 2 told the story of the Perdue program, initiated by Dr. Merrill in the early 1990s. Pitney Bowes is also a company that pioneered many employee-oriented services while most firms were just switching from one insurance company to another.

Without any background in healthcare, except as a third-party purchaser, these firms structured on-site access to health services that ranged from primary care to specialty care to advanced network design and sophisticated disease management strategies. They worked with concentrated employee and dependent bases, whereas firms such as Pitney Bowes experimented with healthcare for employees that were remote and far-flung from a centralized industrial site and residing in any number of locations.

The concept is not a company doctor, but a company-based health clinic that will address the impact that a firm can bring to healthcare once it determines to move the locus of healthcare management on-site. This idea is more about employers attempting to manage one part of their cost profile and assuring that they are making a value-based determination. It is about balancing long-term workforce development against short-term costs and the realization that anything invested in a healthy employee base eventually has a payback. The difficulty is the definition of "eventually" and the ability of a company, municipality, or any healthcare purchaser to challenge the status quo to show some sort of near-term, but not immediate, gain.

If there is any relationship to the old-line company doctor, it is only the feature of accessibility.

There is a medical provider on-site, but now the medical provider is connected to the local healthcare system and to a battery of health, wellness, and preventive tools that benefit employees and their dependents first and the employer in a secondary fashion. The role of the company has shifted from hiring a doctor to buying a benefit plan to managing the benefits

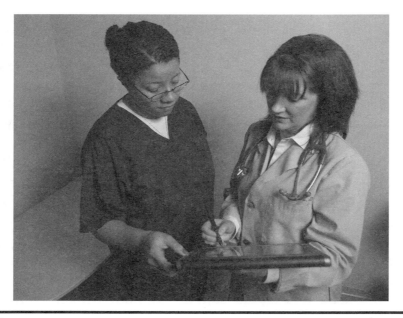

**Figure 3.2  Dr. Mitchell, an employee of Comprehensive Health Services (CHS), confers with another staff member on-site at Hewitt in North Chicago. They are using the latest in electronic medical records technology and, yes, even benefits-consulting firms are recognizing the merit of on-site services for their employees.**

that are delivered under the plan they are sponsoring. If this means a relocation of services from a community-based fee-for-service site to one that is structured as a component of the benefit program and accessible at work, then the result is not a company doctor but a change in benefit and system design.

Later chapters will address the need for including different components on the basis of company-specific research, but firms addressing on-site services are now well beyond just the provision of a doctor. These health units incorporate wellness; exercise therapy; and preventive, dental, pharmacy, physical therapy, laboratory, and radiology services. They are structured for ease of access and focused on customer service. With rare exception, they are also part of a benefit plan that gives the employee a choice in accessing the on-site service or another local provider. They may have modified costs (lower co-pays for the user) and a more advantageous effect on insurance deductibles. They are not mandatory and seldom are they the only source of care that a person can access.

## The Company Doctor Is Gone but Somehow Not Forgotten

When a firm implements an on-site program, it often has to address employee and community concerns about this extinct species and redefine the on-site program as just another place for access to primary care—not any different than a community-based provider. The only similarity is that the doctor happens to be on the company workplace, and they still have the goal of returning the worker to productive activity, but only part of that activity now includes the work environment. Often, they are also involved with population management, disease-state management, prevention, and wellness. Their span of interest and control has transitioned from being reactive to proactive, and the results are both immediate and long term for the patient and for the health investment that the firm is making in their overall health and well-being.

## Reference

1. Colin Gordon, *Dead on Arrival: The Politics of Health Care in Twentieth-Century America*. Princeton, NJ: Princeton University Press, 2003, p. 49.

# Chapter 4

# Components and Complements to On-Site Healthcare: Planning to Plan

One of the most compelling planning scenarios in any literature, popular or business, was penned by Lewis Carroll. It reflects on Alice's encounter with the Cheshire Cat when she asks, "Which way ought I to go?" and the cat responds by stating, "That depends a good deal on where you want to get to." Alice replies that she does not really know or care, and the cat wisely responds, "Then it does not matter really which way you walk." Often, the "Alice approach to planning" is used with on-site clinic implementation.

The fact that healthcare might be delivered on the work site is not a unique or compelling concept; however, the scope of what is delivered and how it is organized can be very different in its conception and delivery. Toyota manages numerous plants throughout North America and the world. By this printing, it may be the world's largest automobile manufacturer. It is certainly, by any standard, the world's most successful. It is also one of the few companies that can boast that a business philosophy or process carries its name. Everyone has heard of the Toyota Production Approach, which is the hallmark of lean manufacturing. Is it any wonder that when it builds a new plant (as it has recently in San Antonio), it studies healthcare and benefits design in the same way?

Toyota staff did not ask consultants, vendors, or health systems what they should do. They knew what the components of the healthcare system were, and they set out to determine which belonged in what environment to provide the best value for their Team Members. They addressed a goal, set objectives, developed a plan, and then contracted for the building blocks necessary to achieve their objectives. The result is a 20,000-square-foot primary care and specialty clinic that serves their own Team Members and many of the on-site suppliers who are Toyota production partners. They started out to build one of the largest production plants in the world using the most advanced technology, making no assumptions that they should use less advanced approaches to benefit design or healthcare delivery.

Their efforts resulted in a departure from the conventional in that it pushed vendors—local, regional, and national—to specifically address Toyota and Toyota Team Member needs. Toyota planning staff, finding little in the marketplace that reflected what they considered to be a "best practices" solution, crafted their own. They did not set out to build an on-site facility—their objective was to design a health system that would focus on the Toyota Team Members and their families. Their efforts did center that system in a world-class on-site facility, but that is only part of the programming. The key to their success is study, planning, objectiveness, design, and implementation. Their process leaves little, if any, room for subjectivity, politics, or tradition.

Toyota staff started by combining a careful study of health system design and corporate needs. They surveyed the marketplace and the national healthcare scene to incorporate best practices from other firms and across the industrialized world. They did not stop there. They influenced change in the Texas state workers' compensation laws to ensure that there would be an even playing field for their benefit program. They were building a new plant, so the challenge of tradition or in-place infrastructure was not a problem. However, the Toyota environment is one of managerial responsibility. Planning, design, projections, and cost comparisons were required, and the question of a capital allocation had to be justified in America as well as in Japan. The team, headed by Dr. Ford Brewer, navigated many levels of review and approvals before moving forward.

## Component Issues and Services to Be Considered in Planning

Not every firm is Toyota, and not many firms enjoy its market capitalization, political power, or access to talent. But all firms can work from the same background information that it used and use the same processes to see what kind of focus and scale their program should take. The approach that a firm (or a municipality or any enterprise) should use needs to come from within and not be guided or influenced by a vendor or by any outside influence—no cookie-cutter solutions here. Planning is never researched on the Internet; it comes from within. Basic planning starts with an inventory of where the enterprise is presently and a definition of where it wants to be. The schematic in Figure 4.1 sums up the process and can be used as a guide for the rest of the discussion in this chapter.

The steps are pretty simple, and some of the goals will be self-evident, but this is more of a balance of ideas than a simple goal setting exercise. Some typical statements or goals used in planning will include addressing costs, achieving improved access, reducing time away from a job site, and improving employee satisfaction. However, these are balanced often by concerns about limiting capital outlay, not wishing to change benefit programs, and avoiding local political snags with hospitals and doctors. The key is to balance the things a firm wants to achieve against the fears it has about change and the effects of change.

A key driver of the process is also the definition of the program. The program should always be referred to as something larger than an "on-site clinic" because this term oversimplifies the process and the challenges the firm should be addressing. Wellness, rehabilitation, safety, intervention, prevention, and behavioral change will all become points of discussion within the on-site clinic planning process. Listing areas of potential impact

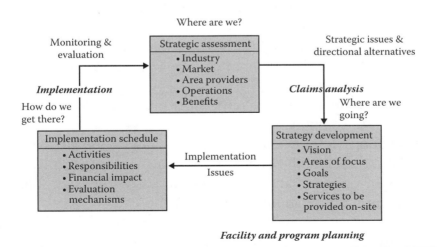

Facility and program planning

**Figure 4.1   This simple diagram outlines everything that a person needs to know about planning. It all starts with an idea of where you are and where you want to go.**

is the first step in the discussion of what might be more correctly labeled "employer managed healthcare."

## What Are the Basic Components of Employer Managed Health?

Generally, the program is an intelligent and thoughtful mix of several factors.

- On-site medical services centered around robust and focused primary care
- Coordination of all occupational medicine, comprehensive, and industrial health with basic primary care
- Coordination of rehabilitation and work-related absenteeism (and modified or monitored work-site presence)
- Routine claims analysis and focus on disease management and disease risk factor control
- Direct contracting for inpatient and specialty services with a local healthcare system that "gets it" and is willing to trade significant discounts for volume
- Narrow channel network development for specialty care
- Reorganization of benefits structure to promote wellness, beneficiary compliance, and selection of the appropriate network services
- Direct management of care coordination and utilization oversight functions
- Coordinated medical record functions that allow recall and compliance monitoring. This implies both an electronic health record (EHR) as well as a personal health record (PHR)
- Structured wellness and preventive programs that articulate with the other program components
- Feedback loops to allow continual quality improvement techniques to be applied to the health benefit expenditure
- Employee involvement and interactive processes to ensure solid communications about program features
- Creation of a learning environment concerning health and the health benefit structure
- Convenience and incentives for employees and their family members to use the system

Each point will be addressed in future chapters and explored in more detail, but the general concept of employer managed care to which a planner should return is that the firm is now going to look at every dollar that is spent on healthcare and try to understand if it is being applied with precision and with some predictable result.

Obviously, this is a lot more than just moving a couple of providers on site, and the employer may wonder if the planning process might not be short-circuited by just going to one of the many "on-site service vendors" and simply buying whatever they are selling. This will normally fall short of the programs being held up as models (Toyota, Quad/Graphics, Perdue, Pitney Bowes, etc.). Why? The vendors of on-site services will miss some of the key components of employee wellness coordination and health status improvement. Most notably, they will miss the electronic medical record. They won't understand the full scope of a focused and robust primary care program. They will omit aggressive care management. They will stop short of the development of a value-oriented specialty network. However, if confronted by a cohesive plan and a compelling client opportunity, most of the program vendors we encountered in the preparation of this book will rise to the occasion and work with the employer to achieve the program design that is required to ensure success.

*Chapter 5*

# The On-Site Program: What and Who Are In and Out? Why?

## Start a "Laundry List"

The planner needs a laundry list, and this chapter will provide it. However, it is first necessary to ask "who" is in. The issue of an employee going to an on-site clinic for a problem that arises at work is rather uncontroversial, but the idea of their child going there for a camp physical can be just the opposite. Also, how are the scope and breadth of services to be defined? Trauma and injury care is pretty well accepted as is "suddenly sick at work" cases, but how about preventive dental or chiropractic care or acupuncture?

The question is not one of size or program scalability, as many vendors will try to tell you, but one of service definition. "Contract with us and we will 'build' the program together." This is a good way to never achieve anything except a contract with a vendor that complements *its* idea of what a program should consist. It is not the way to achieve the goals the employer may be seeking.

The scalability issue should be reserved to the question of what is truly scalable. A facility can be built for an optimum population and then the staffing can be scaled to fit the actual utilization. Build once, after careful study, and then staff to a near-term optimization, which is defined by efficiency and services. However, the program *direction* should not be scaled because there is but one "learning moment" where a firm and its executives

**Figure 5.1 Determining where you want to end up is as simple (and as complex) as figuring out what is going to be on-site. Here is an example of an exercise/fitness area at Briggs & Stratton at their main plant in Milwaukee. Exercise facilities can be extremely popular, but they are space-intensive, and there is a limited ability to predict return on investment (ROI).**

really focus on the idea of moving as much of the programming into a more managed environment. If the clinic itself is sized for the most modest of programming, that may be the start of multiple analyses, justifications, and a patchwork program over many years. If the principles of the program (and its benefits) are to be achieved, it should encompass as much as is practical from day one.

## Sizing and Scalability: Start with "Who"

Scalability can be part of the planning and an important component of the pro forma budgets and projections because there is no accurate way to predict beyond an educated guess about the acceptance of the on-site programming from the workforce (and their families, if they are incorporated within the program). Some factors will help in this process, but the fallback is the adjustment of staffing to allow variable costs to achieve efficient cost profiles. Fewer people mean fewer staff members. Ratios are pretty well understood in the provision of medical care, and they can be referenced against norms reported in the Medical Group Management Association (MGMA) reports on productivity of primary care practices.*

The basic questions align themselves to service lines and the recipients of these lines of service; hopefully, they are easy to address and resolve. The basic premise is that a facility, once built, becomes more cost-efficient when it is used by more people and for more visits. The progression of classes of users is defined by the following listing. This listing is from the simple and straightforward to the more complex and challenging categories.

- On-site employees using the clinic facilities for work-related injuries
- Utilization of the facility for pre-work screening and industrial medicine applications
- On-site employees using the clinic facilities for sudden illness onset (non-work related)
- Employees, from off shift, using the facility for rehabilitation and injury follow-up
- Employees, from off shift, using the facility for sudden illness onset and non-work injuries (urgent care)
- Employees accessing services for preventive and wellness functions
- Covered dependents accessing the services for preventive and wellness functions
- Employees accessing the programming for complete primary care and ancillary services
- Covered dependents accessing on-site programming for complete primary care and ancillary services
- Related work groups (non-employees) accessing on-site services for injury, illness response, safety and wellness, primary care, etc.
- Retirees, pre-Medicare, and Medicare-eligible retirees
- Seasonal workforce
- Employees and dependents of a joint venture partner
- General public

---

* The MGMA annually publishes handbooks that report on various physician and provider productivity issues. The contact information for this group is included in Appendix E. Most references to staffing and utilization are derived from material that they have reported, and many of the projections offered by consultants and on-site providers can be checked against MGMA ratios.

## Sizing and Scalability: Finish with "What"

As one can imagine, the basic thought of providing care on-site becomes more complex as the groups who can access it become more broad. It is also helpful to think about the types of services that might be included. A general listing will help the planning body to clarify its intent. This listing is kept rather broad to foster some basic discussion. Some aspects of service (e.g., electronic medical records (EMR), registration, industrial medicine, emergency response capabilities, etc.) are assumed to be components of any program.

A potential program listing for consideration and inclusion/exclusion in the planning process includes the following:

- Drug testing
- Pre-employment physicals
- Travel medicine

**Figure 5.2    Some things are not really a simple decision. Here a technician studies an image in a clinic environment at Miller Brewing in Milwaukee, but the reader will note that it is a traditional film and not a digital image. Some ancillaries are still too expensive to incorporate on-site. Radiology, for example, requires addressing issues like storage, lead-lined walls, and additional certification for staffing.**

- Laboratory services
- Radiology and imaging services
- Optical
- Dental
- Podiatry
- Rehabilitation (and physical therapy)
- Retail pharmacy, pharmacy benefit management, and clinical pharmacy
- Retail sales of nonprescription items
- Chiropractic
- Medical transportation
- Audiology
- Dispensing of safety and protective devices
- Nutritional services (especially as associated with wellness)
- Employee assistance programming (EAP) and other counseling
- Select specialist access (e.g., dermatology, surgery, orthopedics)
- Expanded primary care (e.g., obstetrics/gynecology, internal medicine, etc.)
- Pediatrics
- Wellness, preventive, and interventional programming
- Work hardening

The only value in making a list of this nature is to have the employer and the program planners consider what the facility will be used for initially and in the long term. At the time of this writing, there is no on-site vendor currently operating with a full complement of these services as part of their product line. However, some employers have put all of the components together and the on-site vendors are learning very quickly to adapt and provide comprehensive services when an employer offers the opportunity to compete for a contract for the provision of on-site services.

## Address the Key Issues before Getting Outside Help

This might also be a time to address some of the other relevant questions that will need to be answered within the planning process. These are the tougher issues to address and resolve, and they will take some focus from top management, human resources, finance, and (depending upon the workforce) perhaps employees or their representatives.

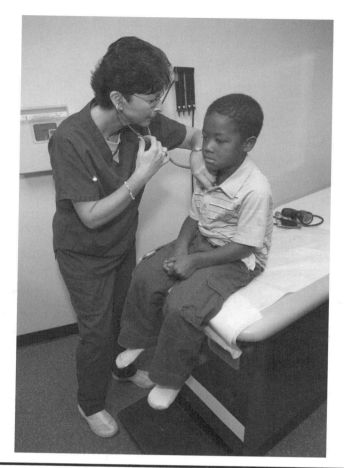

**Figure 5.3  A pediatric patient at a well-child visit at the Quad/Graphics clinic in Milwaukee. The addition of pediatrics requires not only unique staffing, but also some attention to additional detail in the facility design and construction.**

Each issue will have an impact on planning for the facility and for the success of the programming that will take place within it.

1. Are we committed to a robust and functional primary care model?
2. Are we going to move all aspects of health into one chain of command to ensure integration of information and a unity of purpose?
3. Are we addressing this problem from a "population management" standpoint with indicators for success established accordingly?

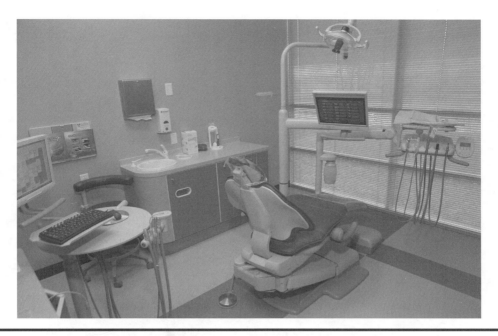

**Figure 5.4 Ancillaries such as dental take skilled planning because it is almost impossible to generalize on the demand for such services. Here is a dental suite at the Toyota Family Medicine Center in San Antonio. They planned for and built four modern suites for primary care dentistry but found that it was impossible to accurately gauge the demand, which far exceeded capacity in the early months of programming. Other programs have found volume projections to be very challenging when employees are initially offered improved access to facilities and services on-site.**

4. Will we change the benefit program to amplify the on-site clinic as a major component of care for our employees and their dependents?
5. Are we ready to implement a value-based contracting process to support the on-site program that would include direct contracting and aggressive case management?

These questions outline most of the decisions that have to be made as part of a change from standard benefits planning to a successful on-site program with effective management of all component aspects. The determinations that need to be made will not always be positive for all issues, but the questions should at least be asked so that the issues that contribute to the final decision can be aired.

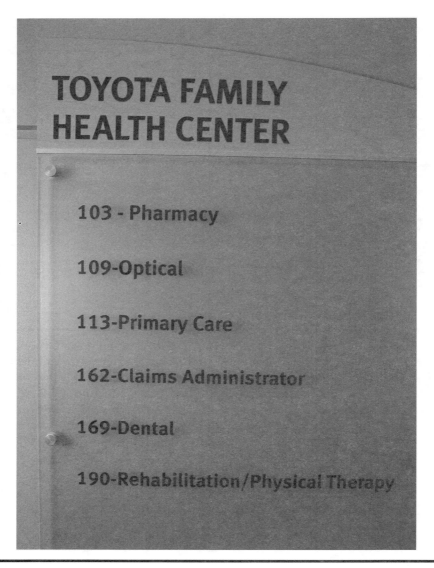

**Figure 5.5** Pictured here is signage at the Toyota Family Health Center that will give the reader more information about the program than a picture of the building. This project was conceived and planned from the inside out. As one can see, this is a complete program that handles everything from primary care to rehabilitation and everything in between.

## Chapter 6

---

# Cost Savings, Cost Avoidance, and Confidence Levels

---

A Birmingham, AL, pipe company that won accolades for its focus on worker healthcare—including an on-site medical clinic—has said it will close its clinic.[1]

Rosenbluth (President of Take Care Health, a division of Walgreens) says every dollar invested in setting up a clinic will return $3 to $5.[2]

Stuart Clark, executive vice president of Comprehensive Health Services in Vienna, VA, says that the return on investment (ROI) for an on-site or near-site clinic can range from $1 to $4 or more for every dollar invested and that his clients usually see a positive ROI within two years.[3]

The Choice Healthcare Center [at the Orangeburg Husqvarna plant] announced it will close its doors Dec. 31.[4]

## The Projection of Savings

Many projections of savings can be made regarding on-site clinics and the cost of benefits. Certainly, any cost savings that can be achieved through program redesign are something that a rational firm would pursue, as long as it does not cause some other form of alternative cost or increase some nonfinancial risk (e.g., employee dissatisfaction, a decline in safety, or employee well-being). A simple process like flu shots will have a cost and a benefit that can be easily quantified. However, the cost is so slight and the benefit so obvious that study is not really required because most would agree that the answer is intuitive.

However, an on-site clinic takes a capital allocation and a budget determination. The related programming might require an alteration to a benefit program and changes in other support contracts such as an insurance carrier or a third-party administrative supplier (TPA). There are legal costs and an evaluation of risk coverage such as stop-loss insurance. Few firms will embark upon a functional and financial commitment of this nature without a formal study of some kind to establish a return on investment (ROI) of some sort. This ROI will not quantify employee satisfaction or the social good of a happier and healthier family. It will focus on cost benefit and the risk associated with not achieving projections.

The industry does not have hard and fast rules on what constitutes true savings as they might relate to the development of on-site health services. There are some readily acceptable terms, but classification of savings might be confused among various categories. In a previous chapter, the concept of near-term returns and programs with a higher confidence level was discussed with the idea that most cost savings programs can be enhanced or improved by the addition of an on-site clinic and the programming that generally is associated with it. To a chief financial officer (CFO), any investment falls into a cash planning scenario and must be defined in a capital needs budget. This type of planning is pretty definitive and it is always "near term." The benefits or the payback to offset a capital outlay must be just as precise.

## Near-Term Savings: Direct and Measurable Cost Avoidance ("Hard Savings?")

What can be counted and what can be counted upon? The savings have to be real and dependable. The following categories can be assessed with a high level of confidence, and the results can be incorporated within a payback pro forma that can be offered to the C-suite without much dialogue. The numbers should speak for themselves.

■ The costs associated with the provision of health services in a site owned and maintained by the company and in which primary care services are made available can be easily measured against outside costs (make or buy).

- The costs related to the development of a select network of specialists and other providers who are connected to the on-site primary care program can be compared easily to alternative contract (or historical) costs.
- The effectiveness of a focused care management team (or concierge nurse), who can assist with the direction of employees and their beneficiaries to immediately accessible and cost-effective health services while reducing duplication and monitoring effective utilization, can be gauged.
- Savings from ancillaries (on-site access to pharmacy, imaging, diagnostic services, laboratory testing, etc.) can be accurately quantified.
- Direct costs for therapeutic services (physical therapy and other rehabilitative functions) can be easily assessed.
- Employee election of more appropriate care scenarios (higher use of generic prescriptions or a therapeutic alternative to surgery) can be projected.

## Longer-Term Savings: Indirect/"Hoped-For" Cost Avoidance ("Soft Savings?")

John Maynard Keynes, the great economist and sociologist, was once quoted as saying that he did not focus on long-term economic analysis because the only thing that was certain was that, "In the long term, we all would be dead." Nevertheless, the on-site clinic industry does focus on longer-term benefits and they deserve mention here. The issues may be important reasons for addressing a change in healthcare programming for a firm, and they definitely will have a benefit for the employees and their families. They are worthy of note and reflection, but they do not belong in an investment-quality pro forma.

It makes sense that, if a new plant is being built, there is always going to be some kind of healthcare benefit that will be provided or purchased for the employees. The same goes for a city, municipality, or governmental unit. They are all here to stay, so to speak, and the construction of programming to develop a longer-term approach to healthcare and the health status of the population is a critical part of the planning discipline. However, CFOs live in the near term and operate on strict project pro forma standards that seldom allow long-term returns to be counted in calculations relating to ROI and project selection.

## Long-Term Savings or the Soft Savings Analysis

There is some risk of confusion in providing this list, but in the interests of trying to justify a program on financial terms, the following is provided for discussion purposes with the caveat, "Quantify at your own risk:"

- The benefit of personal health risk appraisals
- Employee health coaching (except as described as a part of an aggressive care management program)
- Disease-state management
- Preventive programming
- Employee absenteeism
- Employee "presenteeism"
- Health promotion and wellness programming
- Medical records and data mining
- Wellness programming

This is not to say that the longer-term savings and benefits are not important. This classification of program elements is simply to define the confidence level of any predictive value in a presentation to top management when being asked to justify a commitment to an on-site facility that may require a significant capital outlay. Primary care visits can be "priced" and purchased or provided. The cost alternatives can be studied. A wellness or weight loss program has to be estimated and projected using actuarial tables over time. The benefits may be there, but they can only be suggested and never actually projected. Also, the benefit occurs in the long term, and most companies need a payback analysis that is short term.

Simply put, the confidence levels on a program of this nature are tied to the ability of the model to predict the cost of the on-site clinic and to "right-size" it for the employee and dependent base to be served. The key assumption, and the number to which the model is most sensitive, is the estimate of employee and beneficiary utilization. This will be impacted by any number of factors such as employee proximity to the site, site hours of operation, range of services provided, access to alternative caregivers in the community, etc. The employer can have the greatest impact on improved utilization by effective benefit redesign (price advantage), clinic design, and staffing (quality advantage). The manner by which the program is announced and promoted will also play a role in its success.

In presenting this chapter, there were references to clinics closing and to claims by vendors regarding payback and ROI. These are unfair comparisons, but they were used as chapter leads because there are some wild claims being made and some unfortunate decisions being reached on both ends of the spectrum. A more balanced question might be whether these things work over the longer term, and to answer that question the example would have to be from a firm that has used the on-site program for a long period of time and has compared its performance to a cohort of its peers (in a like industry in the same general geographic area).

The chart in Figure 6.1 shows the Quad/Graphics experience and it speaks for itself. This figure depicts the performance of Quad/Graphics on a cost-per-employee basis as compared with other like firms in the Midwest.

The savings are probably underrepresented because the company is reflecting the costs of its on-site wellness, occupational health, preventive, and management programs within its reporting along with basic healthcare costs. This is reported over time, and the trend is upward, but at a slope that does not match that of other companies. It shows lower costs and a slope that is more manageable. This analysis also does not take into account any absenteeism or "employee efficiency" factors, nor does it reflect the fact that Quad/Graphics has a very effective healthcare program that employees

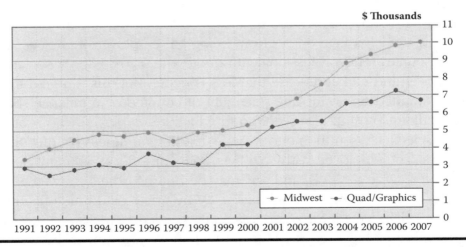

**Figure 6.1** **The Quad/Graphics experience is one of the few programs that can be studied over time. This is a summary of its experience charted against similar midwestern employers under a comprehensive health program that is organized around an on-site clinic model.**
Note: This figure was kindly provided by John Neuberger of QuadMed, which is a wholly owned subsidiary of Quad/Graphics. The material is used with its permission.

reference as a reason to want to work for the company. The quality of the healthcare and its positive impact on the employee population are important, but not easily quantifiable in any pro forma.

## Absenteeism and Presenteeism

To avoid a storm of protest (from other commentators and vendors), there is a gray area that can be quantified and predicted in a near-term time frame. This is the employee work time-loss that can be counted when they are allowed to go off site for services that an on-site clinic might provide. Simple math suggests that a two-hour trip and a two-hour service cycle (waiting at a provider's office) is equivalent to four hours, and a simple trip to the on-site program can be achieved in one hour. The net savings is three hours of productive on-the-job work product. When counted in hourly wage equivalents, this might mean "three hours times twenty bucks an hour" or sixty dollars of "savings."

This is a good thing, and one measure of its "goodness" might be sixty dollars but this is not sixty dollars that can be added to a projection for the justification of an on-site clinic investment. It simply is not a direct cost or a direct benefit that can be quantified along with the costs of primary care and brick and mortar. This is a savings that helps justify a change in programming; however, it falls more in a class of something like a "reduction in turnover," which a firm enjoys from being an "employer of choice." Any human resources (HR) professional can quote a real cost issue associated with turnover and make the case that less is better, but this is a goal that is seldom quantified on an income statement or counted on a balance sheet.

One could also think of a scenario in which an employee who is at work might be selectively sent home to avoid extending an illness or infecting co-workers. The employee with cold symptoms or a flu virus might be at a job site to preserve days off, and this may be putting others, as well as the employee, at risk. There is an old axiom, "Why waste paid time off on days that you are sick? Save it for when it is really needed." This is a cynical viewpoint but all of us have reported for duty when we are "under the weather," coughing, sniffling, wheezing, and on the edge of flu-like symptoms. The on-site medical team is an important interventional tool in cases like this. Just do not try to quantify the cost savings.

These types of savings are real but not projected or predicted in a formal financial model because they are only beneficial for injured-on-the-job or sick-at-the-work-site events. The availability of care closer rather than farther is obvious, but the actual financial effect is only quantifiable if there is a way to predict how many of the incidents actually allow the worker to return to some kind of active role at the job site following the illness or injury and whether their work product can be quantified once they return. There should not be an effort to simplify this by tying the value of an hourly wage to some kind of savings projection unless it can be shown that the wage represents the actual marginal production of the worker.

## Hyperanalysis

These benefits exist, and they are positive and nontrivial, but they are unlikely to be a major factor in the reliable prediction of cost savings for a program of this nature. Similar statements can be made about other long-term benefits. They are real, and they are important but they may not find their way into a pro forma that will be presented to the C-suite.

What is the cost benefit of catching an early cancer or avoiding the onset of adult diabetes? There are numbers that can be assigned, but they should be studied after the programs are functional and when the incidents can actually be counted. Incidentally, the answers offered by QuadMed from its experience of almost twenty years is that an early diagnosis of cancer is worth $550,000 in "prevented" costs, and the early intervention of one person migrating to a diabetic condition is $100,000.[5]

A cautionary note on hyperanalysis: This is a spreadsheet-driven phenomena that has arisen in recent years and reflects every conceivable potential cost and savings figure to the fourth or fifth decimal place. In quantitative physics or chemistry, this level of analysis is crucial, but in the management of populations this is a level of detail that cannot be achieved. Beware of the analysis that depends upon actuarial projections and sophisticated models that normalize data and use complex linear formulas to justify how many examination rooms are necessary. This whole area of projection is fraught with the dual questions of how much accuracy is possible and how much is actually needed. If the payback is in a range that is substantial and incontrovertible, further analysis to define the return is really senseless. If it is a "close one," forget the program because the added accuracy will not allow a real prediction to occur that is worthy of reporting to anyone at the executive level. This stuff is really simple high school statistics, not graduate-level actuarial science.

Projections will allow us to define the need for four or six examination rooms or radiology "in" or "out." Management of the programming allows the project to be effective and the staffing to be matched with the employees who actually elect to be treated at the site. Unless utilization can be projected with some degree of accuracy (it probably cannot be), then the analysis of precise staffing must be left open for managers to be allowed to manage.

To be fair, actuarial projections will allow a firm to project some of the utilization that can be expected as a population ages. If there is a changing gender factor or a shift from one payment category to another, these are areas where financial projections can be more precise with a higher level of inspection of the data and a more scientific financial model. The real question for an on-site project is whether this is needed at the outset or after the program is up and running to fine-tune some of the aspects that might become opportunities once a component of the employee population has committed to direct involvement in the project.

The following chapters will ignore the soft savings and the long-term positive effects and leave these to salespeople concerned with disease management programming. The ROI will be based on the development of an accurate and dependable projection of the actual investment in dollars and what near-term impact it will have on the cost of work force benefits.

# References

1. "American Cast Iron Pipe Company," *USA Today*, November 11, 2005.
2. David Welch. "The Return of the Company Doctor: Medical Clinics Are Springing Up at Businesses—and Savings Are Substantial." *BusinessWeek.com*, http://www.msnbc.msn.com/id/25972415 (August 17, 2008).
3. Bruce Mulligan. "Human Resources and Employee Benefit News: On-Site Clinics Respond to Consumer Driven Era," http://wbrucemulligan.blogspot.com/2007/11/on-site-clinics-adapt-to-consumer.html (November 11, 2007).
4. Gene Zaleski. "Strictly a Cost Issue," http://www.thetandd.com (November 14, 2006).
5. John Neuberger, Presentation to the Membership of the West Michigan Business Group on Health; Employer Options for Collaboration on Health Cost Control, January 10, 2007.

*Chapter 7*

# The Quest for a Dependable Return on Investment: Claims Analysis

There is so much hype out there about on-site programming that the salesperson who is working the crowd of employers is probably only bumping into other vendors and consultants who are trying to sort out the process and see where they can land in the mix of projections and predictions, real and imagined. The field of analysis for in-house management of healthcare and on-site clinics is being shaped by the sales teams of three industries—the on-site vendor industry, the benefits consulting industry, and the brokerage industry. More can be said about each group than would be useful in a chapter dedicated to analysis except to say that each group is missing some basic assumptions, and the client (the employer) is in danger of having too many data and not enough information.

One rule should be that if the analysis cannot be fit on a single page, it is probably too exotic to make sense. The summary of information that should be presented to a client employer can be pretty simple.

- What is the up-front cost of the project?
- What is the near-term estimate of ongoing costs that a firm can expect to avoid (cost savings over the present unplanned, community-based programming)?
- Why should the firm trust you and your numbers?

These answers can be demonstrated in a very simple fashion and with a high degree of confidence if the project starts with background information that is from the employer's own income/expense statements. The reference they need to share is the global cost of healthcare that they encountered in the last couple of program years. That, coupled with the fact that it represents some kind of cost for the population (workers, dependents, and retirees), will give the employer (and the advisory staff) a number that can be derived as cost per year for a covered life or cost per year for a full-time employee. Hopefully, the employer and its human resources (HR) department and benefits counselors have already managed to trim some costs related to the coordination of benefits (this is the exercise of ensuring that they are not paying for covered lives that are also receiving a benefit from another employer or entitlement program). Also, there is the issue of eligibility and the question of how many people are actually eligible for coverage on the program. The inspection of these ratios has to be done with credible numbers to have credible results.

The reader should note I have turned away from the terms "consultant" or "vendor" because there are many worthwhile advisory sources in this process. In each category, some do very worthwhile analytical work, some do very poor work, and some do only work that is self serving. The problem is to recognize the differences. In any case, if the precepts of sound judgment and recognized levels of accuracy are heeded, the employer can rely upon any number of sources for developing sound program financial expectations. Brokers, actuaries, and consulting and vendor groups all have similar data from which to draw conclusions, but there is one aspect of the process that might be questioned and that is the staging of the projections.

In some cases the vendor groups are being asked by consultants preparing request for proposal (RFP) competitive bidding projects to prepare their third-party estimates of the costs and the projections that are being used for the final determination as part of the process. This will not work because the sourcing of the information (at the consulting level) is handed to someone who has to use it to prepare a competitive bid and, perhaps, be judged by the program outcomes rather than their pricing. If the outcomes are good, then they appear to be the more capable among the field of applicants. However, if the outcomes are modest or less aggressive than the other contenders, they are out of the running. This dichotomy in financial planning and program accountability will not produce a result that is credible and the firm will not realize the problem until after they have spent the capital on the workplace clinic and invested years in a program with the wrong vendor. Firms should be wary of program health savings that are derived as part of a competitive bidding process.

## Everything Starts with a Claims File

The best predictor of what the future might be is an accurate measurement of the most recent past. The most accurate reflection of the cost of healthcare is the claims file that matches the healthcare payments associated with the employer's work force. There is a line item in an expense budget somewhere that is a payment for health services, and whoever sent the bill has to have an itemized accounting of why they sent it. Sounds rational, but getting the claims is often a quest that is challenging beyond common sense.

Definitions and data elements are important to understand as the process to better quantify healthcare cost specifics is engaged. The "claims" are defined as a file of unique payments to healthcare providers on behalf of an employer with specific dates of service, type and payment category, provider specificity, and the date and amount of payment clearly delineated. This allows the comparison of employee population numbers (and plan-covered lives) to the body of dollars used to cover the healthcare cost for a discrete time period.

Simple? Not really. The first challenge will be to get a claims file that actually matches an employee listing and then to parse it (pull it into a usable form) so that the claims can be analyzed. For some unknown reason, the data warehouses, data consolidators, and third-party administrators who manage the specific payments for the covered employees do not easily give up the payment specifics to the party with the checkbook. Often, when one is working on an analysis, the first revelation to the employer is the fact that they can request their data, but they just cannot get it. There is a natural feeling among employers that they pay for the health services and they should be able to know—with specificity and not just on a generic level—what they purchased. They are often offered a synopsis, a masked report or a summary of claims, and these are simply not of sufficient detail on which to do a real analysis to the level that is necessary for an investment to be made.

## Why Claims and Why the Need for Detail?*

The claims file represents what was paid on behalf of the employer to providers for the services in a particular period. If the last couple of years are inspected, the history of utilization is there for the comparison to a projection that reflects a "what if." What if there had been an on-site clinic program and an employer managed health initiative in place for the couple of years for which we have actual data? Assuming everyone was doing their job, the best that the employer, the benefits counselors, disease management specialists, and brokers have been able to do has been reflected by the actual costs. No discounts or actuarial analysis needed. Last year and the previous year were the best of everyone's efforts, and the experience is all there for comparison and analysis.

If the pro forma can be developed for a sample year that reflects a comparison to actual historical activity, the chief financial officer (CFO) should be able to have a high level of comfort with any projections. The historical claims can be segmented to reflect various cost categories, and if need be the proposed programming can be compared to these on a line-by-line basis. Spreadsheet programs allow for inclusion/exclusion of specific components of the programming so that each category can be studied.

Projecting historical claim experience into the future has some hazard because a workforce population ages over time and changes with the level of employment. If turnover and the age/sex demographic can be predicted, actuarial science can be used to make a projection more accurate. Epidemiological and public health data can be applied. Trending can be made more accurate by applying risk factors to various scenarios and using sophisticated financial modeling techniques like a Monte Carlo simulation.† All sorts of consulting and data contortion are possible, but there is not much to be gained from hyperanalysis. The additional cost and complexity involved is usually an application of unnecessary precision in which precision is not really achievable.

---

* I recognize the work of W. Jeffrey Beird in this chapter and every chapter that addresses cost, claims, and projections. Much of the material has been directly taken from material he has developed over many years for his clients of advising firms on financial issues related to on-site healthcare and medical access programming.

† A Monte Carlo simulation is one that incorporates alternatives into an analysis that contains predictive ratios that predict (guess?) at the chance that each alternative might be the end result. It is a way to incorporate risk analysis and weigh various potential outcomes. It is only as accurate as the accuracy of the weight offered to each of the potential results, which is to say, probably not very accurate overall. Another approach might be to simply project "best case" and "worst case" scenarios.

Take the claims data and model a program against them. Apply high-school-level statistics, and compare the key categories of cost and benefit. If one feels that additional information is needed, he or she should first compare the cost of obtaining that data and the hoped for results against the increased accuracy desired. Analysts often report dollars and cents in a pro forma just because the spreadsheet can accomplish the calculation, not because accuracy can be achieved at the level that is predicted. Actuarial analysis and exotic modeling techniques are usually overkill and the complex nature of the reporting process will generally produce a result that cannot be achieved or, if achieved, consistently measured.

## The "Claims Request"

To get the right information, it helps to ask the right question. The chart in Table 7.1 is a common request format for claims data and can be used as a guide for helping the "claims repository librarian," whoever that might be, to develop the necessary files. This chart is for regular medical claims, and it could be easily modified for workers' compensation or occupational medicine. A more complete request is included in Appendix B. The one represented here reflects the minimum data set necessary to do a dependable cost comparison or projection.

This is not the only claims file that is necessary. Pharmacy is critical as well as occupational health and, depending upon the service mix desired for study, dental and optical. Additional examples would follow this general model with only the categories changed somewhat to reflect the different ways that each claim might be encountered or paid. For example, a pharmacy claims request would address generic categories or the need for proprietary dispensing. It would also ask for the information about refills and whether the prescription was "on" or "off" the formulary*. Additional detail on a workers' compensation file could include the nature of the injury and any additional rehabilitative factors. The goal is to get *specific paid claims* for a population so that the cost profiles can be accurately studied.

There are a couple of terms in the chart that might require explanation—ICD9 and CPT.† These are billing categories that appear on any medical billing

---

* A formulary is a listing of "approved" drugs within a benefit program, usually defined by a pharmacy benefits manager or program administrator.

† ICD9 (or ICD-9) is the abbreviation for the International Statistical Classification of Diseases and Related Health Problems and CPT is the abbreviation for Current Procedural Terminology. Both acronyms are in general use.

**Table 7.1  Standard Claims Request**

| Field Requested | Notes |
|---|---|
| Claim number | |
| Member ID # | Unique patient identifier |
| Relationship | Subscriber, spouse, dependent |
| PCP medical group | Tax ID# |
| Provider last name | |
| Provider first name | |
| Provider specialty | |
| Provider type | Primary care physician, specialist, hospital, home health, physical therapy, physician extender |
| Type of service | Urgent care, laboratory testing, durable medical equipment, supplies, outpatient, inpatient |
| Place of service | Hospital, nursing home, office |
| Beginning date of service | |
| Ending date of service | |
| Primary diagnosis code | ICD9 |
| Secondary diagnosis code | ICD9 |
| Procedure code | CPT |
| Procedure modifier | CPT modifier |
| Payment status | Paid, pending, rejected |
| Pay date | Initial payment |
| Billed amount | Charge |
| Allowed amount | Covered amount |
| Paid/adjudicated amount | Amount paid to provider |
| Coinsurance amount | Coinsurance associated with claim |

summary to identify the medical symptoms and specific service provided. These references will allow an analyst to begin to categorize claims and related information so that the data provided can be used for projecting the type of service that might be provided at an on-site clinic and which type of provider might be employed. They also identify what services might be made available on-site by primary care providers.

## What Should Be Categorized On-Site and Why?

Medical care records and medical claims are not that complex. They are derived from intuitive sources—hospitals, doctors, and ancillaries. They come from covered employees and dependents. Hopefully (but not always) they come in to the firm that is paying the bills and they are available in a timely fashion. The representation in Figure 7.1 will give the reader an idea of how the claims history is analyzed to begin a projection for the on-site programming. The chart reflects the proportion of claims paid for employees and dependents on a global level. It is further divided to show the hospital versus the provider (doctors, home health, nursing home, etc.) claims.

The proportional nature of the graphic is from a client's actual claims file for a program year, and it is relatively representative of what might be observed in any business environment where the client firm is large enough to ensure that its claims experience is generally representative of the population covered by health insurance products of some kind.

One mistake to avoid in this analysis is to assume that the on-site clinic process only addresses the outpatient "events." As other chapters in the book have (and will) suggest, the on-site programming is part of an overall employer population management program that is driven by robust primary care and thoughtful oversight of the entire healthcare spending pool. The idea of the on-site programming being the only part of this reduces an

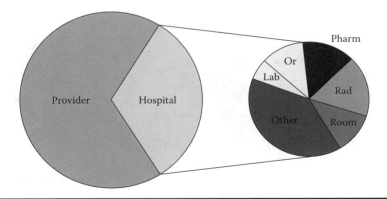

**Figure 7.1** **This pie chart representation is a first cut to define what might be offered on-site. It makes sense that the initial pass will separate inpatient claims from outpatient claims. The area cut out for the inpatient charge history is further segmented into facility-dependent subsets (like radiology and lab).**

on-site clinic to an urgent care or immediate access project with much different analysis required.

The providers supporting the employee and dependent population and their healthcare needs can generally be defined by the type of service that has been identified by the Current Procedural Terminology (CPT) codes reported in the claims analysis (see Figure 7.2). Each claim will specify the type of service as well as the setting in which it was provided. An accurate and complete claim file allows re-categorization of services to begin to understand the composition of physician visits at the primary care level versus those encounters that need to be provided in an institution or speciality setting.

In this part of the exercise, the challenge is to understand which historic events for this population could have been served at an on-site facility. This is the total universe from which a projection can be made. The next step is to determine how many of the potential patients (employees and dependents) will actually elect to have the care delivered at the workplace clinic. This combines what the actual utilization might have been with the program features that will induce the consumer choice of location.

How can this be done? One simple way would be to just ask the potential users. Many firms present programming to their workforce and gauge interest and commitment through a direct indication from the people who

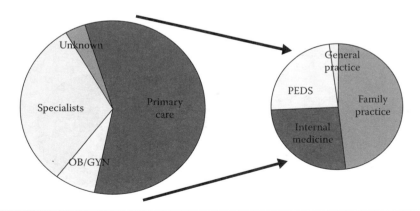

**Figure 7.2 Primary care can generally be organized as male, female, adult, and child. It separates into categories such as pediatrics, obstetrics/gynecology, and adult medicine (family practice, internal medicine, and generalists). Some of this analysis is pretty obvious, but some depends largely on the general categorization of services to be made available on-site.**

are going to subscribe to the programming. The other way is to use like populations and compare the result to the population that is under study when other factors (proximity, benefit design, and program features) are taken into account.

## Projecting Utilization on the Basis of Program Features

Some comments on the likelihood of utilization are offered. Each may seem intuitive, but they are often missed or ignored in planning sessions.

■ The closer people live to the facility, the more likely they are to use it. However, some of the other utilization factors will beat proximity every time.

■ The better the "value proposition" on benefits design, the more that the utilization will be assured. Yes, cheaper is better (from a purely "market basket consumer view"), and this is one of the factors that will beat distance every time. Read that last statement to mean that people will drive out of their neighborhood, and change their doctor, to get care that is value-priced.

■ Value (to a consumer) is not always based on the cost per visit. Consumers recognize higher-value visits as those that offer consistent personnel, qualified staff, access, limited waiting, articulation with other services (laboratory testing, radiology, pharmacy, etc.).

■ If access is limited in a community, the consumer will elect the on-site alternative more readily. Access can be more than the availability of an appointment; it might mean the availability of a culturally sensitive (language-capable) practitioner. It may mean an appointment that is in the evening or on a weekend. It may mean one with a provider of the appropriate gender. In any case, access trumps distance.

■ For medical services, there is a sense that something special is better than something ordinary. Something that is high tech is better than "old tech." If the resulting facility and services seem new and different to the consumers, they will come.

■ Some things are independent of others. For example, dental can be difficult to predict because it is so dependent on the benefit design. The co-pay amount and convenience can greatly impact pharmacy. Optical can be very sensitive to pricing and the availability of eyeglass frames and contact lenses.

**Figure 7.3** Any parent would want to take his or her child to this attractive pediatric unit at Quad/Graphics. The suite is now almost 20 years old but the concept still seems new to the consumer—excellent service in a kid-friendly environment.

Issues like these might be mistaken for common sense but it is surprising how many programs seem to ignore them or fail to understand why people might elect an on-site service (or not elect it.) These factors can be summed up as proximity, cost, value, access, and design. Each will be explored in more detail in future chapters.

# Chapter 8

## The Quest for a Dependable Return on Investment: Key Assumptions and Drivers

We prefer to work with employers who have 1,000 plus employees at one site.

Our firm can develop an on-site program for under $10,000 in a space that is the size of a large conference room.*

## The Employer Has Significant Control over the Success of the Facility

In an earlier part of the book, the issue of utilization was mentioned. The more the clinic is used, the lower the cost per unit of service. This is the simple microeconomics of any facility that produces something—in this case, patient visits. Everything is scalable and so is an on-site clinic. However, the capital and construction decisions are a lot less "scalable" than matching the personnel to the patient demand. If the space is adequate, the addition of a provider or a medical assistant can allow for more services

---

* In the spring and summer of 2008, our staff conducted interviews with every recognizable on-site provider that could be discovered using standard search methodology. These excerpts are quotes from those interviews. The exact commentator's name is withheld to avoid limiting the impression that any reader might have of any one provider.

to be provided on-site. If the space is overbuilt, it will be unused or inefficiently used. If there is not enough space, the services will suffer from the same working problems that face most physicians—waiting time and appointment queuing. This is another problem that can be minimized by careful planning.

Space planning is the key determination in a program because it is the first step in the capital needs request that has to be advanced through the C-suite and defended, in some cases, to various audiences. The determination is made more difficult because it is a building that is being built to essentially accommodate a new business of ambulatory care services in a marketplace that might already seem pretty crowded. The firm is betting more than just capital, it is also wagering on politics and on employee satisfaction. Most programs involving health and benefits considered by a firm or a municipal agency are contract-only in nature. They require a commitment of a moderate and determinate length. By definition, building a facility involves an allocation of land and capital and a significant exposure of corporate identity. These programs cannot be easily changed if they fail, and the facility does not simply go away.

However, most firms know how to consider new business opportunities, and they can apply a couple of different approaches that they probably already use in their standard capital planning tool kit. One approach is to look at the venture as a make-or-buy decision, and the other is to look at the venture as an approach to a new business or a product. The difference is only the determination of how pricing and revenue might be defined in a pro forma. The basics of demand are the same, and they are largely within the control of the firm. This chapter attempts to define the factors that would drive a successful program launch.

## Program Factors That Define Facility Demand

The programmatic options have been described elsewhere in the book. The choice of what to provide needs to be balanced against the actual claims experience. What have employees and dependents used in the past, and what is the likelihood of their use of the services in the future? For the purposes of this segment, wellness and exercise programs are being temporarily ignored. They will be addressed in detail in another chapter, they represent a segment of programming that can be added or modified at a time separate from the development of the on-site medical clinic, and they are easily integrated whenever they are deployed. Also, the exercise areas can be designed to be sparse and rather simple, or they can use spa-like features that might compete with the best of local consumer offerings. Often, there is no direct (immediate) return on investment for an exercise component of programming, no matter what the exercise physiologists and sports trainers claim.

Other programmatic options fare better. The following list is ranked from "top to bottom," with the highest order of program integral value (not payback), or the ones that are most central to program planning, listed first.

■ *Basic primary care space:* This must include capacity for emergency access and initial treatment of the injured worker and the "suddenly sick" employee.
■ *Laboratory testing drawing space:* This is where laboratory test samples are collected, but in some cases, volumes will also indicate that the clinic should dedicate space to simple analytic laboratory services and the processing of the specimens.
■ *Care management services space:* This is dedicated space for the assignment on-site and in-house to special staff (probably a nurse) that can assist employees and dependents with access to care and ensure articulation with other program functions (e.g., disease-state management and inpatient services).
■ *Specialist access space:* More provider services would be accommodated on a part-time basis here to allow employee and dependent access to medical specialists who have been identified as complementary and necessary for program success.
■ *Pharmacy access:* Employees should be able to get (at least) basic prescriptions filled on-site.
■ *Rehabilitation services:* This is typically in the form of physical therapy (PT).
■ *Radiology or imaging services:* Listed last for a reason because this is an expensive service and it is not always able to be cost-justified on volume alone. It could be omitted from many sites without affecting the overall program effectiveness. If employees and providers are asked about the advisability of including radiology, the answer will always be "Yes"; if a financial planner is asked, the first response will be "Unlikely, let me see what volumes there are."

The other program service definitions that have considerable implications for space are optical and dental. If these are added, they will nicely complement the clinic and provide a retail atmosphere; but they should be approached carefully because each can be space and capital intensive, and the utilization is very dependent upon the design of the benefit program. Also, these services are not as basic to a benefit program as primary care might be and generally are the components that are the most subject to change.

If optical is addressed, there will be a need to define the claims volume and the likelihood of program expansion to incorporate retail sales. The allocation of clinic space is simple to project because the volumes will seldom expand beyond a single clinical services lane (with full vision care screening) including the equipment necessary to actually refract the patient (establish a lens power that can be defined as a prescription for glasses or contact lenses). However, there is an issue about what space might be provided to allow consumers to shop "retail" for frames. This is easily understood when one visits a LensCrafters™ store or any other retail, mall-based, outlet. Not so well understood is that an optical service also has an attached laboratory where lens polishing and surfacing might occur. This area may also be helpful for employees who have need of a simple eye-wear repair, a replacement part, or refitting of some kind.

One might ask why chiropractic or complementary medicine programming did not make the list. Complementary medicine is a term used to describe a bunch of care choices that have been called many things—like alternative medicine and holistic medicine. It is not my intent to lump these together with chiropractic but, unlike dental or optical, these disciplines require only the determination of a benefits design team—not a facilities design team. Dental and optical require special spaces and unique room designs that are simply not required for the chiropractors or acupuncturist, homeopath, naturopath, or alternative healer. There is one exception that might be considered and that is the addition of biofeedback services (e.g., psychological, stress relief, hypnosis therapy), which would require a treatment room that has mood lighting, sound-proofing, and comfortable patient seating so that it can be used for a combination of counseling and biofeedback conditioning.

Dental is an analysis that will require extensive expertise and, like radiology, will cost-justify only if volumes are significant. Because of the capital cost involved, planning for on-site dental services is a challenge that requires not only clinical definition of what is to be provided but a specific link to the firm's benefit design.

# The Utilization Equation

In simple terms, the task of defining use of the facility is broadly described by the following equation:

*Workers × Dependent Factor × Annual Visits Per Covered Life = Annual Visits*

This means that if there are 1,000 employees and there are 2.2 family members per each employee family (benefit covered) unit, then the resulting number of "covered lives" will be 2,200. More exotic analysis might be done to further quantify this number from the work that human resources (HR) might do to actually qualify the program participants. Of importance will be the definition of how many employees actually elect family coverage and how many will be adjusted from the numbers because of other "coordination of benefits" issues. Coordination of benefits (COB) addresses the fact that an employee may have a spouse who has healthcare coverage and a more competitive (cheaper) rate for the family coverage that includes the employee. Most overlap of this nature is a well-studied issue by the benefits team, and the gross number of covered lives may need to be adjusted for COB factors.

The annual visits can be checked against population utilization trends that are reported in the managed care literature and by the actual claims file. This number will have a high level of credibility, and it can be an anchor for the facility size because it will only be changed when the size of the workforce changes. It might be augmented by the number of visits made by employees on-site who experience sudden illness or injury, and it could be further refined by adding on-site events such as prescription pickup, preventive visits, pre-employment physicals, etc. However it is derived, the pro forma and the projections can all be documented for analysis and inspection by any third party, and generally they can be considered a credible number for an outside reference on facility utilization.

To continue our "thousand employee firm" example, one generally defensible ratio of "visits per person per year" is somewhere between two and two-and-a-half per person, which is largely a function of age and gender. In any case, for the sake of this example, if a 2.2 or 2.3 visits-per-year ratio is used with our 2,200 covered lives, the result is pretty close to 5,000 visits per year. Knowing this fact, understanding what services will be provided, and making some assumptions on the cost per square foot of construction will combine to allow an analyst to derive a capital cost for the facility.

## The Key Driver of Success: Actual Utilization

However, knowing the need (in primary care visits per year) does not define the use (how many visits actually occur on-site). Most of the programs co-exist with other options that can be accessed by the employees and their dependents. This may be in the form of an open Preferred Provider Network (PPO) or as a choice from among a variety of local providers that are part of an array of services made available through the selected benefit manager (the third-party administrator or the branded insurance entity that pays claims). If a firm like United or Aetna is "managing" the program, the employees and their family members will have a directory of services from which they can choose to access primary care and other medical services. They may already have a primary care provider, and they may be in a situation where ongoing therapy and a high level of trust are already in place.

Why choose the on-site option? Why not honor inertia and stay with an existing provider? Why would anyone want to go to the company doctor? Why do employers like Quad/Graphics, Toyota, and Perdue report 80% plus capture? How can the percentage of utilization be projected and predicted with accuracy?

The potential variance can be minimized by addressing several questions.

■ How concentrated is the employee base, and how close (or far) do they live from the on-site program?
■ How aggressive is the benefit design, and how much economic incentive is there for an employee and his or her family to choose the workplace program under the sponsorship of the employer?
■ How good is the worksite program compared to alternatives in the marketplace?
■ How competitive is the local marketplace? In other words, are alternatives readily available?
■ What promotional efforts have been made to inform and educate the employees about program choices and the quality of the workplace healthcare option?

## Proximity and Access

One of these factors can be discussed and dismissed in a simple fashion. They live where they live and the concentration of their home sites relative to the location of the worksite offering is not going to change, at least in the short term. One can study this phenomenon by using an array of worker households against plant or worksite healthcare location and the result will be a gradient map that displays population density and proximity (or lack of proximity). The result will be a visual demonstration that allows discussion but which probably does not have much normative value. In other words, the fact is that proximity (or lack of it) can be overcome by quality and pricing. The one thing that this may show is the need to adjust hours for ease of access when employees are at the job site and for other factors (quality, benefit coordination, and promotion) to be enhanced somewhat if proximity seems to be a challenge.

Employees can simply be geocoded and, once there is a location that is compatible with a mapping program, they can be placed on a map in proximity to the proposed employer service site. Like most approaches to healthcare projections of utilization, this is an oversimplification. Access is not just defined by proximity. It includes convenience and the perception of service relative to other consumer choices. For example, a person who is located in a rural area may be used to driving many miles for various services, and they will do the same for healthcare. An urban-based commuter may go home at the end of the day and never return to his or her workplace except when there is a shift assignment. Patterns of consumption and behavior must be associated with a variety of features if there is going to be a reasonable estimate of future acceptance.

## Local Competition, Convenience, and Access

The other factor that might be an issue is local competition and access. Many areas have limited access, and one way to gauge that is to simply make some random phone calls and see what type of wait time is necessary for a person to get an appointment with a primary care provider, pediatrician, or obstetrician. If the phone calls are organized around specific questions and the callers are consistent in reporting the outcomes, a study can be constructed that demonstrates with some level of accuracy the absorption rate that a local primary care base might have in a community. This will be very instructive and encouraging if the access is difficult as demonstrated by longer "wait times" for a basic appointment. However, there might be a tendency to be discouraged if every phone contact is met with a receptionist who urges the caller to come right in for immediate access to a doctor.

**Figure 8.1 Employees who are being served by some providers with multiple locations might be able to access other community-based resources like this free-standing Concentra Clinic in Michigan. The key to the consumer is convenience. The caution for the employer is control and the availability of information.**

Geographic proximity and the measure of local access are not the only critical indicators to the determination of actual utilization because they can be overcome by the other three factors. This book devotes a chapter (Chapter 9) to benefits design, which many agree is the most forceful factor. However, quality perception and service delivery may also trump proximity and the perception of access. The real problem is that access is a very difficult thing to study and directly relate to utilization. When combined with other factors, it is found that consumers do not necessarily make their determinations on choosing a good primary care practice simply on the basis of how near the office is to their home. Convenience can also be an overriding consumer choice issue.

Enter then, the factor of retail medicine (offices located in malls, drugstores, shopping centers, etc.). Consumers see these outlets as opportunities to get immediate care for various bread-and-butter healthcare issues. They fill consumer needs related to proximity, convenience, service, and access. If the cost of a visit for a modest service is considered only on its

**Figure 8.2** **Employees at the Quad/Graphics-sponsored pharmacy can pick up their prescriptions on the same day they are issued. In addition, they have a wide selection of nonprescription consumer items for sale on an over-the-counter basis. The key is convenience, service, and ready access, which is what retail vendors such as Walgreens are also providing.**

face value, they may also represent a consumer choice that is a least-cost alternative. Short term, the cost of a flu shot is a market basket choice that can be priced by any consumer who can read a sign or make a phone call. If healthcare professionals are located in a mall or in a drug store, the value of the flu shot is equivalent whether it sells for five dollars or fifteen. If it is free at a county health department (unattractive, long waits, and unfamiliar to the normal consumer) versus five bucks at Wal-Mart (known area, immediate service, and the ability to do some additional shopping), the consumer may elect the Wal-Mart product. Certainly no one can choose locations for convenience and consumer access like the retail organizations that select outlets with sophisticated demographics and modeling. It is no wonder that retail medicine is on the rise. It is targeted at and for consumers. It has been designed and defined by firms that are accomplished in studying and fulfilling consumer wants.

This trend (presently) represents consumer access for the component of medical care that they consider to be "unconnected" to their overall healthcare, such as a flu shot or a camp physical for their kids. However, they do not select these sites for ongoing primary care (or as yet there has been no credible demonstration of that behavior). That is, if they select a doctor for their primary care physician for ongoing care, they will not seek out a Walgreens-based practitioner. As organizations like CVS, Wal-Mart, and Walgreens continue to develop the retail product, the consumer paradigm may change or the service model in the retail sector might become more like the primary care that people associate with their traditional view of a family physician. However, this is unlikely to have an impact on workplace clinic volumes as long as they have been designed around true primary care services.

## Quality and the Perception of Quality

The issue of quality is closely associated with program promotion and consumer information. Any consumer can tell good service as opposed to bad service, but few will be able to define a higher quality of healthcare service as opposed to a service that is of average or lower quality. This should not come as a surprise because even students of the discipline argue about the definition of quality, and there are no real standards for the consumer to apply. As consumers redefine what they consider to be acceptable access (retail medicine vs. traditional primary care), they will also be learning new ways to define quality. They will need a road map and a guidebook.

The firm that uses on-site programming to deliver primary care will need to assist with the definitions and develop the delivery system necessary to help the consumer in the quest for quality and value. This will require a consumer relations program that highlight some of the concepts that consumers do not yet understand and appreciate. These include the value of pooled medical information, access to healthcare information databases, COB design, linkages to disease-specific coaching, etc. They will have to be informed about the true advantage of having healthcare professionals, who are doing their shopping for them; designing networks; and preselecting hospitals and specialists. They will have to be convinced that the employer is working on their behalf when they contract with local healthcare providers for access and pricing concessions.

None of these efforts are intuitively of benefit to a patient who has a cold and wants to get a prescription for an antibiotic. Forget the fact that it may not be a cold and that an antibiotic might not be the treatment of choice. If the provider is available at a site at which there is ready parking and a pattern of access for other items, the fact that they are disarticulate from any access to a combined medical record is not really a problem that is of immediate concern to the average consumer. The perceived need is being fulfilled, and the patient could argue that his or her own doctor probably does not have access to any electronic medical record either. Sadly, they would be correct.

If the employer has a better way, it should be quick to point it out and the value proposition related to on-site care must become part of the "sell" to the consumer. Over time, the program will prove itself, and satisfied customers will sell the service by word of mouth. The key is to ensure the high satisfaction level that is worthy of mention from one employee to another.

# Chapter 9

# The Quest for a Dependable Return on Investment: Benefit and Program Design

It may not seem like much of a revelation, but the fact is that everything related to employee health and employee healthcare is interrelated.

The benefit design aspect has always been singled out as a way to conserve the utilization of healthcare and, in some cases, to shift costs. In a program that comprises an on-site service, it is also a way to ensure that employees consider and use the facility. Benefit design is one of the key factors behind program success and a predictor of program utilization. If there is no commitment of the employer to actually promote the facility that is being designed with advantageous co-pays and deductibles, the projections should be much more modest.

## Benefits Designed to Benefit On-Site Programming

Table 9.1 shows the traditional Quad/Graphics benefits design, which is among the strongest in primary care focused on-site providers. In addition to an excellent on-site experience and ease of access, the benefit program is tailored to encourage in-network participation and utilization of the services designed for the employees and their dependents. Toyota and many other firms have developed similar benefit design features that focus the consumer on the immediate financial benefits of using the on-site facility and its many related network features.

**Table 9.1  This Is the Point at Which "Consumer-Directed Healthcare" Meets "Employer Managed Value"—at the Co-Pay and Deductible Juncture. This Is a Grid That Quad/Graphics Uses to Describe Network and Out-of-Network Options to Their Employees. The Message Is Simple—Use Preselected Network Specialists and Save Money**

| Network | Access | Co-Pay | Deductible |
|---|---|---|---|
| Preferred | Quad/Clinics | $5 Co-pay | 100% |
|  | 400 Specialists | $15 Co-pay |  |
|  | 9 Hospitals | $25-100 Co-pay |  |
| Network | 98 Hospitals | $200/400 | 80% |
|  | 6,650 Doctors | $2,300 Max |  |
| Non-Network |  | $300/500 | 70% |

Access to the on-site clinic has a co-pay that is limited and a corresponding co-insurance coverage (deductible) that is fully covered by the company plan (see Table 9.1). The employer and employee share responsibility for care and have a shared upside in the economic benefit of the decision. In applying this formula of financial encouragement, Quad/Graphics has enjoyed on-site clinic utilization consistently in excess of 85% of all the primary care utilization for their employees and dependents. This also translates into utilization of their selected in-network specialists and hospitals.

The design of the program in this manner also allows the principle of choice to remain as one of the features that can be offered to employees and their dependents, although choice has a defined and near-term cost. This allows a new tool to be added to the programming—steerage. The employer can now use the critical mass of primary care visits to interest and entice the best of area specialists and hospitals to join the network. They can introduce the patients who use the clinic into wellness programs, personal health recordkeeping, disease-state management projects, educational classes, and any other health improvement initiative. Once the patient is under the influence of the primary care provider (PCP), the hope is to use that influence to everyone's advantage.

To be fair to all who provided input for this book, some on-site providers do not use any differentiation of co-pay and deductible and rely solely on the quality of the on-site programming. The rationale is not necessarily flawed. It is just one that might not be using all of the tools at hand. For the consumer, price and access are the key ingredients to choosing where to obtain healthcare, whereas quality and service may contribute more to the long-term ability of the provider to retain the patient. The employer who is embarking upon an on-site clinic initiative should use every means available to entice the employee to try the care and, once they have tried it, to convert to that site as their permanent source of healthcare and health access.

## Projected Savings and Confidence Levels and the Primary Care Decision

Many projections of savings can be made about the cost of health benefits. Certainly any cost savings that can be achieved through program redesign is something that a rational firm would pursue, as long as it does not cause some other form of alternative cost or risk to increase (such as employee dissatisfaction or the avoidance of healthcare). A simple process such as flu shots will have a cost and a benefit that can be easily quantified; however, the cost is so slight and the benefit so obvious that study is not really required. The answer is intuitive.

Benefit redesign, on-site clinics, and complementary programming such as a predesigned network or a disease management project pose different problems. Once benefit redesign occurs, the employees are immediately affected and directly and actively engaged. The on-site clinic has a definitive start-up cost, and a "narrow" network that by its very definition can be described as one that limits choice. One must keep in mind that fewer choices among the providers included in a benefit plan offering might immediately be viewed as a negative design feature by employees and their families, even if the plan components are not being actively used at the time of implementation.

The capital costs of the on-site facility and the operational costs of the staff that provide the care are easily quantified. Visits projected multiplied by the amount of minutes per visit would show a simple hourly room projection and the number of hours in the week for a provider—midlevel or physician—which can then be used to guess the number of bodies needed to staff the clinic. However, one additional factor has to be determined in advance of this computation, and that is the amount of time per visit for the primary care practitioner. This is a factor that the reader can guess at from his or her own experience. How long does your own doctor spend in the exam room on a typical visit or encounter? Probably not too long. Seven to ten minutes might be an average for a typical internist or family medicine provider who is seeing a repeat patient. The time might be increased for a physical exam on a new patient.

This is an opportunity to change the service level from the point of program inception. If the planning calls for a "robust" primary care encounter that is of a higher "effectiveness" level, then the time allotted per patient visit will have to be extended. Mature programs that have a high value for primary care and its role in the delivery of healthcare ignore the conventional time efficiency equations, and they also ignore any measure of the doctors or providers that might be based on productivity alone. The primary care visit time becomes twenty minutes and more with a single provider able to serve no more than 15 or so patients in a seven- to eight-hour work day. (The reduced number is due to the inclusion of longer visits for new patients—up to 45 minutes—and an increased commitment to charting and follow-up.)

In the short term, the pro forma is negatively affected by the new definition of "productivity," and the impact on the "make versus buy" decision deteriorates. At modest levels of utilization and with a program that is focused on a revisionist role for primary care, the simple fact is that the services can probably be purchased in the local community almost as cheaply as they can be provided on-site. If the on-site program uses standard ratios for production, that may not be the case. So, what is gained by the longer visit, and how does it impact program cost?

The longer visit establishes the primary care practitioner as the manager of the patient's health status and allows the patient and the provider to address a complete health status check at each visit or encounter. It also allows the steerage of the patient through a system of preselected support vendors (hospitals and specialists) who can complement the program with improved access, quality, and cost features. It allows encouragement of patient compliance with wellness and prevention programs and the assignment of select patients to specific disease-state management and coaching experiences. The additional focus on primary care is really the design of a program that will allow primary care to emerge as the manager of the rest of the healthcare delivery team.

Turning to the Quad/Graphics experience, again, the on-site clinic, coupled with a select (narrow) network, is supported by both benefit design and a complement of focused PCPs. Selection is limited, but the preselection of the specialty and hospital network has not resulted in employee dissatisfaction. Patients using the on-site programming have a high level of trust in their physician and welcome the suggestion of the specialist or hospital and the assistance in gaining access to a provider that is already "in network."

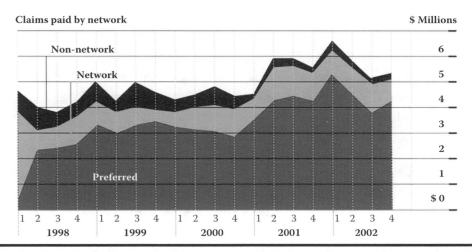

**Figure 9.1  The effect of network design coupled with a strong benefit steerage program is, again, demonstrated with Quad/Graphics data. Even a casual observer can tell when the program was implemented and how it has achieved the selection that the employer has designed.**

## In-Network Savings by Design and Determination

Over the years, as the chart in Figure 9.1 shows, provider encouragement and benefit design have ensured that the selected network is chosen and that the non-network (expensive alternatives) de-selected. Toyota, in its first year of operation (2008), had a similar experience with in-network use well above the 90% level—for those employees who originated their care on-site.

Of course, if steerage works then the issue is to make the steerage work for everyone with a well-designed network to which the employees and their dependents can be directed. Chapter 12 in this book defines a "well-designed network," but for now the idea is simply a network that has been constructed to ensure access and efficiency.

## Hard and Soft Savings, Real and Imagined, Near and Far

Areas in which hard savings can be projected or planned are defined below. In addition, areas in which savings *might* occur are listed. However, the latter should not be included in a formal return on investment (ROI) projection because the savings are actually more long range or "soft" when compared with the immediate cost reductions that should be achieved.

For purposes of clarity, near-term savings and those that reflect immediate cost relief or avoidance belong in ROI projections because they can be easily compared to recent employer experiences. A pro forma can include costs from the following categories, which should be compared to the costs of alternatives from the local marketplace. This is the standard "make or buy" approach that firms use in everyday finance.

■ The provision of health services in a site owned and maintained by the company and in which primary care services are available to employees and their beneficiaries versus the costs of services elsewhere.

■ The development of a select network of specialists and other providers who are connected to the on-site primary care program in such a way that most referrals can be expected to move to them for their specific discipline. (Costs of these specialists and the care they deliver can be compared with costs of general care in the marketplace for like services.)

■ The development of an on-site and accessible care management team (or concierge nurse) that can assist with the direction of employees and their beneficiaries to immediately accessible and cost-effective health services, while monitoring effective utilization. (This can significantly reduce duplication and unnecessary testing and ineffective care.)

■ The incorporation of on-site access to pharmacy, therapeutics, and diagnostic services. (Again, here the cost comparison can be directly compared to the prices generally found in the marketplace and to behaviors like length of rehabilitation, surgery options, and choice of generics.)

## Longer-Term Savings: Indirect/"Hoped-for" Cost Avoidance

These savings are real and can be defined but they do not belong in an ROI because they are long term and have less definitive alternatives to which they can be compared. As an example, wellness is very noble but the payback depends upon many factors, one of which is the turnover of the workforce. It can be argued that high turnover means that other employers will gain the benefit of wellness programs offered for employees, and that this would not be a wise investment from a pure return on investment argument. In any case, the normalization of weight in the workforce and the cessation of smoking are both documented cost-avoiders but probably not in the near term. (Most pro formas go out three or four years, and if there is a cost savings, it has to be documented within the span of those projections.)

The following are complements that should be included in any on-site programming and that have direct bearing on health status but with longer-term positive effects:

- Health risk appraisals
- Employee health coaching
- Disease-state management
- Preventive programming (except for immediate incidents such as flu vaccination)
- Health promotion and wellness programming

This is not to say that the longer-term savings are not important. This classification of program elements is simply to define the confidence level of any predictive value in the model that is being presented. Primary care visits can be "priced" and purchased or provided. The cost alternatives can be studied. A wellness or weight loss program has to be estimated and projected using actuarial tables over time. The benefit may be there, but they can only be suggested and never actually projected.

## Confidence Levels and Program Justification

Simply put, the confidence levels on a program of this nature are tied to the ability of the model to predict the cost of the on-site clinic and to right-size it for the employee base to be served. The key assumption, and the number to which the model is most sensitive, is the estimate of employee and beneficiary utilization. This will be impacted by several factors (many of which have been previously discussed), such as employee proximity to the site, site hours of operation, range of services provided, access to alternative caregivers in the community, etc. However, the employer can have the greatest impact on improved utilization by effective benefit redesign (price advantage), clinic design, and staffing (quality advantage). The manner by which the program is announced and promoted will also play a role in its success.

Some cost savings numbers seem to be tailor-made for an on-site analysis. They beg to be included, probably because they are easy to compute. They relate to absenteeism and time away from work. Less is better = more is worse. The way this is presented seems intuitive ($/hour × lost hours saved = program cost savings). I have not included this in our analysis because it only pertains to "injured-on-the-job" or "sick-at-the-work-site" events. The availability of care closer rather than farther is obvious, but it is only quantifiable if there is a way to predict for these incidents. How many workers can actually return to some kind of active role at the job site after the illness or injury? The benefit exists, and it is positive and nontrivial, but it is unlikely to be a major factor in the reliable prediction of cost savings. Therefore, it is an excellent example of the type of savings considered to be "soft," or indirect.

Table 9.2 shows a series of costs and savings that can be defined for a modest program of primary care and a related select network of specialists. The table reflects the total dollars spent on healthcare for the firm, and it summarizes savings from the clinic as well as from related contracting efforts.

The management fee is reflected to act as a placeholder for the costs associated with any vendor that might be contracted to run the on-site programming. It can be "added back" to a pro forma if the firm elects to develop the program and manage it themselves.

The capital outlay (in Table 9.2 projected at approximately $250,000 in leasehold improvements for space already available at the plant) highlights the need for coordination between standard primary care and occupational medicine as a key to optimizing any investment the firm makes in the on-site program to ensure that the full value for its capital and operations

**Table 9.2   This Sample of Data and Dollars Shows a Simple Make or Buy Alternative. There Are Spreadsheets and Formatted Projection Models That Range in the Dozens of Pages and Use Font Types That Defy Normal Vision, but It All Comes Down to This Page—Near-Term Cost Avoidance Compared with the Capital Outlay. The Reader Will Find a More Sophisticated Treatment in the Appendices**

|  |  | 2006 | 2007 | 2008 | 2009 | 2010 | 5 Year |
|---|---|---|---|---|---|---|---|
| Projected external cost |  | $0 | $3,250,345 | $3,975,821 | $4,992,727 | $6,130,951 | $18,349,843 |
| Projected on-site |  | $247,000 | $2,280,737 | $2,936,550 | $3,479,583 | $3,899,554 | $13,143,425 |
| Project net savings |  | ($247,000) | $669,608 | $1,039,270 | $1,513,143 | $2,231,397 | 5,206,418 |
| Management fee | 3% | $(7,410) | $(77,422) | $(88,097) | $(104,397) | $(116,987) | $(394,303) |
| Net savings |  | $(254,410) | 592,186 | $951,174 | $1,408,756 | $2,114,410 | $4,812,116 |

is realized. In this example, existing occupational health space was simply expanded to allow a wider range of treatment options.

The design of primary care can accommodate occupational medicine; however, an occupational medicine program cannot really accommodate true primary care. If one were to define primary care, the base concept would have to be the full-time dedication of the doctor to the whole patient that extends to the oversight of all aspects of care, including but not limited to prevention, diagnosis, treatment, follow-up, rehabilitation, and all of the custodial aspects of the medical record. Occupational medicine or work-site sickness and injury clinics are more focused on urgent and episodic care that produces a patient record that has to "find" the primary care physician.

The construct of an on-site program begins with primary care. This is a physician who can assume the role of the family doctor and who can inspire the confidence of the work force and their families to a point sufficient to assure that most employees will choose to seek care at the site and from the practitioners based there. This assumes that the site has all the features of a family practice, including access by phone, night call service, access to a full set of patient records, recall systems, relationships with local hospitals, etc. This is more than an urgent care center or a first aid station. It functions as the family doctor for most care given to the employees and their families.

The site can have the features of being "at the plant," but it must be visible and distinct from it to have an image of being a conveniently located doctor office rather than the office of the "company doctor." Branding is important because there is an expectation of service that is implied by one's own doctor and a different level of service that is implied by a doctor that the company might hire to see employees on-site. The brand must be either "manufactured" through artful promotion and informational campaigns, or a local physician with a strong base of support in the community should be recruited to the plant site to demonstrate to the employee base that the services are really high-quality primary care.

*Chapter 10*

# The Healthcare "Buy": Determine What to Purchase by First Figuring Out What Not to Purchase

## Channeling Saves Money

No matter what the scope of the on-site service is, there will still be a need to go to the marketplace and purchase services to augment the on-site practitioners. The more broadly defined the scope is, the less outside services must be purchased separately. This makes sense. However, there is an additional aspect of how the purchasing power of the firm might be applied and that is by coordinating the referral power of the on-site program so that the volume that is being sent to outside services is predictable and of a size and scale that is meaningful to the provider.

The on-site program is perfect for this purpose. The presence of the primary care provider, the information systems, and the power of the benefit design all combine to allow the firm to be able to predict that a certain component of the healthcare will be channeled, or steered, to a preselected and precontracted entity. This will not be a challenging thought when the issue is laboratory services or, perhaps, pharmacy, because these are commodities. They are impersonal and, in a way, apolitical. The challenge may be the idea that the same type of channeling can be done for specialty and hospital inpatient services.

The concept of "steering" a component of the care that is being projected to a certain provider or provider group is known as *direct contracting* for services. It is a concept that originated among the health maintenance organization (HMO) and managed care programs and is not new to hospitals or to most provider groups. It is generally not popular among physicians and hospitals, unless you are talking with a physician group or a hospital that has used this as a business concept themselves. The idea might sound like one that is inclusionary and positive, but the exclusionary aspect of it is so onerous that about half of all states have enacted "any willing provider" regulations. Those laws require contracting bodies to make provisions in their plans so that any provider who wishes to accept a patient at a pricing level that is negotiated or published by a payer can anticipate inclusion in the panel or listing of eligible practitioners for that health benefit plan. However, even this level of regulatory sanction can be overcome by a trusted primary care provider.

## The High-Performance Specialty Network

This component of the project goes by many names. It is a "narrow network" or a "select network," and it is probably defined by a group that is a subset of some other form of employee-wide, company-wide inclusive preferred provider organization (PPO) or managed care network of physicians and providers that has been precontracted to accept the employee benefits at a negotiated fee structure. The selection of a subset of providers is based on several criteria.

- Quality of the provider (reputation)
- Access protocols (priority) for the employer population
- Integration with the medical record system adopted by the on-site program
- Proven patient satisfaction
- Involvement (credentialing) on the medical staff of the select hospitals in the system
- Acceptable fee schedule
- Compliance with care management or other protocols
- Utilization of other sources related to the network, as defined by the primary care practitioners and other prearranged relationships

- Participation with imaging and diagnostic programs related to the select network
- Coordination of off-hours services with quality call coverage

The idea that this narrow network is all about "cost" misses key points related to access, value, and patient satisfaction. A case could be made that the specialist involved in this type of a program could actually be paid more if he or she assisted with ready access and monitored duplicative diagnostics and wasteful length of hospital stay. "Best practices" in this area could have a substantial positive effect on the projected cost savings or cost avoidance, and this feature is one that has significant impact, although only a modest projection has been offered as part of the overall program justification.

This component of the program could also be used for the employees and beneficiaries not electing primary care at the site, although this has not been counted toward any cost projections. The "capture" of patients in the primary care environment is the conduit to the "high-performance network" because the primary care physician (PCP) is the one that steers referrals and utilization of specialists and inpatient facilities; she can only do that if she is serving as the family physician.

## How to Find Specialists Who Are Really Special

Simple—ask the local doctors who are already providing primary care, and they will tell you. They can identify specialists who provide a higher level of consumer-oriented services and deliver referring physician and patient satisfaction. They can tell you who will get the patients in and served with a minimum of barriers and waiting.

There has to be a process to identify these doctors, and it must be credible and defensible. Four features to the selection process seem evident:

1. Identification of the appropriate sources of local information (to make sure there is credibility within the local provider community).
2. Agreement on the standards that will be used and the process to be employed for selection of a provider subset (to assure employees that this process is the same they would use in their own informed decision-making).

3. Collaboration and negotiation with select providers to gain buy-in from them on the standards that have been defined (and to achieve the best purchasing option for the company and their employees).
4. Final contracting with the specialists and establishment of bench-marking standards for continuous improvement and contract evaluation.

There are simple and complex ways to achieve this result. The simplest is to call together local providers and ask them which characteristics make for a good specialist (cardiologist, dermatologist, or whatever). Then, compile the information and describe the perfect type of specialty provider in some detail. Go out again to the provider community and ask which specialists demonstrate these characteristics. Contact the specialists and see if they are interested in a formal relationship.

If necessary and politically correct, many additional steps can be included. Ask employees for input. Source the providers from local healthcare institutions and lists of "thought leaders." Use quality referenced databases. Use information from pre-existing networks.

Whatever approach is used, the goal is not necessarily to find the "best in class," it is to construct a network that avoids the "worst in class." Often, just a simple additional review of the claims history can help a planner to understand which specialists are ordering too many tests or have a higher length of stay or a remarkable incidence of infection. Once the specialists are catalogued they must be categorized to determine if there are hospital relationships that define cost, quality, or access concerns.

After the specialists in each category are determined, meet with them to get them to define their own criteria for hospital inpatient services and for diagnostic and rehabilitation support. They can also help with the design of call patterns and their willingness to perform services on-site at the employer-based clinic.

This process will produce a short list of specialists along with awareness and sensitivity in the PCP community. It will also allow contracting to begin at the specialty level before the final determination of hospital or ancillary service preference is made. This will bring such issues to the forefront as the use of a formulary (for select pharmaceuticals), use of specific imaging, laboratory testing, etc. The discussions can also address the adoption of coordinated medical records, patient registration, and other protocols.

# Case and Care Management

The concept of case management is not new. Most managed care plans have a case manager who intervenes in an admission to perform some sort of secondary review and monitor the processes related to an illness to encourage efficient utilization of resources (or at least avoid waste, if possible). The care management function anticipated here is one that is "on-campus" and directed to support the employees and their beneficiaries. The difference is that the case manager is part of the team and corresponds directly with the primary care provider and the specialists in the high-performance network. The fact that the nurse (or physician's assistant or other health professional) is on-site and involved in only those cases and care processes allows specific input and direction to be shared with the patient and the direct involvement of the care team.

This approach is meant to be very involved and focused, and it moves a patient from provider to provider, especially in a surgical event or an admission, with precision and knowledge of the local resources available. It extends and supports primary care, and it becomes an ally to the hospitalized individual and an advocate for the person in need of care. Once it is established and it has a "face," the employees and their dependents will come to see it as a service and not any form of barrier to care. Whatever national or contracted disease-state management services are available will be complemented by this function and not replaced or diminished by it in any way. However, there may be a need for coordination if the two functions are both in receipt of potentially duplicative reports or communications. Also, these programs frequently depend upon hospital or emergency department notification of patient admission; this is a key event that has to be aggressively managed.

"Case" or "Care" Management?

- Case management
  - ➤ Economic in nature
  - ➤ Episodic
  - ➤ Nurses are oriented by site or by plan
  - ➤ Effectiveness gauged by ALOS or cost avoidance
  - ➤ Hands-off
  - ➤ Protocol-driven and illness-centered

- Care management
  - ➤ Oriented to patient
  - ➤ Nurses focused on patients and assigned to be an advocate
  - ➤ Hands-on
  - ➤ Outcomes and quality and access are stressed
  - ➤ Driven by common sense and the healing process

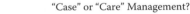

**Figure 10.1    This chart compares standard case management to care management. The coaching and concierge concepts build on personalization of the care management model.**

# Coaches, Concierges, and Consigliere

For the potential benefits associated with program change in the near-term savings projections, the care management model only factors in the on-site clinic, high-performance network, and the direct care management functions. In a similar fashion to the primary care cost analysis, rehabilitation and pharmacy services are included. Again, this is a simple "make or buy" reflection on what was spent and on what might have been saved had the model been in place for the program year referenced. The sensitivity of the model is generally twofold: How many people use the on-site facility and what level of adjustment is made for the care management and the use of the high-performance specialty network?

Improvements in the bottom line can be made most readily by adjusting the economics of the program to enhance selection of the on-site facility and strengthening the adherence to the predesigned network. Even further savings can result from the appropriate use of the predesigned network, but to do that a strong coaching and counseling process must be in place. Much is made of the idea of having care management available, and there are numerous disease-state management programs that use coaches to assist a patient in complying with their treatment protocols. Seldom are these programs as effective as those with designated and available on-duty personnel who are focused on the care management process that has been designed specifically to support the population being managed. This is perhaps a process of facilitation as much as one of medical supervision as anyone who has tried to get a specialist appointment might appreciate.

Coaching is a process of cajoling and urging a person to personally comply with a prescription or a process of some kind. Care management implies that there is some kind of coordination that a third party performs to enable the care of a patient who must navigate among many different choices. In case management, there is a specific orientation to the management of an incident (like an admission). We also want to recognize the term "concierge," which is a new adjective to describe some sort of support mechanism that uses a service process to foster a patient's well-being and sense of being well served as they navigate from laboratory testing to emergency room to admission to discharge.

Actually, these are all somewhat complementary and overlapping terms; and all of the coaching, counseling, and concierge services seem to fade when there is a sudden illness or injury. The patient needs access to a 24/7 locally staffed phone number that is a fulfillment and access point

**Figure 10.2   There are many opportunities to display photos of caregivers and medical equipment, but the most important and impressive technology that can be applied to patient care and intervention is personalized education. Here, a staff person at the newly opened Hewitt program in Chicago advises an employee on how to control cholesterol.**

for all services and is operated by the on-site team. This is not so much a concierge process as one that is at the level of the proverbial *consigliere*\*— a trusted advisor who can be counted on to not only advise but to assist in implementation. There is a partnership here and a level of mutual trust that works to move the patient through the proper steps in each decision-making process, no matter how complex or how simple.

The process is one of a patient or family member in need calling upon a person who has the access information immediately available and who has the power to make an appointment, provide needed information, issue a prescription, or arrange transportation. The phone number should be one

---

\* *Consigliere* is a term that is borrowed from the Mario Puzo book, *The Godfather*. This may be a fictional representation, but the term has come into common usage as a person with whom there is a covenant of mutual trust. The terms *coaching* and *counseling* just do not seem to reflect the strength of the terms needed when employees are being assisted by on-campus staff who know the design and the devices associated with the prearranged healthcare network that has been designed for their benefit.

that is exclusively for the use of the employees and their dependents, and the person who is in charge of the call should have access to the patient information required to assist immediately with the decisions that are to necessary to move within some kind of framework that answers the needs of the patient and their family but within guidelines that will foster effective healthcare utilization.

This process is not the old "gatekeeper" approach that limited care and prevented access, but a patient support and enablement program that encourages discussion and an understanding of whatever problem they are facing. The orientation is one that ensures that the tools that have been developed, including the specialist network and the selected hospital, are used if necessary and that other alternatives are considered when appropriate. The person answering the phone and doing the follow-up must be patient-centered and problem-focused. The attitude they should exude is "Yes, we can."

The person to whom this book is dedicated, Harry Quadracci, started his program with the key concept in mind that the healthcare program was there to be used by the employees of Quad/Graphics, not rationed by protocols that called for second opinions or other barriers to care. He initiated on-site employee support teams to assist employees in the choices they needed to make. His program would fit perfectly within a consumer-directed healthcare model because the consumer was empowered and supported by the staff in the Care Coordination office, not threatened by them. They were on-site so that they could articulate with the primary care providers and follow-up with other professionals who might have a stake in the patient support system. The goal, in Quadracci's mind, was to foster appropriate access by adding an element of consumer service combined with a knowledge base that was integral to the on-site program. At the same time, the employee had a fellow employee to guide them through everything from benefit utilization to hospital choice.

# Chapter 11

# Electronic Medical Records, Personal Electronic Health Records, the Medical Home, and the Medical Homeless

> Google's mission is to organize the world's information and make it universally accessible and useful.
>
> Microsoft's mission is to "Empower people through great software anytime, anyplace, and on any device."*

These two vision statements seem to delineate two separate initiatives: one that is dedicated to software and one that is oriented to the storage and retrieval of information. However, as anyone who uses the two companies is well aware, Google is embarking upon multiple software initiatives and Microsoft is warehousing data. Both compete along many lines, and each is backed by billions of dollars and busloads of talent. If only healthcare information could be "universally accessible" and available "anytime, anyplace, and on any device."

## The Patient-Centered Medical Home

Well-funded and talented corporations are entering the medical record and medical information warehousing business at a time when the idea of

---

* Appropriately, these two references were sourced from *Wikipedia Ask*, which also catalogues information and knowledge for consumer applications.

a medical record and how to use it is changing. It is fitting that employer managed healthcare and work on-site clinics are being redefined at the same time that a traditional idea on the source and use of medical information is being re-examined, refreshed, and rejuvenated. The concept of the Patient Centered Medical Home (PCMH) is being brought back from near extinction and used as a rationale for the rejuvenation of primary care. First introduced (or defined) by the American Academy of Pediatrics in 1967,* this is an idea that might seem to be a basic common sense application of medical information and knowledge but it is actually a key challenge that has eluded the healthcare delivery system for decades. Some say this is an elusive goal with little chance of ever being realized. It is the idea that one primary care practitioner would have at his or her disposal all of the information about a patient in a useful form and actually be connected to the patient through a recognition of some level of interdependence. It reflects the patient being responsible to the practitioner and vise-versa. It implies a team approach between doctor and patient supported by information technology and the information to go with it.

However, this is one of the good ideas in healthcare that has simply not seemed to catch on, although there is little doubt that electronic medical records are more effective at delivering high-quality healthcare than traditional paper records. If there is any kind of debate about this point, it is from healthcare providers who cannot use a keyboard. Even consumers realize and trust electronic recordkeeping and value the ability of an institution to aggregate data. The best example is banking, in which electronic bill payments and ATMs manage people's finances, regularly dispensing data summarizations that are accepted with little question or concern by the consumer. We have our credit scores and bank statements computerized, but not our prostate-specific antigen (PSAs) and cholesterol tests.

The problem is not that the hospitals and the doctors are unable to access electronic media. The bills and payment transmittals from most government agencies and insurance carriers have been transmitted electronically for years. Most of the laboratory and diagnostic equipment that is installed in a modern hospital or physician's office is digital and has the capability of transmitting

---

* The term "medical home" was first introduced by the American Academy of Pediatrics in 1967 in an attempt to organize the medical data and information about children who might be treated in several different environments. It has since been highlighted as a way to empower primary care physicians, and the present debate centers around how an electronic medical record (EMR) might be used in this process and how a practitioner might be paid for using this type of technology and the care that might be associated with it.

information by various transmission methods (including printing information on paper). The real problem is twofold: capital and inertia. It costs money to upgrade to electronic medical record (EMR) systems, and the present system is working okay, so why change? This resistance was overcome with billing and reimbursement for medical care when carriers (payers) began to request the transmittal of charges electronically. At first this was voluntary, and the only benefit to the provider was that the electronic claim would get paid fast and the paper claim would get paid slow. Eventually, there was additional financial differentiation, and most carriers now require electronic transmittal.

In over 80% of the doctor offices in the country, the physician writes the blood pressure on a *piece of paper* and gives the patient a *piece of paper* for a prescription, but his office staff transmit the charge for the patient visit *electronically* to an insurance company or other payment source. This seems silly, but it is also dangerous, because the practitioner can be standing within a few feet of important information about a patient's condition and writing a script for medication while the data on which they might rely to give a more accurate dosage are buried in a paper chart or lost on a desk or in an in basket underneath a fax machine. There is plenty of information available about the patient, it is just presently inaccessible, disorganized, or warehoused somewhere that is protected and secure from both the patient and their doctor.

If one reflects on medical information and its limitations, the definition of a "silo" is soon encountered. A silo is a source of information that is in one place and is unique, independent, and unconnected. In the case of medical data, it exists when the hospital does one procedure, the doctor does another, and each stores the medical information in their own database. Protected there by regulatory standards, tradition, and simply by functional access barriers, the information exists in a form that is disarticulate and only useful to the patient on the next encounter at that particular site. The data are in a silo, so to speak.

The challenge is multiplied when healthcare information becomes personalized with home medical tests, visits to retail outlets, specialists visits, storefront inoculations, emergency room (ER) encounters, changes in physician personnel, etc. Pediatricians encountered this problem with their patient bases early and noted it was a special challenge as kids moved from place to place and practice to practice. Children of migrant families could be seen over a one-year period in various geographic settings, and each encounter would produce a new medical record. Social agencies mounted programs to connect the pediatric patients from office to office as they migrated around the country and accessed healthcare. The idea was that the key to the information was patient-, not physician-, centric.

## Medical Records and Medical Information

The reason that Google and Microsoft are racing to channel medical data into vast storehouses and to augment medical record technology is not entirely altruistic. The result of having billions of bits of medical data means that the company that controls it also has a database of medical information. This can be used for channeling data to health service enterprises, pharmaceutical companies, retail organizations, etc. It can also be coupled with payment information to develop profiles of cost and demographic spending patterns. Google has already demonstrated that information linked to a mapping program can track outbreaks of influenza.* This is an application of collective information gathering from Web activity that was initially collected for one purpose but ultimately used for an entirely different one.

In reality, the information becomes a valuable resource for whoever can catalogue it and put it into a practical use. Predicting the flu and its likely spread seems to be a good public use. Packaging and promoting commercial products for a population that is likely to be introduced to them in a Web search may or may not be a productive public use, but it could be one that has great commercial value.

## The Convergence of the Medical Record, the Personal Health Record, and the Medical Home

In Zambia, what one might consider to be a developing country, the medical record used in rural health clinics is a simple student examination booklet that follows a patient from clinic to clinic and from clinic to hospital, if necessary. Every patient event is recorded in a time-linear fashion. Simple and elegant, the children in Zambia sometimes have a more complete medical record or medical history to present to a doctor than a child in the United States might be able to access who had been inoculated at a health department, seen in a retail clinic, and admitted to a hospital. Quality of care and access to a specialist is one advantage in the United States, but improved medical information integration is not.

---

* As reported in the *New York Times* on November 11, 2008, http://www.google.org/flutrends/ uses consumer inquiries as a proxy for influenza "interest" with the logic that people do not inquire about flu symptoms unless they are having them. Thus, keyword searches in a Web tool such as Google can act as sort of an early warning sign for the spread of a disease. (Miguel Helft. "Google Uses Searches to Track Flu's Spread," http://www.nytimes.com/2008/11/12/technology/internet/12flu.html)

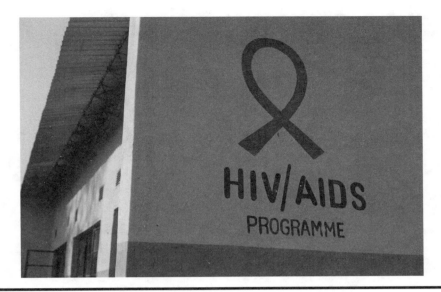

**Figure 11.1    This is the site of a rural healthcare operation in a remote region in Zambia. The site has no running water and only a dozen or so medications. However, each patient has a unique medical history and a record that is transferred with them as they move from one site of care to the next.**

This rural clinic in Zambia does not have running water or a doctor, but it does have a unique medical record that encompasses all of the information on each patient for his or her entire life that is rustic but it is portable across the healthcare system. The healthcare system uses paper notebooks that follow a patient from site to site with all of the medical notes in one place, accessible to any provider. We might think this is crude and backward, but this is the embodiment of the PCMH with all of the information in one place and available at the patient site of care.

What is the barrier? The national organizations that are trying to institutionalize the idea of an EMR are pushing through a bureaucracy that was 100 years in the making. The question seems to be where the control of medical information and its distribution should reside: At the hospital level, the physician level, or at the level of some coordinating body such as an insurance company or government agency? Few thought leaders had ever dared dream that the amalgamation of all patient data might actually be accomplished at the patient level where it could be "assigned" whenever a patient needed it. However, this may be the pattern that emerges as the Web meets the patient record and the patients become more empowered by technology and the growth of massive storage options.

**Figure 11.2   The Cerner Healthe Clinic actually focuses the practitioner and the patient on the medical record as a part of the visit. One part of the patient treatment area, shown here, is a setting that allows the EMR to be displayed for the practitioner and the patient to interact with the medical information available on a large flat screen display.**

## Employers Are the Solution

Just as the employers are solving issues that have arisen with primary care and specialty networks by developing an on-site focus, they can also address the medical information issue. The key is to understand and grasp the basics of the issue and ignore the background noise. The simple way is to deploy an EMR and force coordination through the use of reimbursement incentives with supportive specialists and hospitals.

The PCMH defines the "best in class" approach to a medical record and the following principles define a Medical Home (abbreviated from the literature)[*]:

- The patient has one medical record and it is under the watchful eye of a primary care physician.
- The medical record contains all of the information necessary and pertinent to the management of the individual's health.

---

[*] For the best discussion of the PCMH, the reader is directed to the following position paper: American Academy of Family Physicians, American Academy of Pediatrics, American College of Physicians, American Osteopathic Association. "Joint Principles of the Patient-Centered Medical Home." http://www.medicalhomeinfo.org/Joint%20Statement.pdf.

■ The medical record is compliant with all regulatory standards related to confidentiality and it is patient accessible.

Simply put, the employer should use EMR technology and require any vendor, supplier, specialist, or hospital that wishes to interact with its primary care unit to comply with this requirement and articulate its system with that adopted by the self-funded employer. A simple statement should be added to any contract that will require the choice of an appropriate medical record

**Figure 11.3    As some providers and hospitals in Milwaukee continue to struggle with an EMR, the local printing giant Quad/Graphics has actually completed their second installation of EMRs. On the other side of the wall from this modern printing and manufacturing environment, providers share medical information in a modern health record format that would rival that found in any hospital.**

and, if the site is going to be managed by a vendor, there must be the direction to that vendor to ensure that all resources are linked to the EMR.

It is interesting to note that this is an area where on-site vendors are actually moving more quickly to ensure electronic record keeping than healthcare systems are. The advent of the national healthcare "transformation" may change this process, but with each employer program and with giants like Microsoft and Google promoting medical information consolidation, the trend is obvious and the employer, as the payer, should insist on being part of the process.

*Chapter 12*

# Legal Issues: Contracting and Regulatory Challenges

In a chapter that deals with regulation and legal issues, it is tempting to quote Shakespeare: "The first thing we do, let's kill all the lawyers."\* Actually, the trick is to get rid of the right ones and to keep the ones that can actually help. The problem is that the concept of an on-site clinic combines medical, ERISA (Employee Retirement and Income Security Act), employee relations, real estate, contract law, and benefits issues into one project. It is further complicated by the fact that so many of the regulations are at the state level, and they are overlaid and confused, in some cases by the national legislative and rule-making process.

The solution is to break down the problem into smaller pieces and to address them one at a time. Hopefully, this chapter can assist with that process.

## Legal Tasks Are Twofold: Risk Prevention and Contract Development

During any initial review of the provision of on-site health services, there will be two legal channels that need to be addressed. One is regulatory, and the other is contractual. In one case, the attorneys will be asked if they can ensure, or design a structure that can ensure, a program that does not raise

---

\* *Henry VI*, Part II, Act IV, Scene II.

any potential risk for the firm. If they perceive some level of risk, they will be asked to minimize it. They will then turn to contracting with insurance carriers, third-party managers, hospitals, managed care organizations, and others to provide a legal framework for the program and one that ensures not only minimal risk but optimal performance.

In many companies the in-house counsel is the major barrier to implementing on-site health services. It is simply an issue of familiarity and comfort. The counselors who staff America's corporations are among the best in the world but also among the most conservative and cautious. They sometimes can quote volumes on U.S. Environmental Protection Agency (EPA) regulations or labor relations but know very little about healthcare and its nuances. There is even more confusion about on-site healthcare services because each state has its own regulatory environment, and a firm that is embarking upon a national strategy will find itself faced with state as well as national legal hurdles. Healthcare is pretty basic, in and of itself, but healthcare law is neither simple nor is it intuitive.

Many planners organize their efforts around financial analysis and return on investment (ROI), some address important health status issues. But any plan to move forward with on-site health services, and all that they entail, must include a legal framework. The chief legal counsel has to be considered to be as important as the chief financial officer (CFO) and the chief medical officer. The bottom line for the CFO is the bottom line. The bottom line for a legal sign-off is the control of risk, and to quantify risk, it has to be carefully described, quantified, and, when possible, insured.

Doctors, hospitals, and health maintenance organizations (HMOs) address this matter and understand the implications well. They are in a community of risk-takers. Not so with the standard corporate counsel. They are generally skilled in the direct discipline of their industry, but they may need to be connected with a healthcare attorney familiar with the concept of ambulatory care, on-site clinics, and workplace-related medicine. They also need to develop a comfort level with the reassignment of risk through malpractice insurance and contract clauses that address indemnification and other risk transference mechanisms.

Another way that the firm can move forward with some level of confidence (regarding risk, at least) is to utilize a third-party vendor to provide the on-site services and the general organization of the program. This is a company that can set the program up and act as a surrogate in the provision of services as well as shoulder any legal risks associated with the program. However, the use of a vendor does not mean that the contracting entity can ignore the legal issues. Rather, the problem then becomes how the engagement contract is written to ensure that the selected vendor firm is properly charged with the responsibilities that come with the on-site programming.

We are talking about a set of contracts and a clear definition of responsibilities for the vendor. This is beyond just a recitation of representations and warranties in a standard service contract. Although there is some level of insulation, the way that the service will be provided and the standards of provision have to be described in a contract that outlines responsibility for assurances (as well as a bunch or "insurances") that can satisfy corporate counsel.

The purpose of this chapter is to try to provide a list of legal issues and some guidance as to how the on-site development team might address them. This is not legal advice as much as it is a directive to the reader to get legal advice early in the process and to work with in-house counsel to assist with the programming changes. Hopefully the legal team can become an enabling and constructive part of the team rather than a barrier to execution.

## Start with Structure and Planning Principles

Just as "form follows function" in architecture, the legal form of an on-site health program has to be defined once the business entity determines what it wants to do and how expansive it will be with benefit redesign and service provision. It is critical before engaging counsel (internal or external) to be able to describe the desired outcome and what services and programs are being contemplated. Checklists abound in other parts of this book, but there are some basic questions that should be addressed in the early planning stages before engaging a dialogue with counsel.

- What services will be provided on-site? A simple listing is a start.
- How will workers' compensation and work-related injury issues be addressed?
- Will a vendor be selected to administer the program, will the firm go it alone, or will it partner with a local healthcare provider?
- Which employee and dependent classes will be afforded care at the site (or through the program)?

■ Will there be a value-based contracting process (narrow network or selective specialty and hospital panel)?

■ Will the benefits program be modified to encourage utilization?

Once the program is defined, there is generally development of a document that describes the standards and the scope of work, or deliverables. This might include factors like contract term, a description of services to be provided, and the nature of the form of any relationship. Most of the terms can be found in a provider contract, and there are a couple of ways of learning what is standard for the industry. Consultants are one approach and the use of a request for information (RFI) is another. There is no standard contract that is being used in the industry today, and the choices of working independently, working through a vendor, or working with a local healthcare provider will define how the contract development will take shape.

## Regulatory, Licensure, and Accreditation Issues Go Hand-in-Hand

The issues seem daunting, but—like any project—they are less of an issue when one realizes that others have faced them before and most healthcare and benefits attorneys are from a school used to solving problems and creating business models. That encouragement noted, the following list of regulatory and licensure issues will need to be addressed.[*]

First, it is necessary to recognize that this is both a state and national issue. In each state, there is a set of codes that define the scope of practice that is commonly referred to collectively as healthcare. Each state addresses the licensure of healthcare facilities and any prohibitions against the corporate practice of medicine (or pharmacy, optometry, dentistry, chiropractic, etc.). These laws will dictate the structure under which the healthcare services may be provided. In general, an employer will need to provide healthcare services through employed physicians, a licensed primary care center, or some combination of both. In the case of other medical providers (i.e., physical therapists), they may be also covered

---

[*] I am indebted to Michael J. Taubin, Esq. for assistance with this section. Much of this material was originally included in a white paper developed by him for the original Symposium on Employer Managed Healthcare and On-Site Clinics, which convened in Chicago in 2004, and which has since been updated regularly. Legal counsel should be obtained from lawyers who feel competent in this complex arena of healthcare, employee benefits, and contract law.

under their own unique statutes or the state laws may include them in a generic fashion as "doctors and practitioners."

## Corporate Practice of Medicine

Many states prohibit for-profit business corporations from providing medical services through employed physicians. This prohibition stems from a concern that general business corporations are not qualified to deliver a professional medical service. In addition, there is concern that were a physician to have a financial relationship with a business corporation, the physician's professional judgment may be affected by such financial interest. Instead, in most states, only licensed professionals working through either a professional corporation or an entity licensed under the state's health laws can deliver medical care. Of course, corporations practice medicine all of the time. Think HMOs, hospitals, clinics, group practices, etc. Look at any advertisement for "laser vision" or for weight-loss reduction surgery, or think of Walgreens and Wal-Mart and their on-site medical services. Obviously, there are ways that the corporate practice of medicine issue can be addressed and the issue resolved.

It should be noted that there may be exceptions in particular states for business corporations that are only providing healthcare services to its own employees and their dependents and not the general public. If this is not the case, a corporation owned by physicians can be contracted for services. A vendor group that already "owns" a corporate structure can be contracted to provide care. The real ownership in many of these structures does reside with a physician, but the actual control of the business functions are contracted in a way that allows an on-site program to act, in a sense, like a corporation. However, the spirit behind the law is never compromised. If the law was intended to ensure quality and service regardless of business limitations, this is not minimized and often the firms who are developing on-site services contractually guarantee a higher standard.

## Licensure

If a broad range of services is being provided, the operation of an on-site primary care center may require separate licensure under various state health laws. Any employer who is interested in establishing an employer managed healthcare system must first address the definition and form relating to the corporate practice of medicine and then ensure that licensure statutes are addressed and managed. The reach of these state licensure laws might be very broad, and they may cover individual services such as physical therapy, pharmacy, laboratory, and radiology services. There are licenses within these licensing categories. For example, if there are procedures or tests that use an isotope of some kind for imaging, a separate license will be required just to handle and store the nuclear material. Taken singly, none of these licensing requirements should stall a project, but the list is definitely one that needs oversight and to which an employer must address themselves or which must be ensured through a subcontract with a vendor.

Some requirements may be imposed by state statute that will relate only to licensed healthcare professionals. These are listed as examples that may need to be part of the planning and contracting process.

- *Separate entity incorporation:* The licensed entity may need to be separately incorporated. The entity will need to have a governing body, bylaws, and meetings, etc.
- *Specific policies and procedures:* Many states require the development of very specific policies and procedures governing everything from patients' rights to transfer of patients. Other policies may address reporting requirements, referrals, patient complaints, security, and standards for the maintenance of equipment, among others.
- *Appointment of a medical director and administrator:* Many states require licensed facilities to employ a named medical director and to define how governance is organized and how the site is administered.
- *Policies and procedures regarding personnel:* The state licensure laws may require very specific human resources policies, which may dictate credentialing standards, pre-employment health testing, background checks, etc.
- *Medical records maintenance and policy:* The state licensure law may hold the primary care center to very specific standards relating to medical records maintenance. These standards include retention periods, types of records that need to be maintained, and access. These state laws need to be reviewed carefully against federal Health Insurance Portability and Accountability Act (HIPAA) requirements.

- *Development of quality assurance (QA) program:* State licensure laws frequently dictate the development of a formal QA program as a planned and systematic process for monitoring and assessing the quality and appropriateness of patient care and clinical performance on an ongoing basis. Such programs may include, among other things, the formation of a committee to regularly review outcomes, incident reporting obligations, regular review of medical charts and patient complaints, and implementation of corrective actions.
- *Construction requirements:* State licensure laws may also define healthcare facility construction requirements. State laws may dictate the size of rooms, materials to be used, electrical requirements, etc.
- *Ancillary services and Certificate of Need (CON):* Services such as laboratory and radiology licensing usually have their own regulatory standards, but if an employer is considering the inclusion of sophisticated and costly diagnostic imaging equipment and services [e.g., magnetic resonance imaging (MRI) and computed tomography (CT) scans] in the health center, attention should be given to state regulations that may mandate state approval of the acquisition itself. These regulations are often part of a health planning code that might require a CON before the purchase of any capital item over a certain dollar threshold amount. In some cases, the development of on-site procedural capabilities may also require CON approval.
- *Biomedical waste:* There are specific federal, state, and local laws and regulations regarding the handling of biomedical waste. Compliance with these laws and regulations requires the establishment of mandatory policies and procedures for all healthcare personnel in the primary care center. There is also the requirement to contract with vendors who are in compliance with the same regulations.

## Healthcare Privacy and Confidentiality Laws

This is an area of regulation that might actually work for an employer in that it can be used to assure employees that medical information is not being co-opted in a fashion that allows the employer to access or use personal healthcare data. When an employer expands its traditional employer role into that of healthcare provider for its employees or into an insurer of health benefits, the employer is obligated to abide by the complex federal and state laws governing medical information privacy. The employee/patient has some pretty tough laws on their side.

**Figure 12.1    At Briggs and Stratton in Milwaukee, there is a high degree of separation between the company and the information in the health program. They brand the clinic site carefully to stress that it is managed by an outside provider and they even contract with an outside cleaning firm, rather than company janitorial staff, to keep the premises off-limits to people from the firm and to keep personal healthcare information secure.**

## The Health Insurance Portability and Accountability Act (HIPAA) of 1996

HIPAA is the most formidable of these regulations. Implemented in April 2003, it changed the realm of medical information confidentiality dramatically. HIPAA established a national standard for the privacy and confidentiality of medical information, expanding on a patchwork of inconsistent state confidentiality laws. For consumers of healthcare services, the HIPAA privacy rules offer patients broad access rights and confidentiality protections. For providers of healthcare services, insurers, and health plans ("HIPAA Covered Entities"), HIPAA compliance presents a significant and often costly challenge. When an employer becomes a HIPAA Covered Entity (by providing health services to its employees or by maintaining a self-insured health benefit plan), it will need to demonstrate full compliance just as any other provider.

Compliance will include the designation of a specific privacy officer, development and maintenance of written privacy policies and procedures, provision of initial and ongoing privacy training to persons handling protected health information, establishment of safeguards to protect against improper disclosures of information, and the development of a formal complaint resolution mechanism.

The regulations are very specific as to the development of "firewalls" between the health service site, the plan, the employer, and any other person who might come into contact with sensitive information. All of this requires the maintenance of records and material that documents self-compliance and establishes a formal notification process that informs patients that there are privacy practices in place and how they can access the privacy officer and file confidential grievances, if the need arises.

## State Confidentiality Laws and Special Circumstances

State confidentiality lays and special circumstances may exceed the federal HIPAA requirements, and, where they do, the more stringent regulations must be followed. Certain categories of patients with disabilities and with mental health or substance dependency or HIV/AIDS have special requirements related to how their information is handled and with whom it may be shared.

# Perception of Confidentiality

Beyond the legal requirement governing the confidentiality of health information, the employer will want to keep confidentiality in mind in the physical design and operations of the center. If the center will have a wellness program and exercise areas, those areas should be kept physically separate from the clinical care activities of the primary care center. The center may also wish to have several smaller waiting rooms, rather than one larger area, so that co-workers have limited ability to see one another when they are waiting for their appointment. Appointments should be scheduled to minimize employee contact with other employees and their managers and supervisors. This may also be accomplished by prohibiting management from entry into certain clinical and waiting areas of the primary care center at designated times.

At Briggs and Stratton, the perception of confidentiality extends even to the housekeeping function. They contract with an outside service for the provision of medical staff and they also contract with an independent cleaning service to assure employees that all of the medical service functions have a firewall that is respectful of employee and patient confidentiality.[1]

## Provider Network Development and Contracting

An employer needs to decide how to handle arrangements for healthcare services not provided on-site at the primary care center. These services will include hospitals, specialists, nursing homes, home health agencies, etc. The two approaches an employer can use are direct contracting and purchasing network support services from an existing vendor (third-party administrator, or TPA).

Whether the contract process is direct or through a TPA, the following issues need to be addressed:

- Specifically, what services will be provided?
- Will there be special rates, benefit designs, referral management policies, or other policies created by the employer? (*Hint:* The answer should be "Yes!")
- What performance guarantees/representations will be expected? These might include issues such as claims processing accuracy and timeliness, structure of the provider network, access standards, compliance with benefit design restrictions, etc.
- How will employee complaints and grievances be addressed and resolved?
- What reports and data will be provided to the employer, at what intervals, and in what form?
- How will utilization review and referral management activities be handled?

In the contract form, there should be provisions that set forth the economic terms* agreed to by the parties and several other important provisions relating to the maintenance of all applicable state and federal licenses, registrations,

---

* If the employer shifts insurance risk to the healthcare on-site provider through the contract payment rate (e.g., capitation payments, or target budget arrangements that are becoming more popular among vendors), the provider may be subject to state oversight, and the arrangement may require certain licenses/registrations even though the provider is only contracting with an ERISA-covered self-insured employer.

and certifications necessary to provide the services. The subcontracted entity must accept the payment terms required by the agreement and provide all necessary and appropriate care to employees regardless of whether employer's benefit design pays for such care.* The employer will require that the subcontractor maintain appropriate amounts of malpractice insurance and provide data on health services delivered to employer (or to an entity designated by the employer) in a manner consistent with laws regarding the confidentiality of medical information.

Assuming that accreditation is an eventual goal for the on-site program, the contract will generally require that the providers and subcontracted entities participate in that process and assist with all quality initiatives required by the employer, even when imposed by outside agencies. Contracts with providers ensure participation in disease management or case management initiatives of the employer and compliance with policies and procedures adopted as part of employer's benefit plan and contracting program.

## State Regulatory Network Contracting Considerations

Counsel for the employer must consider whether the project triggers state licensure or registration requirements. In some states, merely arranging for healthcare services can require licensure or registration with a state agency. In other states, an employer's direct provider contracting efforts may need limited registration of some sort. A review of the applicable state law is needed to determine what role, if any, the employer can play in creating a provider network without violating onerous state licensure laws.

Almost half of the states have laws prohibiting health insurers from excluding participation of willing and qualified healthcare providers in their geographic coverage areas. These are known as "any willing provider" statutes and they are meant to allow the doctors and providers to contract without restriction (except the participation in a fee schedule). Although most provisions are limited to pharmacies or pharmacists, several states have adopted broad provisions pointing to hospitals, physicians, chiropractors, pharmacists, podiatrists, therapists, and nurses. These any-willing-provider

---

* To minimize liability for the employer, the provider contract should clearly state that the provider is independent of employer and that the provider, not the employer, will be legally responsible within the provider/patient relationship for providing appropriate care regardless of the employer's payments or other policies.

laws require health insurers (and perhaps those that pay directly for health services) to enter into service contracts with healthcare providers who practice within the general geographic area and who are willing to meet the terms and conditions set forth by the insurer. Consideration of the applicability of the any willing provider regulation in a particular state to a self-funded employer utilizing a TPA provider network or direct contracting should be analyzed before beginning the contracting process and selection of providers.

## Liability and Exposure to Liability

In establishing on-site primary care centers and by directly contracting for specialty and inpatient services, employers may face new risk issues based on various potential legal issues. Employers should carefully analyze these liability risks under the tort laws of any state where they are planning to develop an on-site primary care center and related programming. This is a problem, but not one that is insurmountable. The firm can take several steps to minimize the liability risk. They include the following:

■ Structure the primary care center organization, to the extent possible, to insulate the employer's main business enterprise from any liability that may flow from the operation of the center.
■ Make sure that each entity and each provider has an acceptable medical malpractice history, current coverage, and limits.
■ Seek contractual indemnification in any circumstance in which it might be available to the primary care center entity and/or the employer.
■ Obtain liability insurance to cover any transfer of risk that can be identified and insured.
■ Implement effective risk management and quality improvement programs.
■ Seek and fulfill accreditation requirements that are appropriate for the services being performed.

This is where an attorney with a background in healthcare law in the particular state in which the services are being provided can help. There will be questions about the structuring of the on-site primary care center and various related matters. The center will be a provider of healthcare services and therefore could be potentially liable for the care received by the employees and their families. Hospitals, medical groups, and other providers address such liability with every patient encounter, and there are generally a set of standards in each healthcare environment that have been used to minimize and localize this risk.

This is also where some employers consider the use of an outside vendor to further shield them from risks that they cannot easily quantify. Whether the employer elects to structure the primary care service as an independent legal entity or contract with a third party, it is important to have contracts that obtain indemnification provisions and insurance binders that cover every aspect of care and all of the parties involved. It is equally important that the primary care center actually be operated on a day-to-day basis in a manner that is consistent with its independent status to minimize the possibility of a plaintiff successfully arguing the employer and the center are effectively one and the same for liability purposes.

Counsel will also probably advise that any indemnification clause be as broad as can be negotiated with respect to potential liabilities and that such clauses include an obligation to defend the center and/or the employer because the expense costs of defending even meritless lawsuits are often substantial.

Insurance professionals, or counsel with specific knowledge of insurance matters, should be engaged to explore the insurance options and to recommend a comprehensive program that provides the center and the employer with the appropriate coverage. Not only should the insurance program cover standard matters such as medical malpractice and general liability, it also should provide protection from unique claims like negligent credentialing or other novel theories that might be advanced by creative plaintiff's attorneys.

## Labor Impact

The most significant hurdle an employer with one or more union contracts must overcome is negotiating with the collective bargaining representatives over the conversion of a benefit program to include an on-site provider of healthcare services. This is a new healthcare benefit offered by the employer, and the details of its impact on union members and the collective bargaining agreement must be analyzed. Many programs across the nation have addressed this challenge, and their on-site services have been widely accepted as a program addition, not a limitation. However, each site is unique, and each union experience is one that has a "back story" that may have an effect on implementation. Start by looking at the contract and meeting with the union representatives. It is probably as important to include them in the initial planning than it is to include labor counsel.

The other matter that is unique to a workforce and defined on a state-by-state basis is occupational medicine as a clinical service in the primary care center. Specific attention to state laws and regulations regarding workers' compensation and any requirements for a third-party medical assessment should be part of any program planning, and legal counsel must pass judgment on whether this specific component of care is structured properly. The twin challenges faced by programs that incorporate occupational health events will be record-keeping and the creation of a track for employees to seek care for their worker compensation matters from appropriately credentialed providers.

## Plan Design

An employer establishing an on-site primary care center and direct contracting for specialty and inpatient services will be sponsoring a self-funded health plan under ERISA and the Internal Revenue Code. The plan must be structured to comply with the numerous requirements of ERISA and the Code. The program will have to comply with ERISA's benefit mandates, nondiscrimination rules, claims procedures, and other requirements. Employers should not find complying with these rules to be problematic because all self-funded health plans must already be in compliance under their current plan.

Plan sponsors will also have to decide how they would like to fund the plan. Many employers elect to establish a trust, such as a Voluntary Employee Beneficiary Association (VEBA), to hold employer and employee contributions that pay for plan benefits. ERISA requires that plan assets be used exclusively to provide benefits and pay for reasonable administrative expenses. Additionally, ERISA sets forth so-called "prohibited transaction" rules that prevent a fiduciary from using plan assets for the fiduciary's own benefit. An exception to these rules allows a plan to reimburse a plan sponsor for direct expenses properly and actually incurred in the performance of plan services. Accordingly, if an employer wants to charge its plan for the costs of providing an on-site clinic, it will have to be careful to ensure that the reimbursement complies with ERISA's prohibited transaction rules. These rules can be avoided by having the employer directly pay these costs and by not seeking reimbursement from the plan.

Finally, employers will have to consider how best to incorporate the new plan into its existing healthcare alternatives. For example, will the new plan be the sole medical plan offered to employees or will employees choose from an array of plans that includes the on-site service and related services as well as an indemnity, preferred provider organization (PPO), or HMO plan? What rates will employees be charged to participate in the new plan versus other plans? Although these questions do not necessarily raise legal issues, they do raise important policy questions that might affect employees and the way that plan documents must be drafted.

## Compliance Programs

Every healthcare provider of any substance must have in place a system for preventing, detecting, and correcting practices or procedures that do not comply with the complex and confusing laws governing the provision of healthcare services. The Department of Health and Human Services' Office of Inspector General has published guidelines for the development of compliance programs to address this issue. Compliance begins with the establishment of a written plan.

There are seven basic elements to any compliance plan.

1. Designation of a compliance officer and compliance committee
2. Development of written policies and procedures
3. Development of open lines of communication
4. Appropriate training and education
5. Internal monitoring and auditing
6. Response to detected deficiencies
7. Enforcement of disciplinary standards

Self-funded employers operating a primary care center and providing specialty and hospital services through direct contracting should develop an internal compliance program and plan to implement effective internal controls that promote adherence to applicable federal, state, and local laws. They should also direct their subcontractors to initiate and publish plans of their own.

# Vendor Contracting for the Provision of On-Site Services

Vendor firms, many of which are included in the appendices to this book, are well equipped and experienced in the handling of the factors listed in the previous section. The listing that was offered in this chapter, if the decision is to move in the direction of a third-party manager, can simply be incorporated into the service contract and defined by the legal team as the responsibility of the vendor. Legal counsel for the firm will include representations, warranties, and indemnifications that define the transfer of liability away from the employer, and many of the vendor standard contracts already address these issues.

The other side of the legal challenge is to define the terms and conditions under which the services will be rendered. The conditions of engagement, the scope of work, the provision of special services, and the pricing will all be delineated. No regulations, state or federal, will guide this part of the process. The vendors are the ones who have an advantage here because they do this type of contract negotiation on a routine basis. This section is intended as a guide for the firm so that they can consider what they might wish to include as part of the process of ensuring that their employees and their beneficiaries receive the full benefit of the program they are trying to implement. Regrettably, most vendors have their own standard contract form. Many firms have purchasing standards that have been defined and refined over decades of negotiation with subcontractors. Hopefully some of these issues can be defined as these standards are combined in a final operating agreement.

- *Contract length of term* should be long enough for the vendor to be assured of amortizing its fixed costs but with a period that allows for re-evaluation and revision. One year is too limiting, and anything over five years is too long. Provisions within the agreement should allow for cancellation if there is a material breach (failure to perform, failure to respond to complaints, failure to achieve stated goals, etc.).
- *Contract transitional issues* should be spelled out in fine detail. This should include the ownership (or the transfer of ownership) of supplies, licenses, equipment, service contracts, etc. There is a potential problem in canceling any agreement if the employer is held hostage by a vendor that owns the material and key process items necessary for an on-site program to continue after they are no longer employed as the manager.

- *Personnel and personnel files* should be transferable. There should not be any restriction, restrictive covenants, or noncompete agreements that bind the service staff component of the on-site programming (this is especially important for the professional staff). A lot of effort will have gone into binding the employees with the providers, and any change in management should allow for the continuation of service from one provider to another or from a managed program to one that is internally managed or employer self-managed. This means that there must be guaranteed access to employee lists and a way to transition employees from any status that ties him/her to the vendor to an alternate status that supports whatever form of transition might be called for under a potential organizational change. Otherwise, a firm that wants to end a contract may be held hostage by issues beyond their control.
- *Intellectual property rights* must be defined. The employer should have access to, or own, any of the materials that are associated with the program and the instructions that employees have been given. These materials can be educational material, signage, phone numbers, brochures, advisories, protocols, patient information kits, or whatever has appeared in writing (in whatever form) to assist the employee or patient in their healthcare process. Web addresses, URLs, Internet subscriptions, and licenses need to be part of this discussion.

In summary, there is no one contract form that is generic for these programs. The employer should establish the principles of the program and then define the contract standards. It should not be swayed by a firm that is employing a "standard agreement."

# Reference

1. Interview conducted with Jeff Mahloch, Vice President of Human Resources at Briggs and Stratton, September 9, 2008.

# Chapter 13

# Working with Hospitals Rather than against Them

## If You Have Seen One Hospital, You Have Seen One Hospital

Hospitals and local health systems can represent a challenge for a firm considering an on-site strategy. They contain all of the elements necessary for a program to be constructed but most of the parts are in disarray. Few hospitals have developed systems that emulate what an employer might need to fashion the type of programming described in this text, but most health systems *could*, if they had the political will and the vision to do so. The problem for a firm is to differentiate the healthcare system with which they are working as one that can contribute and complement their program or as one that needs to be dealt with on an arm's length basis.

It all depends on the hospital. Some health systems around the country are pursuing partnerships with local employers to implement on-site programming, and many hospitals have the will and the tools to do so. The challenge is to distinguish between the "desire" of the health system and its actual capabilities as the firm moves forward with programming because there are many areas of opportunity for articulation with local health systems and an on-site project cannot ignore the need to work with them.

This chapter attempts to categorize these opportunities and define what might be required of a health system to further the goals of an employer managed system. However, many health systems might desire an opportunity to manage the whole enterprise and enter into an arrangement with the employer to fully staff and organize the on-site program. This means that the hospital would be the on-site provider and contract for all clinical services. Several examples of successful programs can be found as models, and several more are in the process of being developed. However, in the appendix, there is only one hospital system listed as a formal provider because it is the only healthcare system that we could identify that was providing service outside of their immediate regional area. That system is the one run by Edward Bernacki, MD, at Johns Hopkins. Another program that has gained national attention is the one that is being developed by the Henry Ford Health System in conjunction with Chrysler. As of this printing,

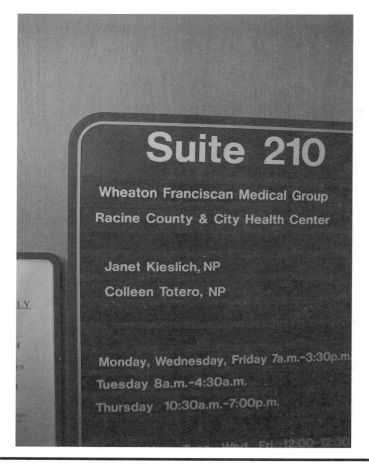

**Figure 13.1    The All Saints Health System, a part of the Wheaton Franciscan organization, offers some care through dedicated clinic space on its own campus. Here, the employees can see their provider at the hospital medical office building, but there is no question about the dedication of the programming. All Saints also operates other employer-based sites.**

the program is not fully operational, but the principles being applied will encompass many of the features defined in this book and it could become a model for other Detroit-area industrial programs if it proves successful.

On a more modest scale, the Wheaton Franciscan Program provides services for firms in the Racine, WI, area, and they have also recently added specialized clinics for the city and the county of Racine. The on-site example that they manage at the InSinkErator Corporation is the classic on-premises model, whereas the city and county program services are provided through a site on the hospital campus. The Wheaton Franciscan Program is unique in that it focuses on the employer and their employees and beneficiaries, and it organizes healthcare around the population rather than being oriented to having each patient access services only provided at the hospital site.

In the longest running nationally recognized program, the Covenant Health Care System (in Milwaukee) has traditionally partnered with the Quad/ Graphics Corporation to develop QuadMed, Inc., the provider organization that has been serving their employees and dependents for almost 20 years.

**Figure 13.2    There is more than one way to work with a hospital, and some hospitals realize there is more than one way to work with employers. Here, the same hospital system that provides care on its own site to the Racine county and city employees demonstrates that it can also provide the care on-site at the plant.**

However, in this example, the Covenant services are more in the traditional hospital role of providing contracted in-hospital services, and the QuadMed organization staffs and manages the on-site programming along with providing services for some of the other area employers who have recognized their expertise and the worth of worksite healthcare (QuadMed, Inc. is listed in the appendix as a regional provider of services).

It is instructive to note that the employers, in these cases, reached out to the healthcare systems and not vise versa. In the case of Quad/Graphics, Harry Quadracci (to whom this book is dedicated) saw a need for a different approach to the provision of healthcare services and structured a joint venture with a health system to achieve that goal. This predated the on-site vendor industry, and most of the firms listed in the appendix under the category of "on-site providers" were not in the business of providing full service on-site care. New ground was being broken, and the result is a continuing relationship between an industrial firm and a health system in which

Proposed delivery model          Current delivery model

## InSinkErator care model grid

| | On-site | Designated InSinkErator community based PCP | Designated InSinkErator specialty provider | All Saints network | MEI network | Out of network |
|---|---|---|---|---|---|---|
| Treatment of work related injury | Tier 1 | Tier 2 | Tier 2 | Tier 3 | Tier 4 | N/A |
| Employee sick visit | Tier 1 | Tier 2 | Tier 2 | Tier 3 | Tier 4 | N/A |
| Employee well visit | Tier 1 | Tier 2 | Tier 2 | Tier 3 | Tier 4 | N/A |
| Work related injury follow-up | Tier 1 | Tier 2 | Tier 2 | Tier 3 | Tier 4 | N/A |
| Dependent sick visit | N/A | Tier 2 | Tier 2 | Tier 3 | Tier 4 | Tier 5 |
| Dependent well visit | N/A | Tier 2 | Tier 2 | Tier 3 | Tier 4 | Tier 5 |
| Wellness and preventive services | Limited to medical | Limited to medical | N/A | Tier 3 | N/A | N/A |
| Diagnostic testing | Limited | Tier 2 | Tier 2 | Tier 3 | Tier 4 | N/A |
| Follow-up treatment | Tier 1 | Tier 2 | Tier 2 | Tier 3 | Tier 4 | N/A |

**Figure 13.3    The InSinkErator programming is more than an on-site clinic. The corporate staff originated this project by defining where each segment of care is best provided. This grid shows the resulting arrangement with various aspects of the health system, including the local All Saints Hospital.**

both have gained direct knowledge of each other's needs. In the case of InSinkErator and Wheaton Franciscan, the healthcare system was chosen as a provider during a request for proposal (RFP) process that was run by the InSinkErator management team, headed up by their vice president of human resources, Drew Abram, in a competitive process. The result of which is now a partnership for the provision of care on-site at their Racine plant.

So, there is a precedent for working with a health system, but it is generally constructed after the firm does its own planning and defines its own goals and objectives. A healthcare system, like most successful entities, is a "learning enterprise" and, when challenged, can adapt to meet almost any conditional offering. However, if the full program of specialty care and selective steerage is to be attained along with the resulting savings, a hospital may be politically and functionally challenged to meet that objective because hospitals and medical staffs that associate with hospitals are, by nature, inclusive. They are loath to rank or qualify any particular provider over any other. Although there are many doctors who might distinguish themselves within an institution, the hospital itself conducts business as a democratic organization of equals. Unless there is a will at the hospital to assist the employer with some of the nuts and bolts associated with the construction of a specialty network and guarantee certain access criteria, the hospital will just be reduced to competing on price with other healthcare systems.

## The Hospital as a Vendor of On-Site Services

If the hospital is contemplating the provision of the on-site services and developing some type of primary care program, the contracting process should be the same as that used for any other vendor. The hospital may either have an advantage or a disadvantage depending on its own philosophy and style. If it approaches the project as a new way to do business, it can add some additional perks to a proposal that an outside, or commercial, vendor cannot—such as contract pricing and preferred access programs. It can also build political bridges for the employer. If the hospital approaches the process as business as usual, there is little likelihood that the organization will be competitive in any meaningful way.

Why is this? Simply, the hospital is a collection of trade crafts and competitive enterprises operating in an environment that is skillfully balanced and integrated through détente rather than collaboration. This is not a criticism, only a reality. The hospital is generally a public utility for independent physicians and other practitioners to practice their art and to see and serve their patients. It is held together by tradition, regulation, protocols, and a class system of licensure and complex professional interrelationships. The hospital is run, generally, by a triumvirate that includes professionals, the community board, and key stakeholder groups. There is no question that this system works, and entire books and collegiate-level courses have been devoted to healthcare organizational theory and management. Graduate-level degrees are granted in this discipline. However, one aspect of healthcare administration that is certain to be agreed upon as common to most institutions is that a health system is conservative in its development processes and that it requires significant buy-in from a variety of groups to maintain its basic equilibrium.

Some hospitals also have to contend with sponsorship from charitable or church-related entities, or they are managed by national firms or by a large health system that is not governed at the local level. These features are not impediments when one considers the charitable and community-minded roles that most hospitals embrace, but they do get in the way of specific contracting initiatives. Religious agencies often put limits on full-service provision (such as women's services or working with projects where key stakeholder groups might be marginalized*). Municipal sponsorship of hospitals can also present a political challenge if there are conditions attached to any public funding sources.

On-site healthcare at an employer's workplace is anything but traditional, and it does not necessarily challenge the basic principles underlying the goals and objectives of the stakeholders in a healthcare system. However, it does challenge the traditional order and the way things need to progress through the planning process. The development of a program that is employee-centered or focuses on the needs of a specific population to the exclusion of a general community good is a change in order (for most hospitals) that breaks the planning cycle and the mode of inclusive/general consensus decision-making that underlies the order in many institutions. However, generalizations are unfair, and many healthcare institutions around the country are very interested in this type of a partnership. The employer

---

* Many health systems are sponsored by organizations connected with Catholic, Methodist, Jewish, and Adventist groups or sponsored in part by tax-supported entities or public trusts. The author recognizes the great achievements of these groups, but also the practicality that many of the groups have specific organizational principles that guide their involvement with women and family medicine, end-of-life care, charity care, working with organized labor, etc. Again, each institution is unique and generalizations should be avoided. If there is a question, the employer should simply let the healthcare system describe directly any restrictive channels of care or service.

is well advised to qualify their own local healthcare system to see if there is potential for any kind of real partnership.

The following issues should be addressed up front in any sort of dialogue with a local healthcare system:

- Is the hospital prepared to submit a formal response to the same RFP that is being developed for other vendors?
- Can the hospital contract for full services at the site and manage it as a truly independent contract, or do they conceive of it being part of a larger program?
- Can the hospital service contract be inclusive to other community healthcare providers (perhaps including some who are competitors)?
- Will the hospital be able to work with the employer in a fashion that allows for programming to be terminated and redirected to another vendor should the contract not meet each party's expectations?
- What is the process of the hospital's governance and for oversight on the proposed contract? Who will be the *one person* in charge?
- What is the hospital's track record with key program components—such as an electronic medical record (EMR), continuous quality improvement, performance-based provider contracting, the Patient Centered Medical Home (PCMH)?
- What provisions can be made to guarantee the ongoing nature of the contract should the hospital change its intent or programming?

A hospital can be a reasonable partner and there are obvious advantages from the political and functional perspective to work with a local provider. However, there are disadvantages to any program that is not vigilant about its own goals and objectives and that does not build in the need for continual evaluation and the ability for program renewal and rejuvenation. The last question that should be addressed if the employer is going to go with a hospital-oriented contract for full service is "What is our contingency plan?"

## The Hospital as a Provider of Support Services

If not a direct manager of on-site services, the hospital is key to any program for support contracting and for specialty and inpatient care. In the following listing, I attempt to define what is needed in a hospital relationship, whether the firm directly contracts with the organization or does so through the assistance of an on-site vendor:

- *Primary care support can include the provision of on-site access* for employees and their dependents. They could also provide staffing on a contract basis. Some firms that are labeling themselves as on-site providers are little more than staffing firms that will provide an on-site nurse or doctor, and this might be a need that a hospital could fulfill if that is all that is required.
- *In the development of the clinic itself,* a hospital might provide consulting advice relating to ambulatory care issues or regulatory and licensing issues. They also might be a source for assistance with suppliers and, if there is a need for equipment maintenance, they often have their own biomedical engineering departments that can be accessed for service and support.
- *Any on-site program will need after-hours support and a call back-up system.* A hospital might be willing to arrange for this coverage and even include the on-site providers within their answering service or paging system.
- *The hospital maintains coverage services for radiology, anesthesia, critical care units (intensivists), laboratory, and the emergency department.* These are areas that are covered by physician groups that are generally contracted exclusively through the hospital. These contracting entities may be best approached in conjunction with discussions with a local hospital to ensure that there is some level of coordination of technical and professional services.
- *Hospitals can assist in identifying specialists for "narrow-network" or "high-performing" network services.* This is an area of political sensitivity for hospitals, but the fact is that they have all of the information necessary to help a firm achieve an understanding of who is really a competent specialist and who is marginal. As such, partnering with a hospital system can often fast-track the development of a select network of specialists that can support the primary care providers on-site.
- *Registration and information coordination can be enhanced with a hospital relationship.* If a person is in a network of some kind, it seems reasonable to assume that they should be able to use any point of the network with the same registration card. Hopefully, the health system can also coordinate access to medical files, appointment information, and other patient care support material. This area represents a very

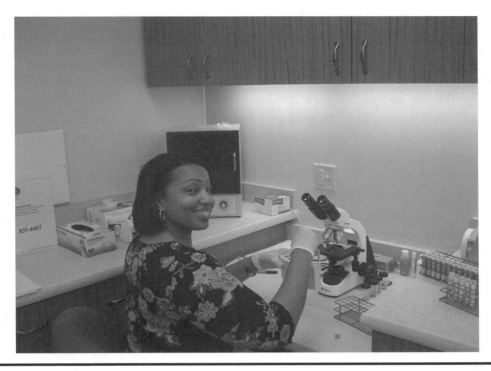

**Figure 13.4    Hospitals would be the obvious choice to provide on-site services in key support areas like laboratory services. The Miller Brewing site in Milwaukee started its project with a full complement of on-site laboratory services. This level of service requires outside contract support for reference services, licensing, accreditation, and oversight. Other areas such as imaging and pharmacy may also be opportunities to collaborate with local healthcare institutions.**

real opportunity to better serve patients by working out coordination problems beforehand. Most health systems and hospitals are not very "consumer friendly," and any opportunity to achieve a seamless transition from outside to inside is going to be met with consumer approval.

■ *Assistance and support with care management, case management, or coaching* (or whatever it is called) can be critical, and it is largely dependent on the willingness of the hospital to allow access for the nurse support team to records of inpatients and, most important, to have a high level of response when a consumer accesses the hospital for care. Great care management, as it has been described in this book, is not possible without a responsible institution that is working with an employer to monitor emergency department admissions and other admission behavior to provide an early opportunity for care management intervention. The importance of this feature of a program is discussed in other chapters, but it is worth mentioning here that the partnership (or contractual relationship) with a hospital is key to the success of any care management program.

■ *The hospital may have some key support programs* that can be accessed by the on-site provider or the on-site practitioners. This might be as simple as coordination with a poison center or articulation with hospital educational and accreditation functions. Sharing of accreditation, regulatory and reference materials, policies, and access to key areas of unique competence cannot be underestimated. Cooperation along these lines can greatly decrease on-site program costs, and at the same time the employer can make some contribution to offset the hospital's fixed costs by coordinating services through them if it is at all feasible.

■ *The hospital is a natural provider for ancillary backup such as reference laboratory services, physical therapy, imaging, etc.* Not everything can be done on-site, and what cannot must be found in the community. Hopefully, through a collaborative hospital arrangement, there can be backup for laboratory services, over-reading service for imaging and radiology, etc. The hospital has to employ a range of special support functions, and it may be very willing to contract these on a part-time or occasional basis to a local employer.

■ *Transfer agreements may need to be negotiated with various areas of the hospital.* These are agreements that may support an emergency department transfer, integration of an admission to social services, transfer from a hospital to an extended care facility, etc. Transfer agreements address the way that the patient care is coordinated and the way that information and medical records are transitioned. They address which practitioner is in charge of a patient and how the patient is charged for services.

■ *Important linkages need to be arranged for a variety of information and support systems.* These can include EMR systems, laboratory and imaging reporting, disease-state management program referrals, postdischarge recordkeeping, and patient follow-up treatment and pharmaceutical prescriptions.

■ *Financial and premium articulation needs to be understood and organized.* The hospital may be required to provide special financial arrangements, advantageous pricing, or any number of coupon-style advantages to an organized and contracted base of employees and dependents. They may have premiums/awards available for members of the program that are admitted or serviced on their premises. All of these programs must be managed, and information regarding them needs to be disseminated to the employees and to the hospital staff.

■ *Coordination with national coverage programs, centers of excellence, and other insurance products* can be fostered through a relationship with a hospital. These programs may not be local, but they all may have linkages to local health systems. Employees and dependents may need to have their care coordinated with transplant programs and other subspecialized care. Also, they may need services from rehabilitation units or nursing facilities managed or owned by hospital systems.

■ *Hospitals often employ hospitalists,* and these doctors will probably provide coverage for inpatient admissions, discharge planning, and other general in-hospital services that the on-site physicians are not structured to offer.

■ *Certification, accreditation, and licensure support* can be obtained in conjunction with a hospital. They have staff and processes in place that can be shared with an on-site clinic that could be very useful in maintaining the standards required to foster confidence in the health services that are being contemplated at the worksite.

## Hospitals as Partners Rather than Vendors

It is impossible to make any generalization about a hospital except that the local hospital has a stake in what is occurring at a healthcare site in a community in which they provide services. It can also be said that most hospitals enjoy some level of community support, and consumers see most as credible vendors in the healthcare service realm. The word to stress here is "most." In a town where there are many hospital choices, there are generally some that stand above the others in any survey of local healthcare consumers.

Hospitals are being graded these days, and there are many ways that the services within hospitals can be judged and ranked. In addition to the national magazine ratings and rankings, most state health departments and some national survey programs (HealthGrades* is one) perform basic ratings of hospital services. This is helpful if there are several choices, but there are many communities in which there is only one hospital provider, and then the choice is not where to send inpatients but how to coordinate other services such as diagnostics, imaging, etc.

---

* HealthGrades is a ranking service that may be arguably the most visible among many that are out there competing for the consumer's attention. It can be found at http://www.healthgrades.com.

In each case—many hospitals or just one—the process starts with a review of the claims file and an understanding of what is being spent in the local healthcare community. Before the employer approaches a hospital or health system, they should know what they have traditionally spent on healthcare at that site. If there are many hospitals, the claims analysis can indicate the employees' preference for care, and it can begin to show the opportunities for steerage or selection that might be achieved by the firm if the plan is to alter benefit design to channel inpatient care to one institutional program over another.

Armed with these data and with the intent to work in a collaborative fashion, the opportunities for coordination with a hospital can be beneficial for the employer and the beneficiaries for which they sponsor care. The idea of partnering with a hospital, although there is an outside vendor providing on-site services, should not be missed because the discussions can include so many areas of advantage, not the least of which is pricing. Other obvious areas include the potential for co-branding a program. If the hospital cares to become involved and if it will lend its name to the on-site programming, that will go a long way in the mind of the employee to assure them of a quality program, and the key to on-site success is the number of employee and covered family members who are electing the on-site services. If a hospital can help, this is one reason to have them be part of the team.

## Hospitals as Competitors

In some cases, by intent or by accident, the local hospital and its programs might be competitive with the on-site programming. This may be especially true with urgent care services, retail medical outlets, industrial clinic sites, primary care sites, etc. The hospital may also take a negative view of the employer-based operation and actively work to entice employees to use their services rather than those offered by the employer. They may also approach other local providers and exert some form of influence with them, constraining an employer's access to services. Most employers will know this lack of cooperation by another name—competition.

However unlikely this may seem, the employer is well advised to meet with the local hospital and explain the goals of the program so that there is an understanding of the ground rules and the stakes in this healthcare initiative. The employer is not competing with the hospital as much as it is attempting to continue a competitive advantage in its own arena of services and products. Healthcare costs are production costs, and the hospital as a community resource and a citizen of the local business community should support on-site programming when their colleagues in the local business community elect this approach.

# Chapter 14

# Utilizing Local Physicians as the Primary Care Anchors

There is always the temptation for a firm to use local physicians and other community-based healthcare resources in the implementation of an on-site clinic program. It just seems to make sense because there is a built-in political advantage and the local doctors may already be seeing some of the employees and dependents for their medical care. Also, this approach allows a program to move forward without contracting outside vendors or engaging in any recruiting efforts.

This could be a mistake, and it could affect many aspects of the programming, not just the recruiting of a provider. Again, if the planning calls for a nontraditional approach and robust primary care, this is probably because these factors were not being readily supplied by the local, fee-for-service healthcare providers.

## Local Physicians Are Traditional Providers: On-Site Programs Are Anything But

Generally speaking, there are counterarguments to this approach that should be considered before spending a lot of time, money, and energy exploring this option. One major barrier is that the local primary care provider is generally working under the philosophy (and business model) of "more care is better care," or at least the business concept that providing more services will generate more income. Another problem is that most primary care providers are at capacity and work hard to keep their offices efficiently staffed, which means there will be scant time available for any additional services. The primary care practices in the United States are generally undercapitalized when it comes to things like electronic medical records (EMRs), but they have usually invested in revenue-generating hardware such as laboratory analysis equipment and other diagnostic modalities. Their staff is trained to optimize these resources because their patients are managed as a fee-for-service enterprise.

This is not an issue of a Marcus Welby style of medicine being replaced by something such as that of Doogie Howser. It is a situation in which the entire fabric of for-profit, fee-for-service healthcare is wrongly suited to the needs of a population management system. The local medical office is oriented to episodic care and events of illness or injury occurring in an individual that presents with a complaint rather than addressing the health status of the individual or an overall plan for health related to an entire population of employees and their dependents. This is an economic reality that forces office and service design that will not easily accommodate any different form of thinking or service design.

## Sometimes the Best Intentions Are Limited by Functional Issues

Local providers with existing practices are involved in ongoing relationships with specialty providers and hospitals that may not complement the employer's efforts to design a true value-oriented system. No matter what a local provider says about independence of thought, if they are used to referring their patients to a particular specialist or hospital that means that their staff is also connected to that system. The relationship goes far beyond politics or camaraderie, and it is a hard cycle to break.

The local provider or physician seems to offer an alternative that is familiar and comforting to some of the patients already in the practice, and this is hard to gauge as a benefit. Patient-provider trust does indeed contribute to a patient's sense of well-being and often leads to higher compliance behavior. The patient is also invested personally with the practice and the staff and has a high level of trust in things like confidentiality. There may also be a comfort level that is gained from the practice already being informed about items of a personal nature. However, these positive factors may be offset by the creation of a new medical record and the fresh look that a new provider can bring to an existing/old problem or issue.

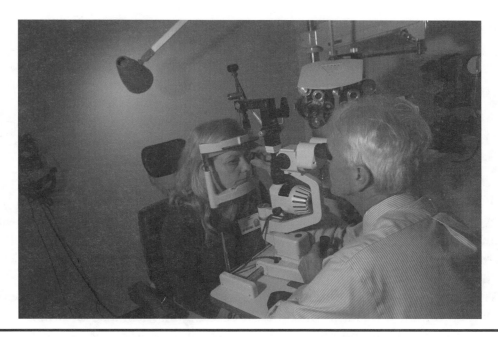

**Figure 14.1    The on-site provider is well-equipped and has access to an EMR and the latest equipment, as opposed to typical primary care practices that can be under-capitalized.**

For the employer, all of the challenges of working with a local provider may not present themselves in the initial negotiation sessions. However, during the planning process, the bias will be toward systems that support the status quo, and this will be where the flexibility of the doctor or doctor group will be evident. The on-site program should be structured around several features that are very nontraditional. Gut-check these points with the local provider and see if they are open or resistant to incorporating them within their care scheme.

■ Each primary care event will encompass a health status check and a review of basic personal health planning criteria. This will mean an investment of time that is three or four times as long as a standard primary care appointment.
■ The basis of any population management system is information. Each enrolled patient will be linked to an EMR. This will require a basic level of technology within the practice.
■ The employer will be working with various groups to define a value-oriented specialist network and support system for inpatient and ancillary care. This will require compliance in referral and follow-up behavior on the part of the primary care practitioner.

■ There will be a feature of the program that addresses access to services and turnaround. This will be patient-focused, and it will be defined and measured on a regular basis. The practitioner should begin to think about an office schedule that is based on no waiting and same day appointments.
■ Provider salary and bonus structures will be comprised of several factors—none of which relate to productivity. These will include compliance with "best practices," patient satisfaction, and 360° staff and peer review.

If these principles are not incorporated within the programming (and the provider contracts), the overall achievement of employer value, population health status improvement, and employee and dependent satisfaction will be missed.

Most doctors operating in the standard fee-for-service mode will recognize these questions as posing a real threat to the way that they have constructed their office and practice processes. Most will also be wary of mixing patients from an employer managed and customer-focused program in with those from standard indemnity and managed care populations.

**Figure 14.2    The real tool that is available to the on-site program provider (when the principles outlined by the employers using best practices are followed) is time. This is a luxury that few community-based practitioners have to spare.**

## Okay, So You Still Want to Use Local Providers (or You Have to)

Programming has to start someplace, and there is a common feeling expressed by many employers that the best way to engage in the on-site experience is to take a path of least resistance with the local medical community. Another argument often expressed is that this is a starting point, and that, as the program grows and proves itself, the doctors can be more fully engaged or a program change can be made to move from the local providers to doctors with unique assignments supporting the on-site programming. (I would argue that you cannot get there from here, but this is an argument that often loses to real, here and now, political barriers.)

Whatever the arguments, there are key issues that will need to be addressed with any local provider group. The listing is offered as a starting point to promote some level of clarity in the planning process.

■ Will care be delivered on-site or at a facility that has been traditionally associated with the local physician practice? If the services are provided at the workplace, who will manage the contracted physicians and employed staff? Which components will be owned and operated by the employer and which, if any, by the physician group? Alternatives have been listed for consideration:
   – Employer owns and manages the facilities and purchases equipment and supplies.
   – Employer hires support staff and nonproviders and contracts with a local entity to provide the physicians and licensed providers (local hospital or a local practice).
   – Employer hires support staff and contracts with a national entity to provide the physicians and licensed providers (national vendor firm or a national staffing agency directed to incorporate local providers as part of their staffing solution).
   – Employer uses a contract management approach to have an outside consulting group oversee the sourcing of staff, providers, equipment, facility, etc., as an owner's representative and pass-through entity (managed to principles and objectives with the outside third party supplying the oversight).

■ If there is no dedicated, on-site facility, is there going to be some locally identified site that is unique to the employees and beneficiaries, or is the benefit program going to be one that merges the employer contract with other local employee bases?

- "Merging" the benefit pool is simply a contract issue and the employer can bid the process or simply negotiate like any preferred provider organization (PPO) might on a fee-for-service or a capitated basis.
- If the choice is to go through several local practices, there would be a requirement that an independent practice association (IPA) be formed in most states. Most areas would have existing local provider networks that might be contracted with directly or "rented."
  - Some of the national PPOs might assist with the development of a local (and dedicated) PPO for a single employer.
  - If one single practice is chosen to serve the employees and beneficiaries, the contract form could be cost-plus, fee-for-service, capitated, or a combination of these methods.

■ Once the contract is ready for review, check for some important issues and items:
  - Who owns the medical records and how can they be transferred in the case of a transition?
  - Make sure there are no restrictions for doctors to leave the employment of the practice and work directly for the employer (or their agent), if the contract terminates.
  - Have all transactions be completely transparent so that there is no wondering about costs and income distribution schemes and other like matters.
  - Retain the ownership of all intellectual property connected with the program so that there is no problem with trademarks, brochures, phone numbers, etc.
  - Have all agreements include the employer (or the agent of the employer) as a preapproved party for full assignment.

## Even with Planning and Consensus, There May Be Problems

Issues and challenges related to the utilization of local practitioners include a few things that might not be evident until the process of development begins. In the first place, providers will have existing relationships with hospitals and specialists and may not be able to easily reorganize their orientation to a newly designed "high-performing network." If they do not have an EMR, the implementation may be a challenge. There is going to be a level of service and care already in existence, and the new ideas posed in an employee-focused and employer-sponsored program will be difficult to initiate.

Practices with multiple providers may not be able to assign them consistently depending on the traditional staffing and coverage models that exist. Also, definitive standards for the providers (and provider performance) may not be able to be guaranteed because of pre-existing contractual and equity structures within the practice.

Employers, especially with on-site programs, have initiatives relating to the application of formularies and prescribing protocols that may be difficult to enforce in a private practice. This may also be an issue when the practice has financial relationships that are predefined between themselves that are inconsistent with the goals of the employer and the model under development. The employer will need to know how the physicians are compensated so that the proper incentives are established for performance. Easy to do if there is independence and complete dedication to the employer programming—otherwise, very difficult. Lastly, it may seem that the election to go with a local group is the best political move, but the selection of any one doctor is the deselection of every other one.

## Aren't There Any Benefits to Working with the "Locals"?

There may absolutely be some advantages that would be gained from working with local providers rather than hiring a new professional staff, if the relationship is solidly referenced against an overall plan that allows for the employer's goals to be met. The incorporation of trusted local physicians would signal support from the medical community for the employer's programming. Also, the doctors selected may already be serving some of the employees and their family members, and these can then be immediately incorporated within any projections. These facts alone may help the on-site program to flourish.

Local physicians already have credentialing completed with local hospitals and managed care programs. If there is a high-performing network that is part of the program, the local doctors can bring some level of "intelligence" to the contracting process to quickly develop it. Hometown providers might also have a good sense of specific resources for disease-state management and for specialty and supportive access points for the employees and their beneficiaries.

On the matter of recruiting and retention, a local crew will be more stable in a community because they have already established residency and there is no cost of relocation and recruiting. Locals are also easier to reference.

Like any program tradeoff, there is no one right answer. However, the planning process and the program goals should be the background against which any final determination might be made. As long as the overall principles of the program are maintained, even a local provider can be part of the solution.

# Chapter 15

# Pharmacy, Pharmacy Benefit Managers, and Other Mysteries

If there ever was a component that deserved its own chapter, pharmacy is it. There are many jokes that people tell about cell phone and cable pricing, and any of them could be recrafted and applied to prescription pharmaceuticals. The price the firm pays for medicine is confused by things like retail pricing, average wholesale price (AWP), and average manufacturer's price (AMP) when all that the company wants is the lowest possible price.*

Of course, entire books can be written about pharmaceuticals and pharmaceutical pricing, but the employer already knows that this is simply a major component of cost under its benefits plan and one that needs direct management. Generally speaking, the issue of pharmacy and pharmacy plan design is so complex that it is impossible for a

---

* There is no acronym for the "lowest possible price" because it is not attainable. Government pricing is probably the lowest, and this is pretty much unattainable unless there is a federal government entity that is directly being served. However, it is important to footnote that some hospitals can establish clinics under a special program that is called the "340B" exemption, which is detailed at http://www.hrsa.gov/opa and addresses unique circumstances for a hospital that is serving a "disproportionate share" of the needy to be able to avail themselves and those they directly serve with pharmacy products at government prices. Could this include a work on-site health program? In all probability, yes. Interested parties would be well advised to explore this cautiously and in the company of counsel familiar with this special type of programming.

normal person to understand it (remember, cell phone pricing), and it is not transparent anyway. The reader is invited to ponder this statement for a few minutes while they browse the Web and try to figure out how to advise their parents on the Medicare Part D (drug benefit plan) that was recently passed to ensure access to drug therapies for the Medicare-eligible population.

Many price lists are available for comparison, but they do not reference significant discounts that bulk purchasers and high-volume purchasers are offered. Mail-order supplies are also priced differently as are program drugs in certain categories of care. Pharmaceutical products can be bundled with other purchases, and there can be stratified pricing if there are many categories of patients under the care of an organization. Another challenge is raised when different classes of patients working for the same employer, using the same clinic site, and taking the same drug, get that drug dispensed at different prices.

Thankfully, there are consultants who deal only with the issues of pharmacy and pharmaceuticals. These are the pharmacy benefit managers (PBMs). They organize purchasing, dispensing, compliance matters,

**Figure 15.1  Toyota has always had a pharmacy benefit for its beneficiaries, and their Family Health Center boasts almost every option necessary for routine primary care right down the hall from the provider who prescribes it.**

delivery, and documentation. They have various ways that they vend their services, and some have adopted some of the same interesting technologies for pricing that have been embraced by the pharmaceutical industry. They are involved in any number of care scenarios, and they are representative of the type of middleman consultant that becomes prevalent when care scenarios become complex. Nothing in this paragraph is intended to disparage this group of advisors and consolidators because there is a basic framework of pricing for pharmaceutical programs that is key to a good on-site project and they may be invaluable for successful implementation.

## Pharmacists as Primary Care Providers?

The only thing that is better than a pharmacist near your home is a pharmacist near your doctor. In the case of on-site managed programming, the access of the pharmacist to the primary care physician and vise versa is a secret weapon in pharmacological efficiency and effectiveness. Furthermore, if the pharmacist is actively involved in the electronic medical record (EMR), they can provide a real backstop against medication errors and prescription drug conflicts. The pharmacist can be relied upon, in many occasions, to offer ideas that are helpful to the patient in complying with pharmaceutical use and reinforce issues related to potential side effects and drug-related complications.

A pharmacist may also have more regular interaction with the employee who is taking prescription medication and therefore greater opportunity to determine if the medications are effective or, of more concern, being abused in some way. If the pharmacists have access to the medical record (and to the physician), they can reinforce healthy behavior and tailor patient education regarding drug use to each special situation. If there are multiple prescriptions and over-the-counter drugs, they can alert the primary care provider (PCP) to compliance issues and the potential for drug interactions. The event of just picking up a prescription can also be used to check health status and things related to disease-state monitoring (blood glucose, blood pressure, serum cholesterol, etc.). Proximity to the PCP and access to the medical record, especially one that is all-inclusive, elevates the pharmacist to a more active and effective role in the delivery of primary care and achieves a true clinical involvement with the patient that benefits the entire program.

# It Is Not Just the Cost of the Drug

The on-site pharmacy, with or without the primary care involvement, can bring several features to the effectiveness of the pharmaceutical benefit. The cost of this component of care is most often confused with the simple cost of the medications. It is much more complex than that. The program managers should be addressing several aspects of the pharmaceutical "buy."

- Are the pharmaceuticals being purchased at a price that is competitive? Could a more cost-effective price schedule be negotiated with a different buying group or PBM?
- Is there a formulary that is well designed and has the appropriate mix of over-the-counter (OTC) and generic alternatives? Was a generic considered and suggested?
- When a pharmaceutical agent is prescribed, is it from a protocol that is evidence-based and under a process that is generally thought to be effective for the present problem?
- When the drugs are prescribed, is there a mechanism to ensure that the script is filled and that the patient is compliant with the methodology for administration?
- Are scripts that are recurring or for which there are refills moved to the most efficient and effective level of dispensing? This is where mail-order drugs and automatic refill processes can be used to lower costs. Are these alternatives in place?
- What alternatives to the pharmacological solution were considered? Is there a longer-term solution to weaning the patient from the medication that is part of the overall care program?
- Is there a mechanism for patient recall and for a feedback loop of some kind to ensure that the drug regimen is fulfilling the goals that the patient and PCP are expecting?

Cost of the drug is an issue, but the overriding issue is effectiveness. From a cost standpoint, generics are superior to proprietary drugs. However, there is also the issue that some alternative treatments can replace drug therapy, and, in some cases, the pharmaceutical agent is not even used or used ineffectively, which does no one any good. This is an area where a community-based primary care physician or an urgent care (episodic) provider may not be able to be as effective as the patient-focused provider in an employer-sponsored program. The way that the benefit is designed along with the way the pharmacy event is coordinated with primary care will have a lot to do with effectiveness. It should be obvious to the reader that this is another argument in favor of the patient-centered medical home approach outlined in a previous chapter.

## Drugstores as Providers: Retail Emerges as a Development (or Distraction?)

Arguably, the most interesting and far-reaching event in the last few years concerning on-site care has been the acquisition by Walgreens of two of the most visible and successful on-site vendors—CHD Meridian and Whole Health Management. Each of these providers had a solid reputation and an impressive stable of clients. Each had pioneered several innovations and was developing, along with their clients, to become more integrated and to embrace a broader definition of on-site care that could have moved the industry on to another level.

Along with pioneers like Dr. Len Quadracci, who developed programs in Milwaukee for Quad/Graphics, there were other initiatives being developed by Jim Hummer (former chief executive officer of Whole Health Management) and companies like Perdue Farms and Florida Power & Light. Like any good idea that is pushed along by the environment, there is no true inventor of "employer managed care" or "on-site workplace health access." Scott Paper and Harrah's Entertainment allowed and encouraged vendors to experiment and expand services. Occupational medicine providers like CHS, IMC, and Concentra, Inc., modified programming to suit client needs and launched new program features as the benefits became evident to their management and to the management of the firms they served.

Jim Hummer* was among the first to recognize that the issue of the healthcare benefit had to move from the human resource (HR) department to the desk of the chief financial officer (CFO) if there was going to be a capital contribution by the firm that would change an organization from a purchaser of vended services to a manager of a healthcare process (and population). He pushed the envelope with the concept that healthcare could be an investment and not just a cost center.

There is a new "envelope" that is emerging, and Walgreens seems to have recognized it and capitalized upon it. They have a division called

---

* Mr. Hummer is the founder and CEO of Whole Health Management, now owned by Walgreens.

**Figure 15.2** **This is a Duane Reade outlet in New York that has an on-site service provided by a Manhattan-based hospital. Consumers can find healthcare and pharmacy under one roof. However, this model may not be the most effective overall in complementing an on-site program.**

Take Care Health, which is a retail healthcare asset providing minimalist primary care services to consumers in locations combined with, and within, Walgreens locations. Their business model seems simple, and, in this simplicity is compelling. The consumer can get low-cost access to a provider in their own neighborhood and, if they need a prescription filled, the pharmacist is right down the aisle. The chapter started with the statement that a pharmacist near your home is a good thing. A pharmacist right next to a provider writing a prescription (and near your home) seems even more attractive.

Where Hummer and others recognized a need for on-site integration, Walgreens seems to have been the first to approach the industry with corporate service-line integration. They can provide on-site services to a firm along with an on-site pharmacy, coupled with local access to other providers who are retail-based and, generally, also located in convenient shopping destinations in communities where the consumer lives. Their idea of "integration" is not patient-focused but product- and sales-oriented and, although this may not run exactly parallel to the idea of a care system coordinated around the employer's needs, it may get there as Walgreens absorbs the intelligence they have purchased from Mr. Hummer (Whole Health Management) and Dr. Ray Fabius (former Medical Director of CHD Meridian). Actually, the real transformation of knowledge will probably continue to be from the companies served by Take Care Health as they continue to analyze the effect of the on-site programming that the employees are receiving in the client bases they purchased.

Where Walgreens goes, Wal-Mart, CVS, Kroger, and Target are sure to follow, and there are sure to be other initiatives and alliances that form between on-site service vendors and retail pharmacy chains. Like any industry that is emerging and defining itself, there are successes, near-successes, and failures. Meijers, which is a large midwestern-based chain of big-box stores, launched a retail program that was coordinated with a large physician independent provider association (IPA) and supporting hospitals. It was modeled along lines that emulated the best thinking in retail medical service lines, but it closed a few months after it was launched. Whether this was a product or a planning failure will probably never be known, but the moral of the story is that the retail relocation of medical care next to a pharmacy is not always a guaranteed success.

## Pharmacy: Conclusions?

The fact that pharmacy has such a high impact on the cost of care is based on the reality that there are many tiny events with high cost, the floor space commitment is relatively small, and the cost impact immediate. Compare this with wellness, in which there is a huge space and facility commitment and rather indeterminate payback, and one can see why the pharmacy is often the first on-site service considered and the one that is quickly added as an ancillary.

This is an area where claims are often confusing and disarticulate from the rest of the medical information. It is a zone where consumer health savings dollars are often not captive and where compliance is in question. Retailers are emerging with low-cost options that, frankly, will be attractive for many. In western Michigan, for example, many prenatal drugs and pediatric generics are "sold" for free at the local big-box stores. Many other scripts are just a couple of dollars and, somehow, this type of pricing needs to be worked into the healthcare cost equation by the firm because it is definitely being contemplated (and elected) by the consumer.

If there is a conclusion to this conundrum of pricing, access, and effectiveness, it is the fact that this is an area that merits continual oversight and that lends itself well to a primary care program located in proximity to the pharmacy access.

## Chapter 16

# Employees, Consumerism, and the Illusion of Choice

The consumer has voted and the Internet is now being used primarily for two things—accessing to information on healthcare and finding pornographic pictures. Functional matters also come to mind like using the Web as a replacement to the Yellow Pages and finding movie times. Add these trends to the fact that more and more responsibility for health management and the management of healthcare dollars is being put in the hands of the consumer and the result is the perfect storm of too many data in the hands of people with an inability to process the information. Economic behavior only works when the consumer has choices along with the knowledge and power to make intelligent determinations. With advertising and Internet searches, there is no real differentiation between truth, half-truths, fiction, and outright falsehoods.

## Consumers Have Too Much Information, Most of It Useless

A Google search returned almost 10,000,000 options for "ED" (erectile dysfunction), but only a little over 3,000,000 for "shortness of breath." The number of information sources is not as important as the way the information was offered. The ED banners offered the standard links to the common drugs that are being touted for anxious males. However, the "SOB" page will take one to paid banners that are sponsored by firms specializing in chronic obstructive pulmonary disease, pulmonary embolism, asthma, or pulmonary arterial hypertension. To be fair, there is also a Google option to refine the results you have been served, and there are some general sites to which a person can be directed to search for general medical information.

However, by the time the consumer is able to find his way to a general site, the "specialty sites" have him convinced that he can be suffering from some sort of outrageous malady that can be resolved by the click of a mouse. There is even a name emerging for this consumer tendency to overreact to Web material and to latch onto the most outlandish and anxiety-producing information as opposed to that which is most pertinent—*cyberchondria*.[1] Research indicates that there is a clear danger of consumers using the Web in a fashion that escalates their opinion or concern about their symptoms. The search engines function to move people to develop a more acute idea of whatever problems they are having, and the effect of this on a population of Web users is yet to be determined, but the results can only be more consumption of unnecessary and duplicative health expenditures.

The Web and Internet search engines are becoming a new source for advertising and for promotion of healthcare products and services, the effect of which is unknown. Just as television carries advertisements for prescription drugs, the Web is carrying advertisements for things that match "keywords," and the content is geared to what the advertiser thinks the searcher might wish to buy. This is not health-related information; it is health-related hucksterism that might be likened to the days of the old medicine show. There is no effective filtering or ranking that protects a consumer from an advertiser willing to pay more for a higher rank in a search results window. There is no quality score that can be assigned to a Web search to allow consumers to get an answer that has some level of guaranteed professional expertise or even a guarantee that they are getting information that is pertinent to their condition and needs.

There is also the danger that the consumer might use a website to self-diagnose or to avoid engagement with the medical process of diagnosis. Home remedies aside, there are lots of promises being made on the Internet that, if pursued, will delay a person's access to medical care while they attempt over-the-counter cures. Every school child knows that a person with shortness of breath is a potential heart attack candidate, especially if this condition is one of rapid onset. Most of us would assume that the way to better understand the condition would be to seek help from an emergency department, not from the Web. However, there are many gradual onset conditions that do allow for an otherwise intelligent consumer to try the

Web remedy route. As more and more information is categorized about each of us, the advertisements will become more and more targeted (and effective), and more consumer spending and effort will be directed through seeking Web treatments or practitioners who have connected with them by way of a social network or medical website.

The consumer needs to have some of this information categorized and its content "graded" and linked to local resources if it is to become useful. The way to do this is to channel medical source information through an employer managed program that can link the employee or the healthcare recipient to quality sites that have a linkage to the network of services that have been "prequalified" by the employer programming. This sounds like a judgment call—and it is. Someone has to have the responsibility to judge the worthiness of a website and use this judgment as part of a Web strategy to augment the employee's understanding of their health benefits and where they should best be accessed. This means that there should be Web access to programming that is fundamentally organized around the benefit structure and the health services that are being developed. As more consumers seek Web options, they should be able to choose one that has the credibility of their own healthcare program behind it rather than being forced to access local search options that offer unqualified alternatives.[*]

## Consumers Cannot Shop Price for the Fear That They Will Choose Based on Price

With consumer health savings accounts, co-pays, coinsurance, and deductibles, the consumer is directed to make "market basket decisions." That is, they will look at a healthcare expenditure and form an opinion on the basis of price or on how the expenditure will affect their overall savings balance. If they are running out of "savings" dollars, they must weigh the purchases against other consumer goods. However, price in healthcare has never been an indicator of "value," and it is certainly not connected to quality. If the consumer were trying to understand some value proposition in a large durable good, she could go to *Consumer Reports*, and if she were using a household good, she would look for the Good Housekeeping™ Seal of Approval. There are ratings on insurance, mutual funds, banks, and plumbers. There are

---

[*] There is one organization that is attempting to qualify Web content related to healthcare. It is URAC, and it is not yet a recognized brand name among consumers. Its consumer advisory material can be found at http://www.urac.org/consumers/resources/accreditation.aspx.

no qualified ratings or rankings for medical services, hospitals, doctors, medical testing, etc. Most of the services that call themselves rating systems are limited in their scope, undependable, or inaccessible to a consumer who is really shopping for value. Until some form emerges, the employer becomes the consumer's best source for information because the employer and the employee have similar objectives. However, the employer must act to earn the employee's trust in this matter and truly develop a program that is based on quality measures.

Advertising either promises a cure or it focuses on pure pricing. The issue of shopping for price from a consumer perspective, without having any reference for value, will not produce an overall healthcare result that is predictable. In planning the Toyota Family Medical Center, the author drove by a vendor that sells contact lenses. Figure 16.1 is a real picture from a highway in San Antonio. As one can see, the purveyor of turkey legs and hot roasted corn is selling contact lenses. Just down the street, along the same highway, was another site selling various sundries—and contact lenses. At least with respect to eye care, the consumer had a choice and, chances are, the choice could be predicated on price. The idea of competition on the Web, in the Yellow Pages, or on television is not much better than the two roadside optical options in San Antonio. Consumers, as they are forced to bear more of the healthcare expenditure, will need to be informed about value and its relationship to the investment that healthcare

**Figure 16.1   This depicts an actual "provider" on a highway in Texas. Just down the street is another offering the same mix of retail products. One must assume they are competing on price and drive-by convenience.**

represents for their own well-being. They will need a trusted resource to be able to direct and confirm their choices.

The Toyota Family Health Center, a few miles down the road, organized an on-site offering for vision care that is being used by the employees and dependents of that plant, and they may or may not sell contact lenses at a price competitive to these vendors, but the patients are receiving a dependable service from a provider that is linked into their own healthcare system.

## Consumer Health Savings Accounts Can Be Part of an On-Site Program

The concept of consumer health savings accounts and consumer-directed health plans are here to stay. The idea of developing an intelligent and committed consumer with some investment in their own healthcare is attractive to industry and business and appealing to the workforce. The way it is presented and implemented is important. From one perspective, it can be described as "cost shifting," and it does transfer some cost from the employer-sponsored health component to the control of the consumer. In another sense, it can be empowering and allow the consumer to choose options that fit their lifestyle and needs.

Again, needs and wants must be balanced against what is practical and useful. The employer, in any consumer-directed partnership, is still carrying the brunt of the healthcare spending and is in the best position to bargain on behalf of the consumer base for advantageous pricing with predictable levels of service and quality. Consumers are not prepared or organized to be able to negotiate contracts or to establish access points in the healthcare system in a fashion that will actually be useful and bring them to any kind of rational choice. Healthcare is too complex a process for any single consumer to amass a body of knowledge sufficient to make appropriate choices. Information about service and quality is guarded and not easily accessible. Rating services are still in their early and formative stages. Where available, they are incomplete. The perceived needs of the consumer must be balanced by a primary care provider (PCP) who can assist with their choices, and this PCP must be backed up by a system of care that is also programmed to support their choices and complement their decision-making.

The consumer health savings account must be linked to the employer program in a way that assures the patient that the funds are being accurately accounted for and easily accessed. Many plants and industries have a

**Figure 16.2   A psychologist specializing in cardiology or a cardiologist with an interest in psychotherapy. The consumer must evaluate and decide.**

cafeteria program in which an employee slides a debit card in a lunchroom and has their lunch or snack charged against a cafeteria account. There has to be a similar program in the on-site model that allows the employee health savings plan to be accessed by a simple card-swipe to allow a direct connection between the employee's choice of healthcare and their economic involvement. If the co-pays and deductibles have been designed to allow a significant savings over other options, so much the better.

This consumer-oriented payment access program has to be organized in some way by the employer.* There is no other way to accomplish this task unless it is through a local broker or in partnership with another component of the healthcare system that has the flexibility to develop a program that can mirror what is needed by the employees and their beneficiaries. Few such programs exist, but one could recognize the benefits of such an offering if it was comprised of specialists and a supporting hospital, all of whom were tied into the same medical record system, with access guaranteed and a prearranged pricing advantage. The employer's challenge is to find such a system—or to build it.

---

* Some employers, most notably Nissan, are giving employees a fixed annual sum for their healthcare purchases. This type of programming can also be organized to take advantage of an on-site access point for services and service choice.

The issue of consumer choice is one that is directly related to consumer cost, and the idea of health benefits, which have long been cost-confused (or cost-shielded), now coming to the forefront of the consumer spending equation, is a great opportunity for employers to use one more tool in promoting better use of the healthcare "spend." However, employers must first define what that better use is before trying to entice consumers. This is part of the on-site clinic story and the planning for the specialty and hospital networks that need to be connected with them.

# Reference

1. Ryan W. White and Eric Hovitz. "Microsoft Research Cyberchondria: Studies of the Escalation of Medical Concerns in Web Search," 2008. http://research. microsoft.com/apps/pubs/default.aspx?id = 76529.

# Chapter 17

# Ambulatory Care Nuts and Bolts: Site Design and Function

On-site programs have their own set of issues regarding location and site design. Because they are generally found on a work-site campus, they generally do "double duty" as a resource for occupational medicine and rehabilitation. There is also a possibility for the facility to serve on-site, in-house, workforce demands. This begs the question of on-site response to emergency and disaster situations.

The process generally used to plan a facility starts with the anticipated throughput and utilization. How many patients and what kind will be served on-site? What will be the hours of operation? Where can the site be located to best serve the needs of the population? If we have planned for the patient flow, we can define the number and type of practitioners needed to work at the site. Defining the practitioner complement allows us to define the tools they need and the types of spaces necessary for their workflow.

There are two other factors that must be considered before the planning process can begin, and these are related to consumer access and consumer attitudes about care and where they receive their care. The consumer knows what a typical doctor's office is and what type of service they can expect. They do not know what a work site service might be like. Is it oriented to family medicine or plant medicine? Will there be other children and spouses or only co-workers or employees with injuries and illnesses? The image can be defined by the building and the premises. The location has to be accessible and welcoming. There is a need for security, but also for proper signage, parking, good access, and egress, if the project is going to serve dependents as well as working employees.

## Size Matters

Back to the plan and back to the claims. The development of the pro forma will provide a certain number of on-site visits. These may grow as the program grows in acceptance by the workforce. They may be changing based on the change in the actual workforce numbers. In any case, the facility needs to work flexibility into its design but, like any brick and mortar structure, it needs a specific footprint. The size should probably be planned for full utilization at program maturity. The program should mature in a three- or four-year period. Simply stated, if the project is going to be successful, it will be at maximum penetration (of the workforce) sometime during the fourth year after the doors open.

This is not a complex process. It is one that is worked through in steps that are pretty intuitive once they are outlined.

- Take the number of claims that produce primary care visits.
- Estimate the percentage of employee on-site utilization.
- Determine claims will result in on-site events.
- The number of encounters will provide an idea of the number of doctors needed. This is simply encounters per hour and hours per provider (which can be derived from MGMA or other clinic/staff ratio sources).
- There is a clear ratio of staff to physician.
- Knowing the number of staff and doctors will give one an idea of the rooms.
- Add the number of exam rooms to the other spaces and the result will be "facility scope."
- Size the rooms and the scope can be converted into total square footage.

Table 17.1 suggests three "sample" sizes for some representative facilities. Note that there are some program design features added in the larger employee base example. This suggests a very modest program for the smaller site and a more aggressive program for the larger example. The space needs to correspond to program design and number of employees. This type of chart can assist in the transition from service needs to capital planning.

**Table 17.1   On-Site Space Needs Projection**

| | Employees | | | | | |
| --- | --- | --- | --- | --- | --- | --- |
| | 1,000 | | 2,191 | | 4,413 | |
| | # | Square Feet | # | Square Feet | # | Square Feet |
| General rooms/areas | | | | | | |
| Examination rooms | 3 | 300 | 5 | 500 | 8 | 800 |
| Treatment room | 1 | 153 | 1 | 160 | 2 | 340 |
| Medical records | 1 | 150 | 1 | 90 | 1 | 90 |
| Administrative office | 1 | 100 | 1 | 121 | 1 | 121 |
| Provider's office | 1 | 100 | 1 | 90 | 2 | 180 |
| Nurse station | 1 | 80 | 1 | 108 | 2 | 216 |
| Staff room | 1 | 100 | 1 | 400 | 1 | 500 |
| Toilet | 2 | 72 | 2 | 690 | 2 | 690 |
| Storage | 1 | 100 | 1 | 300 | 1 | 400 |
| Reception desk | 1 | 150 | 1 | 150 | 1 | 210 |
| Reception area | 1 | 150 | 1 | 400 | 1 | 680 |
| Corridors | 1 | 120 | 2 | 160 | 2 | 240 |
| Medical | 1 | 1,575 | 1 | 3,169 | 1 | 4,467 |
| Laboratory | 1 | 120 | 1 | 120 | 1 | 120 |
| Rehabilitation | 1 | 625 | 1 | 581 | 1 | 696 |
| Wellness | 0 | | 0 | | 1 | 1,000 |
| Radiology | 0 | – | 1 | 340 | 1 | 340 |
| Pharmacy | 1 | 300 | 1 | 500 | 1 | 500 |
| Optical | 0 | – | 0 | – | 1 | 685 |
| Examination rooms | | | | | 6 | 838 |
| Sterilization room | | | | | 1 | 84 |
| IT storage | | | | | 1 | 70 |
| Director's office | | | | | 1 | 120 |
| PANO room | | | | | 1 | 56 |

*(Continued)*

**Table. 17.1** (*Continued*)

| | Employees | | | | | |
|---|---|---|---|---|---|---|
| | 1,000 | | 2,191 | | 4,413 | |
| | # | Square Feet | # | Square Feet | # | Square Feet |
| Reception desk | | | | | 1 | 154 |
| Reception area | | | | | 1 | 312 |
| Corridors | | | | | 2 | 480 |
| Dental | 0 | – | 0 | – | 1 | 2,648 |
| Care management | 1 | 225 | 1 | 300 | 1 | 400 |
| Total | | 2,845 | | 5,010 | | 10,856 |
| Contingency | | 285 | | 501 | | 1,086 |
| Projected total | | 3,130 | | 5,511 | | 11,942 |

With the project total square footage determined, there are several other pricing issues associated with the design of the facility. One that presents a conundrum is the issue of "available" space versus acquired space. The cost of acquired space is, as one can guess, the actual price of the space, whereas the cost of already available space is whatever anyone says that it is. If it is unused, there is often the inclination to work the number into the pro forma projections as zero. Actually, this is an advantage to those "selling" the program but there is always an "opportunity cost" to assigning a resource like land and a building to a fixed and unique department.

A firm may have an internal overhead allocation that might solve this issue, or they might have a clear definition of space allocation costs. Whichever the case, the cost of the space should be defined by the firm's chief financial officer (CFO) or accounting staff protocol, and the analyst should not allow a projection to be presented with the cost of land and the facility left blank. The accounting staff at the firm should also define several other variables for the projections. These include, but are not limited to, overhead allocations, facility maintenance costs, janitorial factors, depreciation schedules (for the facility, facility improvement costs, and fixed equipment), security costs, internal cost of capital, etc. If these are not in line with the other standards that the financial people anticipate for other capital projects, the analyst may have to rerun the numbers (and may lose credibility in the process).

Common things that are missed in the cost side of the facility planning are exterior and landscaping costs, waste disposal, medical waste disposal, certification and permit fees, loan closing costs, site preparation, inspection fees, construction site cleanup, and disposal of construction-related materials. The goal in the development of any pro forma is to be accurate and to inspire confidence in the audience. A simple mistake, even an error of minor omission, can cause the whole presentation to be called into question and the project to be shelved.

# A Doctor's Office with Special Needs

There is a temptation to think that this is just like any other ambulatory care facility, clinic, or doctor's office, except it is not. The following points may be helpful in developing the site and in thinking through how this project might better serve the workforce consumer. These are offered with the understanding that the architect designing the facility has healthcare experience and that the basic functional points of construction associated with a doctor's office (sinks, patient flow, special lighting, special storage situations, privacy, etc.) are all being dealt with as part of the general design. If the architectural team is not familiar with healthcare design and construction, they should be checking their work with someone who is.

If pediatric patients (and their mothers) are to be served, there should be special areas for the little patients and for nursing mothers. Some facilities have separate areas for well children and for sick children. If there is a childcare center on the worksite, there has to be some thought given to how the medical facility and the childcare facility will co-exist. How will kids be transported between the facilities and how will their security be assured?

If there are ancillary areas (wellness, dental, physical therapy, laboratory, pharmacy), there will be special design requirements. Wellness and physical therapy often require shower and changing facilities, and they may have an access point and registration process that is not linked to the care site to allow patients (or employees who are just involved in exercise and preventive programming) to access an area without going through a doctor-office environment. Will security cameras be needed for general exercise areas? Will there be a need for computer kiosks so that employees can access their personal health records? Is there a plan for a classroom or for group

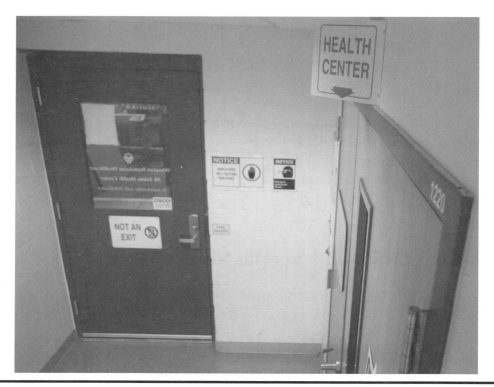

**Figure 17.1   This picture depicts the obvious but it reflects a challenge in many installations. How close can the clinic services be to the plant? What are the barriers or advantages to proximity? What about security (both ways)?**

meeting areas? All of these questions (or the answers to them) will change the nature of the facility from that of a standard medical office to one that is truly a health center.

If safety services are to be included, there needs to be special emergency access and, in some industries, this may include detoxification facilities or at least an emergency shower area. If this is a true decontamination issue that is combined with medical intervention, the facilities must address U.S. Environmental Protection Agency (EPA) standards as well as those associated with the Occupational Safety and Health Administration (OSHA) and with the medical protocols. Ambulance access must be considered, and the transition from the industrial or work setting should be separate from the regularly scheduled patient traffic areas.

Some employers incorporate wellness and exercise areas, and this type of planning requires a background beyond that of a normal medical office. This is a consumer orientation that is common to health clubs and fitness

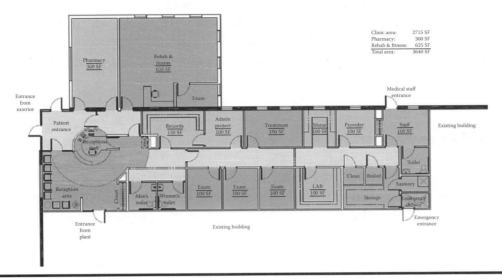

**Figure 17.2** **Shown is a conceptual floor plan that matches some of the material in this chapter. This is a primary care practice site with access from two different zones for public and workplace support.**

centers, and the only articulation between the exercise area and a medical site may be registration, the transfer of information, and monitoring. If rehabilitation is to occur in the exercise space (especially pulmonary or cardiac rehabilitation with patients who are fulfilling exercise prescriptions),

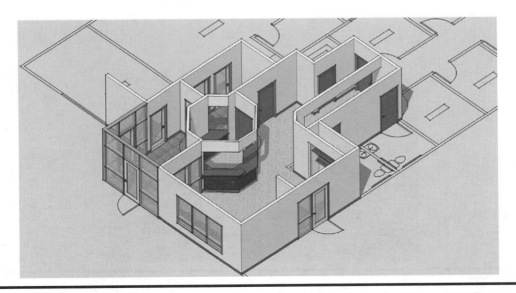

**Figure 17.3** **This is another view of the same floor plan shown in Figure 17.2 that shows spatial relationships and reflects the basic functionality of the space. The reader might note that this is a simple space program that meets the needs of primary care but does not accommodate many of the "extras."**

this space may need to be equipped with patient physiological monitoring equipment and emergency call mechanisms. It should also be staffed with appropriately trained technicians qualified to recognize patients in trouble and prepared (and equipped) to intervene if necessary.

## The "Wow Factor"

Employees initially choose a site for service on the basis of cost, convenience, and maybe curiosity. They return because of service, confidence, and the features that they experience. This is another area in which the facility can be a factor in program success. The only place to which a patient can compare the on-site experience is their own doctor's office or to a hospital environment. If the employer has taken the initiative in making the clinic look and feel different, the employee will not only react positively, they will share their positive impressions and experience with others.

There are many environments that house on-site programming that really induce the customer to have an experience that is different than the typical doctor visit they have known in the past. The architect should be encouraged to build in some features that distinguish the project. These may be functional design factors or merely interior design, but the goal is to have some part of the facility that is unique and inviting.

**Figure 17.4   A facility built to impress patients, their family, and visitors. This is the Cerner Healthe site at its home office in Kansas City, Missouri, which has been engineered to avoid any space for waiting or patient staging before arrival in the examination area.**

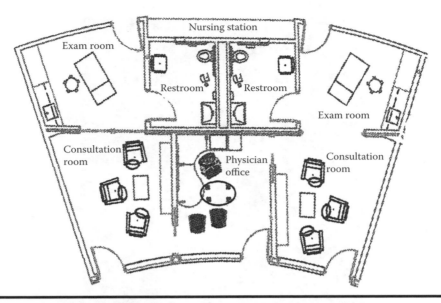

**Figure 17.5** **This is the clinic floor plan for the Cerner operation that reflects provider efficiency, consumer service, and comfort levels not generally found in the standard doctor office.**

# The Architectural Process May, or May Not, Involve an On-Site Vendor

This is an area of contention, especially among the vendor community. Most vendors would like to be involved in the planning process and the provision of services. Depending upon the timing and the confidence level in the vendor, this may be suitable and very appropriate. However, a fast-tracked project must often move the facility and program planning ahead without the vendor or implementation staff on board. Also, many firms have facility planning staff available, and they are either working with available space and land or they have the confidence that they can develop the facility that might be used by whatever vendor is finally chosen.

This goes back to the issue of planning that has been stressed throughout the book. If the program waits for a vendor or a consultant to plan the project, it probably will be an "off-the-shelf" product, and it may not exactly fit the employer and employee needs. The employer should plan the project and then choose the vendor. If the approach is one that is determined externally, it will probably work as well as all of the other programs that have been adopted from outside vendors to attempt to address healthcare costs and issues. Also, each design is unique to the grounds and the nature

**Figure 17.6   The Toyota Family Health Center reception pavilion, obviously built to welcome (and impress) potential patients.**

of the employer's existing structures and plant facility. Depending on the region of the country, it may also have unique features defined by geography, weather, and soil conditions. The employer may not have staff who feel comfortable in designing a medical facility, but there are many architects well versed in medical matters, and few will be challenged by the fact that this is a medical facility at a work site.

The process is pretty simple.

- Define the size and the scope of the needed facility.
- Determine the actual site location on the basis of available space and proximity to the end users—the employees and their beneficiaries.
- Determine basic levels of construction finishes and interior standards.
- Plan for patient access that complies with site-security issues.

- Study and define parking ratios and estimates for surrounding buffer areas.
- Have a basic architectural rendering prepared with information and assumptions available suitable for general estimates on cost per square foot.
- If the cost per square foot and the overall project cost are achievable, utilize the architectural renderings along with a specification sheet (based on location, finishes, and service lines) for inquiries to qualified contractors.

## Capital and Timing

Unlike medical contracts and those for vendors for on-site services, the contracting of architects and construction services follow a predefined path that is pretty well known to most enterprises. Architectural firms use standard American Institute of Architects (AIA) process steps and contract forms. General contractors likewise have standards for pricing and contracting. Fees can generally be pretty easily determined and are very negotiable. The advantage for the firm in getting this process started is that it will define two important factors for the project—capital need and timing. These are the two critical elements that turn a strategic plan into a project plan.

Return on investment (ROI) cannot be defined unless there is an investment on which to base it, and the test of a program is in which quarter the capital will be allocated. The timing process also allows definitive contracting with time-sensitive objectives for any vendor. If a vendor is not going to be utilized, it establishes the hiring process and determines when personnel should be engaged in the process of program implementation. A solid time frame also allows the employee information campaign to begin because the facility will become a major part of any "awareness" process.

Fast-tracking might be done if the employer is committed to the program and if it has access to a site and an architectural firm with medical experience. The facility does not, and will not, change but on-site providers would be replaced for a variety of reasons. If there is a high level of confidence in program commitment, the facility can move forward without a contracted provider.

# Chapter 18

# Workforce and Population Analysis: Prevention, Intervention, Wellness, Disease Management, and the Care Management Team

[D]isease-state management can be described as an integrated system of interventions, measurements and refinements of health-care delivery designed to optimize clinical and economic outcomes within a specific population.[1]

Overall, disease management does not seem to affect utilization except for a reduction in hospitalization rates among patients with congestive heart failure and an increase in outpatient care and prescription drug use among patients with depression. When the costs of the intervention were appropriately accounted for and subtracted from any savings, there was no conclusive evidence that disease management leads to a net reduction of direct medical costs.[2]

# Value, Volume, Pricing, and Cost

When one leaves the realm of the individual patient encounter, the question of the management of a series of encounters becomes an issue. The right choice can be made by a patient and a doctor for one event, but the disease process and the behavior that might have exacerbated it is drawn from patient lifestyle, the social situation, family heredity, social situations, etc. The focus of health benefit program construction has traditionally been to manage the event and not the process. Enter "disease-state management" and the process of defining the environment and the background behind the event for which the patient is seeking healthcare treatment.

This is where leaps of faith can be suicidal or where they can lead to a giant leap forward in the management of a population. Some definitions are important. First, forget "quality" as an indicator. There are really no indices of practitioner and facility quality that apply. There are certifications, credentials, and accreditation, but very little to suggest that once a provider (institutional or individual) is deemed to have the appropriate background and licensing, they have any better or worse skills or capabilities than the one down the street. However, this does not mean that there is not any way to qualify services to the population under management.

If we forget quality, we can concentrate on value. This takes into account effectiveness and pricing. However, the price of health services is often confused with employee contributions and muddled with discounts. The true price is the actual cost, and this can be derived from the claims history. However, the story does not end there, because the cost of an event is different than the cost of a particular service. Can the event be defined from an occurrence or an outbreak? A heart attack may be identified as a process that begins with chest pain and ends with cardiac rehabilitation (hopefully, because the only other outcome is death). However, the real beginning is poor diet, lack of exercise, and bad genes. I am under the assumption that there is someone else out there writing a book on preselecting employees with good genes. So this chapter is limited to the idea that the heart attack event can be defined by a treatment plan that addresses lifestyle, prevention, early risk identification, diet, exercise, and (where needed) correct diagnosis and treatment.

Some of these things are pretty simple to address because the person who is most at risk of having a heart attack might be easily picked out of a crowd because of weight or a smoking habit (for example). This could be helpful overall because the overweight person is also linked to many other disease states such as diabetes, depression, pulmonary problems, joint problems, back ailments, hypertension, etc. The congruence of health and lifestyle seems to follow age, weight, and behavior, and because we cannot address age, the program planning should try the other two categories.

Thankfully the disease-state management crowd has already laid out a pretty good road map to identify categories of concern and care intervention. However, one clarification is important in this process because even the term is misleading. Disease-state management is not about the disease (or only partially about it), because the thing that is really being managed is the population that is prone to the disease and the individual patients themselves. This is more targeted than simply addressing the idea that a workforce that exercises is healthier than one that does not—it relates to identifying those employees and healthcare beneficiaries who are at risk and moving forward with a plan of education and intervention that will reduce that risk.

Some conditions (or categories) readily present themselves and seem to be the main areas on which disease-state management (DSM) is focused.*

- ■ Asthma and allergies
- ■ Cardiovascular diseases such as coronary artery disease and congestive heart failure
- ■ Depression disorders and disorders dealing with chronic compulsive behavior and addiction
- ■ Diabetes
- ■ Digestive diseases
- ■ Infectious diseases such as urinary tract infection and community-acquired pneumonia
- ■ Chronic pain
- ■ Matters relating to women's health issues

Why these categories? Pretty simple, they are all chronic disease or health incidence arenas that are easily predictable. They all have potential for high cost and high pharmaceutical utilization. Each can be approached with a variety of treatment options and each is known to be somewhat controllable or reversible with early recognition and intervention. Obviously, what is needed is an integrated system of some kind that measures the impact of different initiatives and optimizes the various resources necessary to control the disease itself and the behaviors that lead to the symptoms and misdirect patient energy, causing additional risk and cost.

---

* For the purposes of this chapter, employee assistance programs (EAPs) have been ignored, but not forgotten. There are targeted programs for substance abuse, alcoholism, and other chronic physical and behavioral maladies that are associated directly with healthcare but often handled discreetly.

## Systems Are Good, but What Is Really Needed Is Someone in Charge

The concept of "case management" is not new. Chapter 10 introduced this concept as a constructive part of the "high performance network." Most managed care programs have some form of a case manager who will intervene in an admission, perform some sort of secondary review, and monitor the process related to a procedure to encourage efficient utilization of resources (or at least avoid waste, if possible). The care management function that is anticipated here is one that is on campus and directed to support only the components of the employer's program and its beneficiaries. The difference is that the care manager is part of the treatment team and interacts directly with the primary care doctor and the specialist in the high-performance network. The fact that the primary care provider (PCP) is on-site and dedicated to this particular population allows specific input and direction to be shared with the care team (as well as with the patient and his or her support team).

This approach is meant to be very involved and focused, and it moves a patient from provider to provider, especially in a surgical event or an admission, with precision and knowledge of the local resources available. It extends and supports primary care and becomes an ally to the hospitalized individual and an advocate for the person in need of care. Once it is established and it has a "face," the employees and their dependents will come to see it as a service and not a barrier to care. Whatever national or contracted disease-state management services that might be available will be complemented by this function and not replaced or diminished in any way. However, there may be a need for coordination if the two functions are both in receipt of reports or communications and if there is a notification function that is developed and coordinated with the inpatient healthcare institutions.

How does "care management" work and how are the savings projected? First, it works as a facilitator or a conduit for care for employees and beneficiaries, not a gatekeeper (except for knowledge about providers). The main areas of focus are

- Prevention of unnecessary admissions
- Attention to admissions to ensure that they are minimized in length
- Support of employees in making decisions that steer them toward more efficient providers, but especially away from those that are inefficient or wasteful

- Prevention of unnecessary and duplicative testing
- Prevention of unnecessary emergency department visits
- Assessment of "best and most optimum" care locations (hospital, home or extended care facility)
- Assistance to employees and patients in the consideration and evaluation of health service options and how and when they are necessary
- Provision of health coaching support to frequent health system users (the frequent fliers)
- Development of relationships with providers to ensure immediate access and timely reporting processes

In a previous chapter dealing with the concept of care management and coaching, the idea of a healthcare consigliere (or something like it) was introduced. This was tongue-in-cheek but not so far off. The on-site care manager is the person who meets the patient when care is engaged and who provides an important feedback loop. Combined with the rest of the team members, this can be a very effective part of the program, and it can complement almost every other aspect of program design.

## The Team? One Component Is the Incentive Program

Every piece of healthcare usually works independently. One reason for this is the concept of fee-for-service payment because it invades every aspect of the health system. In the case of disease-state and population management, the team members all need to understand that their key responsibility is to address the needs of the population, the individual patient, and to support the efforts of the other team members. This is best done when incentives are aligned. Incentives mean money, and the idea of a consumer having an adjusted co-pay should go hand in hand with that of a vendor having a certain amount of their fees associated with population well being and health status improvement. It goes hand in hand with the doctor being paid for effectiveness, patient satisfaction, and compliance with protocols. If these important pieces are missing, the entire program is reduced to a simple staffing plan for an on-site clinic.

This is still a process that is emerging, and everyone has a different answer or approach, which means, of course, that there is no one answer. However, in the unique arena of an employer-based program, the search for the answer starts with data, and data start with claims and a computer system that can track them. This is more of an issue of data aggregation and management of data points than one of billing or reporting. All of the components of the care cycle should be connected in some way and each should commit to share demographic, enrollment and event data.

This type of aggressive data mining and follow-up is the only way that return on investment (ROI) will move from a cost-per-clinic visit to the analysis of the total cost of an untreated illness and the cost/benefit of addressing different forms of intervention early. This is the only way that wellness and health promotion programming will survive hard times and hard chief financial officers.

The idea of tracking a population or group of patients is a simple concept that suggests that the employees and dependents in a population that use services in any one year will probably be those that use services in the future. This follows also the Pareto Principle (80% of the cost is associated with 20% of the healthcare-covered group). However it is described, the fact is that there is a subset of any working population that has a propensity to use care and to consume healthcare resources. This is a group that can be identified and, once identified, assisted in finding ways to avoid unnecessary utilization and fostering appropriate and efficient use of health resources, if the care is actually necessary.

## Developing and Adopting Treatment Guidelines

Choose the team, align the incentives, and define a baseline level or pattern of care. Hopefully, by now, the specialists who are high-volume users of diagnostics and procedures have also been identified, and there is a network of "preferred practitioners" to which people are being directed.

The protocols can be obtained readily from literature associated with national organizations, national expert panel recommendations, and managed care groups. Many hospital and health plans have endorsed protocols and care plans. They can be purchased in algorithmic form and in preloaded software formats.*

Success is achieved by agreeing on the protocols and by using the standard total quality improvement (TQI) process for implementation. The physician

---

* Some sources include the America Board of Internal Medicine, the American Heart Association, the American Lung Association, and the Joint National Committee on Detection, Evaluation, and Treatment of High Blood Pressure, to name a few.

is the key and the patient has to be the focus of any program. The patient's incentive seems to be evident—better health status—but this is not enough. That is why many programs are developing incentives that align more with a reality show mentality than the idea of total health being its own reward. Trips to Disneyland are often coordinated with savings bonds and discounts on healthcare premiums to reward body mass index and lipid panel improvement. Whatever works is fair as long as everyone is on the same playbook and has the same set of goals.

## This Is Not Actuarial Science and These Are Not Gatekeepers

Very sophisticated disease management models and actuarial prediction strategies can be used to verify this concept and to help manage a program, but at the start, this is usually overkill. The reason these services exist is that primary care services are often disconnected from the patient base. This is a factor that does not exist with an on-site program in which the employer is taking an active role in managing the process of healthcare delivery and purchasing.

It may help to define a couple of terms that are used and misused in discussing patient care and the management of disease processes in a population of patients. Case management is a term that is most often associated with the management of an admission process by a healthcare professional (generally a nurse) who is notified at some point in the disease or injury event and who then directs or channels the care once the patient has engaged the healthcare system. This is another form of "gatekeeping," a term that fell into disrepute in the health maintenance organization (HMO) era when the "gatekeeper" was a doctor who acted as a primary care conduit to other healthcare access (such as tests and specialists) and who (in the minds of many consumers) was incentivized to restrict access to care. In the approach suggested and fostered by the most successful programs, the "case management" process is redesigned to assign the patient, who is navigating the healthcare system, a facilitator who can intervene to ensure that the healthcare experience is coordinated and efficient.

The care manager (who has replaced the case manager) is engaged when the patient first encounters the healthcare system. He or she manages the many competing forces that buffet the patients in their most vulnerable moment—when they are sick or hurt. The care manager can prevent duplicative tests, get the patient into an environment that matches their care needs, assist in the access to specialists, arrange for discharge support, etc. When paired with a primary care physician who is also focused on the patient's well-being, the care manager is the person who can often supply the organizational muscle to force the system to work when there is a roadblock or a problem with simple matters of communication. Anyone who has dealt with phone trees and answering services can appreciate that just getting an appointment or a form to authorize a test can be a daunting task.

In the case of "care management," there is an adoption of a patient-focused approach. This is not a reaction to a healthcare need as much as it is a proactive focus on a patient's need for planning when the patient actually has a healthcare challenge of some kind. It is sort of a wellness and prevention program for someone who is already sick or prone to a sickness of some kind. This type of service is less about responding to the crisis as much as it is recognizing that a crisis is looming and preplanning for the event. This is not really disease-state management as such. It is much more the understanding that there are some individuals within a company's covered population who have a predisposition to healthcare events and the fact that the nature of these events can be predicted. If this is the case, and the PCP and patient recognize this fact, why not go ahead and prepare for the event?

Examples are easy to find in any of the current literature references to disease management. The top vote-getters in any healthcare managers' poll for "most likely to be admitted" would include conditions related to heart disease, diabetes, and asthma. Depending on the population, there might be an additional category added for prenatal care and some musculoskeletal (back) ailments. This is not to say that there are not other opportunities for care management. There are several, but each firm should be working with their medical and analytical team to identify their own costs and opportunities and tailor the response to their unique situation. Again, the best predictor of future health system use (hospital and emergency department admission) can be the most recent use—simple, not complex.

What would a "care manager" look like, as opposed to a "case manager"? The care manager is probably going to be a nurse and he or she would be a member of the healthcare team and closely allied with the primary care physician. However, the PCP would not necessarily be the only guide because the care manager would have the entire population as a focus of intervention, not just the population served on-site. The care management nurse would work with the analytical process to identify the covered beneficiaries who might be considered most prone to require care in the immediate future.

There might be a tool set provided by a disease management firm or identification through a simple review of patient claims. (It is not a challenging process to find the patients who will be most likely to be hospital and emergency department consumers in any upcoming period.)

The following questions can define a pretty good subset of the population for the care manager to assist:

■ Which patients have been admitted in the past for disease-specific care?
■ Which patients have been prescribed medications for diseases or conditions that complement the care management model?
■ Which beneficiaries were admitted to an emergency department in the last 24 months with complications or crises associated with one of the health conditions under review?

The challenge with this approach is that there is a need for access to specific claims data and a level of access to the patient's primary care physician to ensure that privacy rules are not compromised in some way. One cannot just sift through data and begin calling people about their health status. There must be a process that respects Health Insurance Portability and Accountability (HIPAA) regulations and fosters employee confidence rather than concern or anxiety. Like any program component associated with an on-site clinic, the standard for implementation is higher than that faced by an HMO or independent third-party administrator because this is an employer-sponsored process.

The care manager can become the ally of the beneficiary for any kind of health access or coordination. The best care managers become aware of the lifestyles of their charges and can work with them toward not only effective utilization of the healthcare system but also a higher level of prevention. The chronic asthmatic, the family with a number of children with allergies, or a sufferer with emphysema can come to rely upon a care manager to assist with medication, access to support services, enrollment in informational programs, etc. Coordination at the care services level might involve a home site visit and assistance with personal monitoring and lifestyle changes. Whatever form it takes, the care manager will also be a "first line" call when the member needs assistance with access to health services because of a crisis or a change in their condition. Successful and effective care managers are on call and available for patients and families that they serve.

The care manager should not be confused with the old "gatekeeper" mentality. The care manager is not incentivized to any endpoint except efficiency, effectiveness, and patient satisfaction. The care manager may suggest alternatives for access, such as an appointment with the PCP rather than a visit to an emergency department. She may be armed with access to a special list of specialists and diagnostic services who have guaranteed access or who link to the on-site electronic medical record (EMR). She may know of approaches to receiving medical services that are participating providers within the employer healthcare network. Whatever she knows, and has access to, it is meant to be in the benefit of the patient and not a barrier to patient care in any way.

Firms that embrace Lean Programming and TQI will find that population management is analyzed the same way that production controls might be. One is not prone to use the word "defect" in the same sentence with "employee benefit programs," but the fact is that some of the inefficiencies in the system can be worked on in the same way that other processes are studied. However, it has to be in conjunction with solid data and informed and empowered providers.

## References

1. Mary C. Gurnee and Robert V. Da Silva. "Constructing Disease Management Programs." http//www.managedcaremag.com/archives/9706/9706.disease_man.shtml.
2. Soeren Mattke, Michael Seid, and Sai Ma. "Evidence for the Effect of Disease Management: Is $1 Billion a Year a Good Investment?" *American Journal of Managed Care,* 13, no. 12, 2007: 670–676.

## Chapter 19

# Special Situations and Some Solutions (Middlemen, Brokers, Third-Party Administrators, and Consultants)

## Advisors Do Not Come Cheap

The firm is well advised to pick its helpers carefully. As with any purchase that is managed by a procurement strategy, these relationships should be occasionally tested for fit and for price. Strangely, most firms settle into a zone of comfort, and there is seldom any evidence that they re-price or rethink services on any kind of routine basis. Healthcare is a special situation, and middlemen come in various forms. The danger in an on-site care process is in creating an additional level of management at the firm site (which adds overhead). This may include a vendor that becomes a broker of services and conduit for healthcare dollars. The goal is to see where there is an ability to apply the health benefit dollars directly to the need and the purchase of the services without having additional fees tacked on as purchases are consolidated, managed, billed, reported, and otherwise re-sold from level to level.

How much play is there in the healthcare middleman/broker arena? In one often-reported case (Southern California Edison), direct contracting saved over 20% of the total healthcare cost profile for their employees.[1] Most of the self-funded firms could use the process of direct contracting, but that would only provide a portion of the savings that the network development processes described elsewhere in this book could produce. The contracting may not even need to be "direct," if the choice of the providers can be managed. Someone has to perform this task. In addition to that "someone" who is doing the contract development, bills need to be prepared and reports need to be generated. Many firms will find that they are still going to contract for specialty services from national groups that allow employees to receive care when they are out of the area [national preferred provider organizations (PPOs)]. Also, there is going to be a need in most cases for stop-loss insurance coverage, and this must articulate with the on-site program and the manner in which cases are managed.

## The Smarter the On-Site Management Team, the Fewer Middlemen

The trick is not necessarily to get rid of any of the advisors or consolidators, it is to make sure there is no overlap and that the pricing is transparent. If there is a standard and conventional process for pricing, check that against what other firms are paying. If there is not transparency, then the goal is to achieve it somehow. This gets tricky with pharmacy benefit managers (PBMs), discounts, and commissions. The on-site vendor or on-site management team must be charged with the overall management of the entire healthcare "spend," and one of their goals has to be to replace the past practice of "business as usual" with the standard that no relationship is guaranteed and nothing is sacred. Everything is up for review.

Some points to consider:

- The on-site managers should be charged with annual comparisons of all costs relative to market alternatives and comparisons of internal benchmarks. These should be reported through the clinic and its on-site operations because these managers—from whatever source they draw their knowledge—touch every aspect of service and performance.
- Each subcomponent must be evaluated to see if there is transparency and an ability to review the service and, where appropriate, re-bid it.

- Each service vendor should sign an ethics statement and ensure the firm that they are reporting complete costs including (but not limited to) commissions, premiums, rebates, bonuses, volume riders, prizes, concessions, etc. Complete means everything. This may need to be explained a couple of times to some vendors.

## What Is Needed for Operations?

There is no way that a healthcare program can launch without the assistance of any number of support functions, some of which will bear the burden of being called "middlemen." Some may be organized through an on-site provider, and some may be actually contracted through that provider. A listing is offered (with some comments) for planning purposes.

- The PBM has been discussed elsewhere in this book. This will be a different process if one is contracting with Walgreens versus another (non-pharmacy-based) provider. The firm should watch this relationship carefully because it is one that has a great deal of built-in premium rewards related to volumes and discounts.
- The third-party administrator (TPA) is necessary to process claims and adjudicate payments. This is a critical function if several groups are going to be involved. Most of the pricing has to do with the payment of claims and, in a self-funding situation that uses on-site care, one must

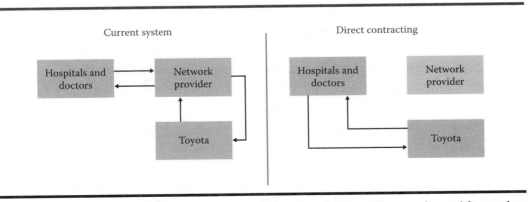

**Figure 19.1    Before and after. Toyota deals directly with suppliers and providers using the same procurement methods honed over years of prudent purchasing. Why should there be a middleman?**

ask if the cost of claims processing is the same if there is no check being issued and a final adjustment process being made. The TPA would say "yes," common sense says "no."

■ The insurance broker (for stop-loss) is a key player for many firms. The broker has a lot to do with pricing and program features. With an on-site clinic, everything is up for redefinition. There is a newly contracted price structure with hospitals (reduced premiums?), and there is a more active role in direct management of patient care (redefined coverage?). In any case, the clinic presence and the construction of the contracting network should change every premise on which traditional premiums were based If there is stop-loss or re-insurance in place, re-bid it.

■ Benefits counselors and other consultants, where needed, may actually be a cost that increases (in the short term) with an on-site program. This is because the benefits program is being changed and reorganized. The idea of paying anyone on a commission basis, in this regard, should be questioned. This area is all straight hourly fee consulting, and it should be clarified in some way through a pre-project proposal to keep a lid on the costs.

■ Networks like independent practice associations (IPAs), PPOs, and service contracts related to laboratory or disease management or employee assistance programming (EAP) and any other support modality can be lumped into the middleman hunt for value. Are these still necessary? Are there alternatives? Can they be redefined now that there is an on-site management function?

■ There may be a program component for the analysis of claims and comparison of the claims information to a data warehouse or to standards provided by mining (or borrowing) data from other firms. This may be done by an insurance company that has a base of information or by a business coalition or, in the future, by emerging organizations called Regional Health Information Organizations (RHIOs). This is *important* information to have if it is in a useful and applicable format. However, sometimes it is constructed and disseminated on a one-time basis (like a consultant would provide it), and sometimes there is a requirement for the firm to use a subscription of sorts or to sign up and engage in the services for a period of time. There is not much that can substitute for information access, and these programs make sense if they are structured to actually provide it. Many times these service bureaus just aggregate a bunch of data without really suggesting ways to find (or to apply) the knowledge contained within the data. The message here is to continuously re-evaluate the need for these vendors and to challenge what they provide.

## What Is the Role of the On-Site Management Team, Again?

They should know the costs of every aspect of the program and how those costs bring value to the table. They should know the alternatives available to the firm and be the catalysts for rechecking and rethinking each and every contract. Their role is to be the one who stands up and takes ownership of a relationship when someone asks if a specific component or contract is of value and if it is priced correctly.

The addition of the management body in an on-site program allows the middle part of healthcare that is involved in coordinating delivery (but not actually in delivering anything) to be continuously reviewed. It does not matter if the program is managed externally. This is the firm's means to rethink each and every step in the process of organizing healthcare, what it means to the employees, and to confirm the role of every subcontractor.

## Reference

1. David Wessel, Bernard Wysocki, Jr., and Barbara Martinez. "Spending Bypass: As Health Middlemen Thrive, Employers Try to Tame Them." *Wall Street Journal Online*, http://online.wsj.com/article_print/SB116732697745661660 (December 29, 2006).

*Chapter 20*

# Working with the Vendors: The Request for Proposal and Its Application to the Development Process

## Requests for Proposal, Requests for Information, and Cost Savings Competitions

The idea of implementing an on-site program may be daunting, so many employers will choose to go the "vendor route" and subcontract the effort to a firm that specializes in this type of healthcare provision. The problem then becomes how to choose the appropriate vendor and, once chosen, how to execute a contract for on-site services. Although nothing is standard, the common approach would be to go through some kind of planning process, often with the assistance of a consulting group or benefits management firm. Once this is done, the consultant or someone in purchasing or human resources (HR) develops an request for proposal (RFP) and the process of selection is engaged.

With more vendors coming into the industry, and more firms morphing into on-site providers, the process is changing somewhat. Now, many vendors are offering analytic services and performing the cost-benefit analysis. The process is changed to one in which the vendor interests the employer; a pro forma is done that shows considerable savings potential, and a consultant is engaged to check or validate the vendor's work product. In some cases, the sales process of the vendors themselves will initiate the RFP process. Variations on the theme include situations in which a request for information (RFI) is developed, and various vendors are matched against each other, each vying for the top spot as the healthcare cost savings winner. A consultant is generally engaged to sort out the responses and to keep the information internally comparable so that a determination can be made, comparing like categories and performance criteria.

There are differences in the process, but the same components are always present. First, there is a decision to go with (consider, expand to, adopt) an on-site program. Then, somebody does a projection on costs. There is an active or passive determination that there is a need for an outside vendor to provide the services. Deciding that there is a need for a competition, somebody thinks of an RFP and, after the selection, there is a contracting process. This is simple, straightforward, and probably similar to other contracting and purchasing processes the employer already uses.

Differences occur when a firm has a pretty good idea of what they want to do and how they want to accomplish it. If there is just a general idea, and the important thing is to form a process for deciding if this is a go or not, then a vendor sales representative will probably emerge who will offer a free analysis, and this may become the focus of the planning process. This is about as effective as choosing insurance from an agent that calls your house in the evening and offers a free analysis of your insurance needs and a plastic portfolio in which to store your policies. The planning becomes marginalized by a sales process that is embodied in a business analysis. If the firm has a plan, an idea of the direction they want to pursue, and the place they want to be, the process can be much more effectively completed by getting the appropriate vendor (or a couple of them) to fit their programming to the goals that have already been determined rather than the other way around.

If there is a need to create a final plan with all of the detail necessary on the basis of the vision of the employer, this can be done with the assistance of other firms who are consultants focused on the project development, not long-term implementation and management (therefore, less potential for conflicts of interest to play a role in the development phase). Many of these are listed in this book. Contacting firms who have already made this journey, most of whom are eager to share their experiences, can also assist in this process. The best approach is introspection and planning that is self-directed and results in a unique set of goals and objectives that are driven by the nature of the work force and the firm that uses them.

# RFP or RFI?

An RFI is a request for information and it is generally, well, pretty general. It asks about the firm and does not get into many specifics. It is looking for some basic information that might include the willingness of a firm to respond to a more formal RFP and matters that may include references, performance, general approaches to pricing, etc. It is a part of the process that can usually be dispensed with if there are limited vendors and a pretty clear scope of work to be done. The example of the choice of an electronic medical record (EMR) comes to mind. As of this writing, there are over 200 EMR purveyors jockeying for the market among doctors, hospitals, and everyone else out there providing medical care. As of the printing of this book, who knows how many there will be. For a person choosing a medical record for their office or hospital, there is a real reason to start with an RFI that might help narrow the field.

In contrast, a firm looking for an on-site service has an algorithm that goes something like this:

- Are we going to do it ourselves? If not,
- Are we going to use a local hospital or medical group? If not,
- Which of the national or regional vendors will we choose?

In looking over the universe of vendors, there are only a handful that will come to the forefront. If the employer is national, they may wish to align with a vendor that can become a national partner and provide services for every installation. If they are local, they may have a choice of regional partners or even look to a firm that is already providing services on-site and see if they can piggyback somehow on their program. All of these options deserve consideration, but the fact is that there will probably not be an enormous field of choices if the firms have been vetted properly beforehand.

Vetting means simply checking them out. Many of the firms are privately held, and they are minimally capitalized. Simply stated, they are probably not very dependable, and they may have, like many firms that are startups, a pretty thin management team. Can the firm back up their promises? What is the risk of performance if the principal of the firm is hit by a bus or just loses interest? Can the firm perform in any kind of economic and/or political turmoil that might arise in the healthcare environment? Small is not bad, but a more modestly sized firm may be able to provide a higher level of guarantees and back up a contract with more contingencies. Bigger has its own problems, and the firm doing the contracting will quickly figure this out when the national firm presents a contract and the concept of flexibility and fit is explored.

## A Sample RFP for the Firm with a Plan

For the firm that "gets it," there is an approach that moves the RFP to a level of collaboration and insight that will short-circuit the RFI process and get to the core of the project. The approach is to simply state the program goals (which we have done in sample format) and then to go right to the firm's strengths and weaknesses. The goals of the program are simply pass/fail. If a vendor firm needs to explain an answer that requires a simple "yes," then they fail and the firm conducting the RFP simply moves on to another vendor.

The core issues are focused on just a few "essay questions."

- What distinguishes your services from others?
- Who is going to be our contact person and program manager?
- Take us to a place where you have already done this type of a program.
- Tell us about your EMR.
- Tell us about your ability to manage a narrow network of preselected specialists.
- How will your services be priced on this project?

Again, if there is waffling or an extensive/vague answer on these questions, move on. Each question is designed to assist an employer in qualifying a vendor on the basis of criteria that will absolutely generate differences from provider to provider. The mature firms are the ones that can breeze through this process and give a simple and direct answer to each of these queries.

The following is a more formal RFP that includes these questions as well as the information for a "sample firm" that has decided it will move into the on-site service provision arena. The pass/fail component bears review because it encompasses what the employer (in this case, the fictional firm Ajax) has decided it needs as basic program components. The "essay questions" are highlighted along with the "pass/fail" components.

## Section One: Firm Background and the Intent of the RFP

Ajax Incorporated is a 1,000-employee firm with a self-funded PPO program for healthcare. It has an industrial base and it is located in Goshandgolly, Utah. The organization spent $8 million on its healthcare-combined programming in the most current calendar year. The intent of this RFP is to establish a partnership with a firm that can provide on-site services to its employees and their dependents in the form of an employer-sponsored health (ESH) program to be located at its primary manufacturing facility.

Ajax intends to obtain proposals from qualified firms interested in providing their employees and the dependents covered in their healthcare plan with a broad range of on-site primary care, occupational health, and overall coordination of all healthcare services. This RFP is being distributed to your company for consideration of services.

The goals of the ESH program at Ajax include the following:

- Increase quality and appropriateness of primary care and occupational health service goals
- Enhance access to care for employees and dependents
- Increase employee satisfaction, retention, and recruitment
- Coordinate services with local healthcare facilities and providers
- Promote healthy lifestyles and disease prevention
- Improve worker productivity and absenteeism
- Lower annual healthcare expenditures

Project Scope: Ajax recently completed a detailed feasibility study to define the benefits of an ESH program for its workforce. As a result of that study, Ajax has committed to initiating programming not later than January 1, 20___.

Key aspects of the program will include the following:

- Eligible employees totaling approximately 1,000 lives
- Eligible dependents totaling approximately 800 lives
- Renovation of approximately 3,000 square feet of existing plant space into Class A medical service space
- Service components including primary care, laboratory testing, rehabilitation, pharmacy, and care management

- Benefit design promoting enrollee use of on-site services
- Narrow network of high-performance specialty care and facility providers
- Robust information system, care management services, and reporting capabilities

Key projections of the program include the following:

- Year-one medical office visits of 2,200 increasing to 3,300 in year four
- Year-one therapy cases of 100 increasing to 120 in year four
- Year-one prescriptions of 5,000 increasing to 6,100 in year four
- Year-one laboratory draws of 2,500 increasing to 2,800 in year four
- Medical suite including three exams rooms, one treatment room, laboratory and rehabilitation space, and pharmacy
- Clinic hours ranging from approximately 50 to 60 hours per week

INSTRUCTIONS:   If you intend to respond to this RFP, please submit your Intent to Respond to _____ via fax by May 20, 20 ___, prior to sending in your response. A total of three (3) original copies and one electronic copy of your response and supporting material should be sent to _____ at the specified address. Final responses are due by 5:00 p.m. eastern standard time on June 1, 20 ___. Responses that are not delivered on time will not be considered.

Please prepare your response to the proposal requirements listed in the following section using the same format presented here. Your response should be brief and factual and should contain a minimum of preprinted marketing material.

Please note that all potential vendors, regardless of response, should treat the information contained in this RFP and obtained in follow-up communications as confidential. Vendors should not refer to Ajax in any media release or public announcement without prior written consent. All responses will be held by Ajax and remain the property of Ajax upon receipt. Ajax may distribute, reproduce, or photocopy the response and any supporting documentation for the purposes of internal evaluation.

This RFP is not deemed to be an offer by Ajax, and any response to this RFP by the participants shall not form any type of binding agreement between the parties. At any time, Ajax reserves the right to cancel this RFP at no cost or penalty to Ajax or any of its agents. Further, Ajax reserves the right to edit, alter, or modify the requirements of this proposal. Any changes will be communicated with all vendors that notify Ajax of their intent to respond to this RFP. At any time, Ajax reserves the right to negotiate with any potential vendor. Ajax shall not be liable for any costs associated with the preparation and/or the presentation of any vendor's response. Ajax reserves the right to request additional information for clarification from vendors during the evaluation process for this RFP.

Any potential vendor who discloses, shares, or distributes information related to this RFP to anyone outside the potential vendor's company will be immediately disqualified. Any potential vendor who attempts to contact Ajax through an unauthorized channel will be immediately disqualified.

Potential vendors must agree to provide and release necessary authorizations for Ajax or its representatives to verify any claims included in their response. Misstatements of experience and capabilities will be grounds for disqualification.

## Proposal Requirements/Responses

[*Essay Test*] (Each question should be addressed in not more than 200 words.)
Briefly describe three attributes that distinguish your firm from others in the marketplace that may also be responding to this proposal.

Please provide the *curriculum vitae* of the on-site manager that would be assigned to this project if your firm were selected as the management vendor for the project.

Please provide details and contact information for two similarly prepared sites (currently under your management) that would be willing to host members of the evaluation team for a day-long operational review session.

Please provide details on the methodology that your firm would utilize in establishing a reasonable price for the services requested through this RFP process.

Please provide a brief description of the EMR, practice management system, and data warehousing capabilities that your firm would use if selected as the management vendor for this project.

Please provide a brief description of your firm's experience in developing and managing a narrow network of specialty and facility providers.

Please indicate your commitment to the guiding principals of the Ajax ESH program. (*PASS/FAIL component*)

- The program will deliver the highest quality care available in accordance with established clinical protocols and evidence-based medicine.
- The focus of the ESH program will be the integration of health services across all spectrums of required care.
- Patient satisfaction will be a priority and continuously monitored and reported.
- The foundation of the ESH program will be the attributes represented by the Patient-Centered Medical Home model.
- There will be strong commitment to primary care and personal responsibility for health and wellness.
- Care management services will be an integral part of the programming and seek to effectively manage chronic disease and promote wellness.
- Positive relationships will be developed with local specialty and facility providers.
- A culture of continuous quality improvement will guide the operations of the program and the parties charged with overseeing it.
- The program will rely on a narrow network of providers committed to the goals of the ESH program and selected based on reliable quality data.
- Related services provided by third-party vendors such as disease-state management and workers' compensation case management will be integrated and coordinated through the providers of the on-site clinic.
- Confidential information will be handled according to industry standards and applicable laws and will not be used for any purpose other than for the benefit of Ajax and its employees/dependents.
- Health records and data will be collected and monitored utilizing state-of-the-art electronic records and management tools.
- Regular hours of operation will be established to reflect an appropriate balance between patient access and operational efficiency.
- Patients will be processed in an efficient manner with wait times far less than those currently experienced in the typical office setting.
- Time with provider will approximate between 20–30 minutes per visit and focus on acute needs as well and chronic conditions and lifestyle choices.
- Provider staffing ratios (MD/midlevel) will be established and reflect an appropriate balance between patient need and operational efficiency.
- The ESH program will provide and maintain a formulary with emphasis on cost containment.

- Adequate commercial and professional liability insurance will be maintained at all times.
- A dedicated on-site manager will be provided to oversee the operations of the ESH program.
- An account manager will be provided to serve as the liaison between the vendor and Ajax to address and resolve all issues identified.
- A designated backup to the on-site manager will be provided to cover regularly scheduled absences.
- A designated IT (information technology) professional will be provided to work cooperatively with Ajax and its representatives to implement and support the IT requirements of the ESH program at Ajax.
- Management fees will be fully documented and submitted monthly for review and processing.
- Performance clauses will be developed and utilized in the execution of any agreement for management services.
- The initial term of the management agreement will last for a minimum of three years with options for renewal based on successful negotiation between the parties.

As an authorized agent of [enter company name here], I acknowledge our commitment to guiding principals of the Ajax ESH program indicated above.

_____ (Signature)

_____ (Printed Name)

☐ Yes, we intend to submit a proposal for the Ajax ESH program as outlined in this RFP.
☐ No, we do not intend to submit a proposal for the Ajax ESH program as outlined in this RFP.

Contact Name (Signature): _____

Contact Name (Please print): _____

Company Name (Please print): _____

Street: _____

City/State: _____ Zip: _____

Phone Number: _____ Fax Number: _____

E-mail Address: _____

If this RFP is used, or some process like it, the firm will have all of the information it needs to get comfortable with a vendor that can actually provide the services it is seeking. Once the firm has been chosen, and they know that they are not one among many, but "the one," additional specificity can be achieved. The management team can be further defined, and an organization chart can be developed. A chart showing tables of authority can be developed. A sample contract can be requested and reviewed. Formal contingency planning can be discussed and a timeline for implementation jointly developed.

In a collaborative fashion, the employer and the vendor firm can further refine the appropriate levels of staffing and define standards that will determine sufficient and efficient staffing ratios and response to peak loading demands. A strategy for dealing with local political issues can be explored. The firm and the vendor can also develop a common lexicon of terms and really understand what "integration" is and how it is going to be defined and measured at the site. If there are other vendors for corollary programs [disease management, chiropractic, physical therapy, employee assistance programs (EAPs), dental, optical, etc.], the planning for integration of these important features can be addressed so that they will not only cohabitate the space and share the patient base but be involved (integrated) with meeting of the employer and employee needs through articulation with the medical record.

Because every program struggles with standards and with evaluation, this would be the time to also jointly agree on how the success or challenges will be measured. Demonstration of the ability to provide services is sometimes indicated by accreditation or licensure. The demonstration of effectiveness and quality must be shown through process measures and total quality improvement (TQI) programs. Getting these measurements (along with others such as accounting and other financial reporting issues) resolved up front is key to good program management and maintenance.

The assumption has been made that there has been a site visit, or two, by this time to other programs under management by the vendor. Therefore, discussions can reference what was remarkable or remarked on at the other sites. Because the program manager who will be responsible for the site has been identified, he or she is present at all of the planning and contracting functions and is involved in defining the scope and purpose of the program and in understanding the key elements of success. Details can be handled by staff that will actually be fulfilling each party's expectations.

Some challenges will still exist in program planning, and these include the development of wellness, workers' compensation, and ancillaries. There needs to be some benefit redesign and an employee awareness campaign. Of course, there is the issue of local network development and contracting.

There must be a clear understanding of the approaches being planned for utilization review, case management, care management, claims administration, and adjudication of claims from outside vendors and providers. In each case, standards have to be defined for the administration function to demonstrate proficiency. "Best practices" for delivering pharmacy services within the ambulatory services site and for the program overall will have to be defined.

## Do's and Don'ts

This approach will determine the best vendor and use that vendor's talents in a process of joint planning rather than through rug market bidding to attain a final result that is derived through a third-party-managed RFP process.

Some don'ts include the following: Don't force the vendor to contract or compete on "savings" projections. This is the type of health maintenance organization (HMO) style of contracting that will only produce program shortcuts, gatekeeper activity, and the type of cost savings that have been tried (and failed) in the past. Don't use the vendor standard contract. If it has only one approach, then it is not the vendor that can be in a flexible and learning program. Don't force a vendor to use resources that are precontracted or predetermined. Rather, make them responsible for program success by making them accountable for all aspects of the program.

Some do's include the following: Do involve legal early in the process (as an observer) to make sure they know the overall plan and its hoped-for result. Do make several trips to other sites and service environments to see what the end result should be. Do put everything on the table and force the re-examination of each part of the programming. Do stick to the principles and goals that are behind this process and make the vendor understand the importance of each. Do include the narrow network, value-oriented contracting, and a robust approach to primary care backed up by an EMR system.

## Some People Will Not Like This Approach

Among this group will be some vendors, some of the firm's existing on-site providers, the existing occupational medicine team, local benefits consultants, the local healthcare providers, and existing medical staff. As the firm responds to the criticism, it should consider the source.*

---

* Frankly, as a consultant who has proctored RFPs, this material will replace much of what I might do. Can a firm do this by itself? Definitely. Should it do so? Probably.

*Chapter 21*

---

# Political and Functional Barriers to Establishing an On-Site Medical Service

---

Having read all the literature and after meeting with several vendors who are promising employee satisfaction, savings, and improved productivity, the firm is convinced—an absolute trifecta! So what is holding up the program?

## "Let's Initiate On-Site Healthcare"

For those familiar with on-site healthcare and its many permutations, this seems like a "no-brainer." *"Stuff costs money. We can do stuff cheaper and better. Let's go."* The problem is that the decision-making process is different when it involves risk and requires capital. The following obstacles must be overcome in the on-site decision process:

- This is something we (meaning the host firm) have not done before. It is outside of our area of comfort.
- This is something that could have unquantifiable risk because it involves employee benefit issues and medical services.
- This program has political overtones.
- If it fails, this program is not easily reversible.
- This program requires significant capital.

The first two issues are derived from the fact that the firm considering the implementation of on-site health services (unless it is a hospital) is generally scared of healthcare. If it is not scared, the term might be cautious or respectful. Their staff people, attorneys, and advisors are not used to dealing with healthcare issues, and they are not comfortable with the regulatory environment or with the risk-limiting features of insurance products that might help address their concerns. One solution is always to relocate this risk to an outside vendor, but that comes with some cost and effort. The way to address this issue is to move it up front and either seek counsel from a legal group that has a grasp on this matter (probably not the corporate legal counsel) or decide that the program will be implemented by an outside vendor to whom the risk can be transferred.

There are also political overtones for every project, and these are different for each installation. In some cases, firms have a high regard for (and interrelationship with) the local healthcare community. In some cases, this is less of a problem with the healthcare community and more of a problem with labor groups, existing vendors, internal stakeholders, and present providers. The problem, like any political issue, can be moved from "insurmountable" to "surmountable" once the groups are recognized, listed, and addressed with some form of communication and commitment strategy. Once the overall decision is made, the issue of how these groups might be involved will arise again. If they can be part of the implementation scheme, their concerns might be channeled. If not, they may need to be ignored for the program to move forward.

When listing these political constituencies, each should be categorized as to their "rank" because any program that is truly revolutionary is not one that will be embraced by structures that benefit from the status quo. Employer sponsored on-site health is definitely not the status quo, and change comes hard to people who might feel marginalized, threatened, or part of a reorganization. The simple question is: "With whom must we work and which ones are important versus those that are not essential?" Because there will be some change, it is best to address the impact up front and decide if the opposition can be minimized, or if not, if it is something that anyone really cares about anyway.

Working with political groups and stakeholders, there is always the possibility that they may have a growth opportunity in the implementation of on-site care. Can they fit into the emerging program? Will their role survive, although it may be altered? Will they have an opportunity to continue to provide service (be involved) in a different fashion? This is where early identification and a written implementation plan might help. This is also where commitments from any vendor to incorporate existing staff, networks, and advisory functions into the on-site programming could make a political process less of a stumbling block.

Program "reversibility" is a challenge. Once an on-site clinic and the related structures are initiated, there is little chance of going back. This is not something that a firm can try for a while and then abandon. The benefit programs will likely have been altered, there may be a building, and employee policies (and expectations) have been recast. This "irreversibility" is one reason that firms linger so long over the idea and why it is one that generally has to move from the human resources (HR) venue to the "chiefs"—the chief executive officer (CEO), the chief financial officer (CFO), and, maybe, to the board.

Thankfully, this is getting easier with the general press concerning these programs listing the successes and general satisfaction of firms and their employees. Conferences have emerged, the literature is beginning to take note, and there are many "reference firms" willing to share endorsements of this type of programming. The challenge is to move away from the "vendor assurances" and on to a realm of objective information that can be used to show the feasibility and the practicality of this type of programming. It also helps to place this decision within the overall framework of the cost and changes occurring in the benefits area. Certainly, the background of cost-shifting, general fear of benefits loss, and the competitive problems created by benefit costs are a good backdrop against which to challenge status quo solutions.

## Irreversible?

Yes, but it is also a dramatic step that is being taken by the firms that can see beyond the near term and whose executives are planning for a competitive cost environment for the long term. The advent of on-site programming provides leverage that can be used for many other changes and program tweaks that could only be accomplished by a firm that is in touch with services and information the likes of which can only be directly managed by being in direct contact with the provider and the employee recipient.

One can also look at the challenge of reversibility in context. There are a lot of changes that are occurring without the firm's direct involvement. Healthcare costs are going up. Employees expect to be more directly involved financially and in their choice and payment of plan features. Reversibility is a relevant thought.

The issue of reversibility is less of a factor for any firm that falls within one of the following categories: (a) a firm committed to being an "employer of choice," (b) a firm that is already involved in on-site employee services such as childcare or exercise and health preventive programming, (c) a firm that is a technology leader or a clear "thought leader" in its industry, (d) a firm that is in a growth and acquisition mode, and (e) a firm that has a bunch of other unconsolidated healthcare cost control programming efforts.

## Capital

Capital is another matter. The idea of a new program that is merely an add-on contract change to a benefits constellation is a simple one. Try it; if it works, keep on doing it. There is no need to allocate space or capital. However, once the space and the capital needs are introduced, the whole equation for decision-making changes. We are including "space" in this discussion because very few firms "overbuild" space or "overbuy" on the prospect of expansion for anything but production. The allocation of space or facility capacity, to most industrial firms, would be a determination that is of similar (or even greater) gravity than capital. We are now in the realm of the chief financial officer and, the chief of facilities, and we are back to the concept of ROI (return on investment, return on capital, or whatever the firm wants to call it).

Hopefully, this section will offer some ideas about how these issues can be addressed and their effects mitigated. As a consulting firm, we work through issues like this with clients on a regular basis, and we probably have seen every factor that fosters success. We have been involved with some clients for almost 10 years in various stages of planning, planning, and more planning. The programs go through evaluation and often the data "times out," through re-evaluation. Our experience looking at successful programming is pretty much that of the industry. There are market leaders, innovators, and "early adapters." They are implementing, or about to implement. The "on-site" adventure is one that they have determined is well worth taking.

## Study the Process before Beginning It

As mentioned at the beginning of this chapter, on-site health programming is almost a "no-brainer"—unless the exercise becomes one of hyperanalysis and multiple layers of decisions. Then, the program hunt may actually cause resources to be misdirected as the various constituencies and stakeholders jockey for position.

One factor that is often not reflected as a cost is the opportunity cost of the administrative team assigned to this project, which may be a significant time and energy commitment. Use the following steps as a guide:

- Review of the analysis and correction of any assumptions related to the project.
- Administrative study team meeting to define program goals and objectives and to finalize basic design features (program as well as facility).
  - Location of the clinic
  - Benefit redesign
  - Assignment of implementation staff
  - Determination of final structure (self-managed or contract managed)
- Site visits to like programs in similar industrial settings to confirm objectives and to seek references for any additional project imperatives.
- Refinement of the pro forma with any additional staff projections or employee base adjustments. (This is also an opportunity to use actual space and construction costs on the basis of the facility choice.)
- Reformat of the pro forma to fit within the company budget and book-keeping standards for depreciation, HR reporting, benefits reporting, etc.
- Attention to any issues with benefit design, network design, claims administration functions, HR infrastructure, etc.
- Review of legal environment in which the site will be operating to define any issues that might need to be refined because of regulatory concerns.
- Establishment of a timeline and engagement of a consulting firm to assist with the selection of a vendor to provide services or to act on behalf of the employer to develop the services in-house.
- Engagement in discussions with the employees concerning their perception of the proposed changes and initiation of discussions with local providers to better understand the incorporation of the high-performance network and the articulation of care management with their institutions and practices.
- Initiation of facility design, equipment selection, and recruitment. (These are steps best done secondary to the choice of consulting and/or an intermediate provider.)
- Establishment of final timelines and budgeting, engagement of a PR program, and scheduling of benefit design change dates.

All of these steps have subpoints and, as any project planner can tell you, sometimes the best ideas get bogged down in the decision-making pipeline or in the implementation process with the result that the entire business enterprise suffers. One must remember that all good ideas do not have the same value and that most of the businesses out there are focused on avoiding risk as well as pursuing good ideas. The more complex a program is or the more foreign to a business enterprise, the more risky it seems. Can there be anything more complex or more foreign than getting into the healthcare business? Could we make it even more risky by including our own employees? Maybe we could add to the confusion by incorporating occupational health, employee assistance programs (EAPs), and pharmacy? Could there be added complexity by working with another firm?

The firms that have overcome these issues are the ones that are now enjoying the cost savings and the improved employee relations that are associated with the well-designed on-site program. There are barriers and challenges, but many firms have successfully surmounted them.

*Chapter 22*

# Involving Other Businesses as Customers of the On-Site Program

The involvement of others in a clinic operation and workplace healthcare solution just seems like a natural step and a rational economic move because anything that raises the use of a facility ends up lowering the cost per unit. If the outside world (or part of it) can access the clinic that is being created, it stands to reason that the cost will be less for the original sponsoring employer. Like almost everything that seems simple, this is more complex than it sounds.

Several challenges present themselves. The first is that the set of values that were originally embraced when creating the on-site programming has to match exactly the values of the new participants. Assuming that there is an on-site product that involves robust primary care, an electronic medical record (EMR), a value-defined specialty network, etc., the challenge may be in simply comparing the plans of the clinic creator with those of the firm (or group) that wants to avail itself of the services. The next issue is that just one additional group or business will push the process of registration, coordination of security matters, segmentation of data, reporting processes, cash handling, etc., to a new level. Once that barrier is crossed, the development of these additional processes can then be used for the next group of participants as well, but the transition from one population under the care of a single site to "more than one" is a giant step.

Furthermore, the recipients of the clinic services [and the primary care provider (PCP) care] all have to be organized around the same ancillaries, the same care protocols, the same disease management processes, and a lot of other stuff that is internally program-consistent. Simply put, the program will have to cover all employees with nearly identical benefit programs.

## If It Is So Much Trouble, Why Do It?

Sometimes, it just makes sense. For example, an employer can be using temporary-to-permanent labor solutions; there may be a large segment of these temps on the premises and they may wish to access the programming (especially if they are eventually going to become part of the permanent work force). If there are on-site suppliers (Toyota has more than thirty such firms at their San Antonio site), they may wish to become involved on the tail of the larger firm. In any case, the on-site supplier costs eventually become the costs of the firm that is buying the supplies from them (the "host" firm). Lastly, the issue of reducing costs or achieving cost-offsets from the "sale" of services is pretty tempting. The fixed costs are "in," and the more top-end revenue that is generated, the better.

One additional matter must be dealt with in healthcare. More and bigger is not necessarily better and cheaper, but proficiency should come with volume. A healthcare environment that is running at capacity, like most production operations, just runs better; and it produces fewer errors and makes fewer mistakes. However, although optimal capacity is good, optimal sizing is better.

## Putting It All Together

There must be an agreement on how costs will be allocated. This may be as simple as the creation of a surrogate bill that represents a cash transfer of some kind or it could be as complex as an assignment of a proportional allocation on the basis of utilization. In either case, a schedule with some utilization predictions must be developed to ensure (first) that there is capacity and (second) that there is a reasonable and rational way to offset the cost of the original sponsor of the program.

This might be where a local joint venture sponsored and managed by an intermediary or a broker could be desirable. This might be a third-party

**Figure 22.1  In Milwaukee, the QuadMed program allows employees of one firm to access the network and the facilities of other firms. In this case, the cooperating firms include Quad/Graphics, Miller Brewing, and Briggs and Stratton.**

administrator (TPA), on-site vendor, or even a managed care organization, and it will vend services to everyone in the care matrix. Depending on the number of suppliers and covered employees, there may be an opportunity to form a special group or an employee benefit trust to gain preferential pricing from insurance carriers. There may also be an opportunity to pool experience and to be more effective in purchasing stop-loss coverage.

Some care may be necessary to ensure that the plan for on-site services is offered to the same classes of employees and dependents. It is difficult to structure something for an entire employee base for one firm while another just uses laboratory services. The organization of services should probably be around a preferred provider organization (PPO) "point of service" plan that specifically uses co-pay features to support the employees' choice of the on-site services and the related contracted network. This will allow some kind of projection of utilization. It would be necessary also to give employees and their beneficiaries a special card that identifies their involvement in the program so that they can use the card to access the on-site services and, if appropriate, to present when registering at other healthcare sites.

The brokerage (or managed care program or TPA) will process claims as they do with any other client firm (with the guest firm's employees being the client, in this case), and they will recognize the on-site facilities as a PCP. They will pay claims against standard billing rates pre-negotiated with all parties. There will be no distinct cost advantage to the purchaser (the firm that is sharing the services) because the host firm charges to the managed care intermediary will be at some fee structure that is fair market value for the services rendered.

The host employer's contracted network will be treated as "first tier" or preferred providers by the intermediary, and the guest workforce will be afforded reduced co-pays from these providers as well. All program components will be designed to ensure efficiency and to optimize access. This implies universal registration; coordinated medical records; process, form, and protocol consistency; coordinated recall programs, etc.

This is not without cost or additional effort. The on-site programs must now process insurance-style paperwork; however, this is minimized by predesign. The clinic must deal with different levels of privacy and reporting, although this is minimized because only one outside carrier is being contracted. There may be additional legal work involved, but this is again minimized because only one option is being designed and offered, and it is one that is developed to articulate with the overall program concept.

## Politics, Anyone?

A political issue may arise with the selection and qualification of the broker or intermediary that provides the single insurance product to the cooperating firms. The idea is that the originating firm (the host) will be developing (or causing to be developed) the "one best healthcare" access and insurance product, to the exclusion of other competitive alternatives. Of course, pricing of the product and the success of the enrollment is going to be somewhat preferential, and it is probably going to preclude any other competitive products. If there is a local intermediary involved, they may face issues concerning "most favored nation pricing," which can only be given to the "most favored nation" and not to everyone. Confidentiality and precision in contracting can resolve this type of an issue.

The intermediary should also be able to manage this process as a consultant to all of the firms involved. If the intermediary chosen is an attorney, they should be free of any conflict issues so that they can act on behalf of the group and not be aligned with any one member of the contracting firms.

If the best broker or attorney in the area is working for the competition, that is okay because everyone benefits when healthcare is made more affordable and more efficient. If they are working for the "dark side" (so to speak), such as the hospitals or the local business coalition*, there could be a problem. Confidentiality on pricing and program performance is key, and this entire contracting process is one in which a few key players are taking advantage of market arbitrage, in some respects. That being the case, a good price for the client cannot be really shared among the entire purchasing community.

---

* The author apologizes to hospitals and business coalitions, but the definitions here have to be stark. Only firms that are willing to move ahead of other firms aggressively can achieve the arbitrage that flows to the "best in class." These firms are naturally competitive with their partners in the general business community and they often challenge hospital pricing patterns.

*Chapter 23*

---

# The Future of On-Site Services and the On-Site Industry

---

Several things should be considered as inevitable, and some others have started to emerge even as this book is being written. As a firm considers on-site services and taking more responsibility with their own benefit management structure, they should address the following future trends, each of which is certain to have some impact on future programming.

## Consolidation in the Industry Will Continue

The acquisition of I-trax and Whole Health by Walgreens has set the stage for further consolidations and acquisitions within the industry. There is nothing to suggest that a fully capable regional firm cannot deliver services to an employer and, as a matter of fact, the local firm may have some advantages over a national operation. However, if local is small, then the employer should be on the alert for the firm to merge, expand, be purchased, or expire. This is another area where size matters, and talent is going to be moving to the firms that have the scale to command that talent.

Employers should prepare their contracts with keen interest in the clauses that relate to transition, termination, assignability, and restrictive covenants. In any contract, there should be a provision for the change of ownership (or management) of the provider and a preclusion that allows a replacement form (or the employer) to directly engage staff and transition key items that are program-critical from the vendor to its own purpose and ownership.

This includes leases, databases, computer licenses, intellectual property, subcontractor arrangements, equipment, supplies, and so on.

## New Forms of Access Will Mature: Think Retail

The new kid on the block is now "retail medicine." As discussed in a previous chapter, this is a term applied to medicine that is provided in the retail environment. Walgreens, CVS, and Wal-Mart are becoming key providers, and their presence will have a great impact on local urgent care centers, emergency departments, and—some say—on prescription sales. The consumer is being targeted with immediate access and low-cash pricing for a garden-variety examination, advice from a midlevel provider, and a prescription that can be conveniently filled in the same location. What can an employer do except buy stock in a pharmacy chain?

Depending on the local area and the penetration of these types of retail functions, join them. They will be used by the employees and dependents on your plan anyway, and they might have a way to articulate with the plan design as long as there is a way to develop standards that include recognition of some kind of information interchange and compliance with referral and prescribing protocols. The specialty networks and hospital contracts described elsewhere in this book are of little use if the employee is sent by the drugstore or big-box store practitioner to a specialist outside of the network who will then refer the patient to a hospital that has not been contracted in the selected network. Retail medicine can be embraced if it can be incorporated intelligently into an overall integration of service with the on-site clinic and its supporting system of providers and protocols.

The best integration would be to link the on-site clinic with a system of midlevel providers that share the registration function (health savings account, benefit articulation, and qualification) along with the Patient-Centered Medical Home [PCMH; electronic medical record (EMR)]. As this book is being completed, several companies are exploring this approach.

## New Forms of Access Will Emerge: Think Remote

There have been several recent attempts to address the patient with equipment, cameras, monitoring, and communications, all of which are designed to complement (or replace) direct access to a provider. The Cisco-Cerner partnership is certainly one of the important teams to watch, as will be the GE-Intel collaboration. These efforts have yet to earn an acronym or a standard name, but some are using remote patient monitoring (RPM) and remote patient services (RPS). Actually, in a patient-centered program, it is the provider that is the "remote" part and the patient who is accessing services using a tool, rather than a personal visit.

These applications will range from direct monitoring of vital signs and biologicals to personal webcam and direct video linkages between sites. Think of your scale or home blood pressure device hooked up to a Web access point that a doctor (or a robot!) could monitor. Now think of remote testing for diabetes (finger sticks), and then imagine the possibilities for home monitoring on exercise equipment and on every other bodily fluid and physiologic process. Update your dermatologist on your rash using a webcam. Use a thermometer on your child that is communicating to a pediatric nurse practitioner. Have your treadmill transmit a basic electrocardiogram to an exercise physiologist. Monitor your walking and stair climbing calories, and use a debit card at a cafeteria to add in the nutrition content of your lunch at work. These are not futuristic ideas; they are already in place and in use. The only question is how widespread will they be and what impact can they have on costs and health status. If one adds access to specialists and specialist access to the EMR, who knows how the model will emerge?

The implication for on-site clinic operations is the ability of the remote site to augment a program at a workplace that does not have enough employee volume to actually merit a full-time provider. There may also be disease-state management and wellness implications, but the idea that Cerner and Cisco are exploring is to have a clinic that is a combination of a medical assistant and a remote monitoring station linked to on-site, live physicians and coordinated through a sophisticated EMR. With this type of an application, even a temporary job site might be able to have some level of medical access. If one adds access to specialists and specialist access to the EMR, who knows how the model will emerge?

## Companies Will Change Vendors

There have already been instances of companies switching vendors, and this trend can be expected to continue. As the industry matures and more vendors enter the marketplace and begin to distinguish themselves, the information available and the comparisons between vendors will increase with the result that companies will benchmark performance related to vendor performance. This might not always reflect negatively on any particular vendor. For example, Nissan changed the management of one of its on-site programs from Whole Health Management (prior to the Walgreens acquisition of that company) and now has an ongoing relationship and management contracted to CHS. Both are very competent providers but each had, at the time, different philosophies and approaches to the delivery of services and to contract implementation.[1]

Future changes might be based upon philosophy, price, firm consolidation, performance, or other factors. Whatever the reason, changes are on the horizon for on-site providers that will result in changes affecting patients (their employees). Firms who are considering entry into the provision of on-site care should strive to ensure any transition, expected or unexpected, will be transparent to the workforce and their dependents.

## New Pricing Practices Will Emerge

We are already seeing some differentiation of price methodologies among vendors in the current marketplace. The stable "cost-plus" format has been joined by flat-rate approaches and even some in which the vendor is willing to move to a bonus structure or some kind of shared risk methodology. This one area has the greatest potential for change and for the emergence of a true partnership between the employer and the vendor. However, the line is pretty narrow between a vendor that accepts some kind of risk and a health maintenance organization (HMO) that is a risk-bearing vehicle. This is also an area in which the vendor could move from employee and patient advocate to a cost-oriented provider that has to depart from the basic premises of good service and good medical care to some kind of prioritization structure (read that as rationing care or restricting access in some way). Haven't we been there before?

Pricing and price transparency are the keys to great employer/vendor relationships, but the real key issues are the program drivers—access, program effectiveness, employee and dependent utilization, and patient and consumer satisfaction. If these factors are lost in a pricing scheme, the program will be reduced to yet another transitional program that is doomed for replacement.

# Specialized Accreditation and Licensing Will Evolve

Anytime there is something new in healthcare that is outside of the box, the accreditation and licensing bodies move to define it and regulate or classify its existence. This is not really to be feared, and, in some ways, this may actually help the industry. It will certainly help the vendors to define their roles and to standardize contracting. The issues of confidentiality and the "company doctor" were addressed through regulations that specified who may and may not have access to an employee's healthcare information. If there were no regulation, the concept of an employer-based program would still be muddled in a suspicious fog that might have impeded many program installations. The regulatory initiative makes privacy a moot point.

One could argue that the addition of standards will only confuse an already complex set of issues because ambulatory healthcare sites can now gain licensure for things like radiology and laboratory services and the accreditation bodies (The Joint Commission and The Accreditation Association for Ambulatory Health Care, among others) will certify such sites. If the site is going to encompass a specialty network and perform third-party administrator (TPA) functions, or incorporate safety or dental or workers' compensation for the employees, it is a special case. Should there be one central body that can understand what an employer is trying to do with its employee population and foster these goals rather than try to fit them into a set of standards designed for the general public and the status quo? Probably.

In addition, these programs do not fit the mold of the normal risk pools that are regulated for HMOs, and they are more expansive than most ambulatory environments in that they are inclusive of secondary and inpatient contracts. They can encompass the management of consumer fund accounts and wellness and preventive programming. They incorporate patient and employee incentives. There are issues with emergency preparedness and transportation. Security issues and human relations matters can also be involved as well as exotic healthcare initiatives such as travel medicine, environmental surveillance, and ergonomics. This is a different type of healthcare, and someone with a stake in accreditation will soon realize the need and the opportunity to begin to certify and standardize its operation.

# Standardization Will Occur, Company to Company and Vendor to Vendor

With accreditation and the discipline that it implies, there will be a set of standards and best practices that will emerge. The companies that are involved in this are already settling on common nomenclature and benchmarking, although it is occurring in an informal fashion. Medical directors of programs are meeting in the hopes of sharing information simply on a "what works" and "what does not" level. Soon, this dialogue will become more structured, and there will be a scribing of activities and results. Some of this will be borrowed from the managed care industry, and some will be original to the on-site workplace clinic environment.

The standards for a simple on-site health access service for suddenly ill employees will be much different than those for a full-blown medical site with the features of the Medical Home and a consumer-driven health plan coupled with wellness and dependent care. The industry is waiting for a set of guidelines, definitions, and standards, and they are probably evolving as this book is being written.

Another area on which there is certain to be convergence is on benchmarks for judging the effectiveness of these programs. This will include not only cost-control measures and return on investment (ROI), but also program effectiveness and measures related to population health status. One would also assume that there will be a movement toward some kind of common medical record system and, if not that, then an agreement that there should be a common medical record and data repository. Google and Microsoft come immediately to mind, as does Cerner. The future will be defined by successes and failures.

As the industry and the idea matures, firms will continue to look to their peers for guidance and ideas. The promised transformation of the U.S. healthcare system seems headed for a speed bump rather than a U-turn with conventional forces prevailing to keep the system that exists with some adjustments and tweaks. Successful businesses will continue to move care of their workforce into an environment where value matters.

This is a trend that has not yet hit a plateau and that will continue to attract managers who have responsibility for self-funded populations well into the next phase of healthcare reform. They will be building on the successes of other firms that have led the way, and attempting to insulate themselves from the failures of the conventional healthcare environment in which they must operate.

# Reference

1. Interview with Jim Hummer, former President and CEO of Whole Health, July 1, 2008.

# Appendix A

# On-Site References and Reading List

In this section, we have tried to provide a brief listing of pertinent books and articles that would support a reader who might wish to delve further into the concepts in this book.

Bailit Health Purchasing, LLC. "Value-Driven Health Care: A Purchaser Guide." Version 1.0, February 2007.

Berry, Leonard L., Ann M. Mirabito, Sankey Williams, and Frank Davidoff. "A Physicians' Agenda for Partnering with Employers and Insurers: Fresh Ideas." *Mayo Clinic Proceedings* 81, 2006: 1592–1602.

Boulton, Guy. "Companies Forming Own Clinics: Cost, Convenience, Personal Care Pay Off." *JSOnline-Milwaukee Journal Sentinel,* October 7, 2007, http://www.jsonline.com/story/index.aspx?id=671917&format=print.

Burns, Lawton R. and Wharton School Colleagues. *The Health Care Value Chain-Producers, Purchasers, and Providers.* San Francisco: Jossey-Bass, 2001.

Cassedy, James H. *Medicine in America: A Short History.* Baltimore and London: The Johns Hopkins University Press, 1991.

Collier, Samantha. *Healthgrades Guide to America's Hospitals and Doctors.* New York: Sterling, 2008.

"Connecting Health Communities for Positive Health Outcomes." *Microsoft HealthVault,* http://clients.metia.com/2877/files/HealthVault_Fact_sheet_0708.pdf.

Davis, Rich. "Toyota's On-Site Pharmacy Lets Workers Save on Meds." *Evansville Courier & Press,* November 5, 2006, http://www.courierpress.com/news/2006/nov/05/cutting-health-care-costs.

Decker, Eric. "Corporate America Looks at Quad for Alternative Health Care Model." *Small Business Times Milwaukee and Southeaster Wisconsin Business News,* May 2, 2008, http://biztimes.com/news/2007/10/12/corporate-america-looks-at-quad-for-alternatives.

Dunn, Philip. "Can Big Business Save Health Care?" *Hospitals & Health Networks,* January 2007, http://www.hhnmag.com/hhnmag_app/jsp/printer_friendly. jsp?dcrPath=HHNMAG/artic.

Eddington, Dee W. and Alyssa B. Schultz. "The total value of health: A review of literature." *International Journal of Workplace Health Management,* 1 No.4, 2008.

Enthoven, Alain C. and Laura A. Tollen (editors). *Toward a 21ˢᵗ Century Health System.* San Francisco: Jossey-Bass, 2004.

Fishman, Charles. "Record Time." *Fast Time,* April 6, 2009, http://www.fastcompany. com/magazine/104/cerner.html.

Frauenheim, Ed. "Going from CEO to HR Minder at Kohl's." *Workforce Management,* August 28, 2008, http://www.workforce.com/section/00/ article/25/73/61.php.

Freudenheim, Milt. "Company Clinics Cut Health Costs." *The New York Times,* January 14, 2007, http://www.nytimes.com/2007/01/14/business/14clinic. html?r=l&ei=5087%0A&.

Geisel, Jerry. "Survey: Health Plan Cost Hikes Slowing." *Workforce Management,* September 25, 2007, http://www.workforce.com/section/00/article/25/13/37_ printer.html.

Goldsmith, Jeff. *Digital Medicine-Implications for Healthcare Leaders.* (ACHE Management Series) Chicago: Health Administration Press, 2003.

Goodale, Anne McMillin. "Clinic Assists Employers in Keeping Employees Health." *Reno Gazette-Journal,* January 27, 2006, http://news.rgj.com/apps/pbcs.dll/ article?AID=/20060127/FALLON/601270330/1.

Groopman, Jerome. *How Doctors Think.* Boston: Houghton Mifflin, 2007.

Herman, Roger and Joyce Gioia. "Onsite Clinics Reduce Healthcare Costs." *The Herman Trend Alert,* August 23, 2006, http://www.hermangroup.com/alert/ archive_8-23-2006.html.

Herzlinger, Regina. *Who Killed Health Care? America's $2 Trillion Medical Problem—and the Consumer-Driven Cure.* New York: McGraw-Hill, 2007.

Hewitt Associates. *Employers Implement On-Site Health Clinics to Manage Costs* (White paper). Lincolnshire, IL: Hewitt Associates, 2007.

Kenney, Charles. *The Best Practice: How the New Quality Movement is Transforming Medicine.* New York: Perseus, 2008.

Kessler, Andy. *The End of Medicine: How Silicon Valley (and Naked Mice) Will Reboot Your Doctor.* New York: HarperCollins, 2006.

Kleinman, Wendy K. "On-Site Health Clinics Are Making the Grade for Tulsa's Union Schools." *NewsOK.com,* June 22, 2008, http://www.newsok.com/ article/3260448/?print=1.

Langreth, Robert. "Where to Get Checked Up." *Forbes.com,* December 24, 2007, http://www.forbes.com/forbes/2007/1224/074b_print.html.

Levin, Doron. "Toyota Can Teach GM a Thing or Two about Lipitor: Doron Levin." *Bloomberg.com,* January 24, 2005, http://www.bloomberg.com/apps/news?pid= 71000001&refer=columnist_levin&si.

Liddeck, Betty. "Sick over Health Care Costs, Companies Get Some Relief with On-Site Medical Centers." *Workforce Management,* May 2005.

Lizuka, Izabella. "Information Aggregation—Safe Harbor Allows Companies to Model Strategies that Drive Value." *Managed Healthcare Executive*, July 2008.

McCarthy, Michael. "Can Car Manufacturing Techniques Reform Health Care?" *American Society for Quality*, January 27, 2006, http://www.asq.org/quality-news/2006/01/27/20060127cancar.html.

Miles, Anthony R., Kaylynn S. Yoon, and Ruth E. Granfors, "Convenient Health Care: Legal Considerations for a New Consumer-Driven Model." *Metropolitan Corporate Counsel*, March 2007.

"More Companies Opening In-House Clinics for Employees to Help Reduce Health Costs." *Medical News TODAY,* September 11, 2006, http://www.medicalnewstoday.com/printerfriendlynews.php?newsid=51544.

National Business Group on Health and Watson Wyatt Worldwide. *12th Annual Business Group on Health/Watson Wyatt Survey Report. Dashboard for Success: How Best Performers Do It.* Washington, DC, 2007

O'Donovan, Diarmuid. *The State of Health Atlas.* Berkeley: University of California, 2008.

"On-Site Clinics Market Overview." *BusIntell Report from Knowledge Source, Inc.,* March 2007.

Porter, Michael E. and Elizabeth Olmsted Teisberg. *Redefining Health Care: Creating Value-Based Competition on Results.* Boston: Harvard Business School, 2006.

Starr, Paul. *The Social Transformation of American Medicine: The Rise of a Sovereign Profession and the Making of a Vast Industry.* New York: Basic Books, 1982.

Terry, Ken. *RX for Health Care Reform.* Nashville, TN: Vanderbilt University, 2007.

Tu, Ha T. and Paul B. Ginsburg, "Benefit Design Innovations: Implications for Consumer-Directed Health Care" (Issue Brief no. 109). Center for Studying Health System Change, February 2007.

Watson Wyatt Worldwide. "Staying @ Work 2003/2004: Designing Targeted Programs to Improve Total Health and Productivity." 2003/2004, http://www.watsonwyatt.com.

Watson Wyatt Worldwide. "Global Medical Trends 2008 Survey of Medical Insurers." 2008, http://www.watsonwyatt.com.

Watson Wyatt Worldwide. "Realizing the Potential of Onsite Health Centers." 2008. http://www.watsonwyatt.com.

Wells, Susan J. "The Doctor Is In-House." *HR Magazine* 51, no. 4, 2006.

"Worksite Clinics Reduce Costs, Provide Health Stat." *Insurance Newscast*, January 11, 2007.

# Appendix B

# Claims Request (Complete Listing)

Chapter 7 contained an example that reflected those categories represented below in bold typeface. These are the categories that would be considered a minimum data set necessary to begin an analysis. This claims request table does not include request information that would incorporate pharmacy, dental, optical, occupational medicine, and a few other categories that might contribute to the overall analysis.

| Field # | Field Requested | Notes |
|---------|-----------------|-------|
| 1 | Claim/Record Type | Facility Or Professional |
| 2 | **Claim Number** | |
| 3 | **Member Id #** | Unique Patient Identifier |
| 4 | Member City | |
| 5 | Member State | |
| 6 | Member Zip | |
| 7 | Date Of Birth | |
| 8 | Patient Age | |
| 9 | Patient Sex | |
| 10 | **Relationship** | Subscriber, Spouse, Dependent |

*(Continued)*

(*Continued*)

| Field # | Field Requested | Notes |
|---------|-----------------|-------|
| 11 | PCP Id Number | |
| 12 | **PCP Medical Group** | Tax Id |
| 13 | Line Of Business | |
| 14 | Network Status | In Or Out Of Network |
| 15 | Provider Group Name | |
| 16 | Provider Group Number | Tax Id |
| 17 | Provider Id # | |
| 18 | **Provider Last Name** | |
| 19 | **Provider First Name** | |
| 20 | **Provider Specialty** | |
| 21 | **Provider Type** | Primary Care Physician, Specialist, Hospital, Home Health, Physical Therapy, Physician Extender |
| 22 | **Type Of Service** | Urgent Care, Lab, Durable Medical Equipment, Supplies, Outpatient, Inpatient |
| 23 | **Place Of Service** | Hospital, Nursing Home, Office |
| 24 | **Beginning Date Of Service** | |
| 25 | **Ending Date Of Service** | |
| 26 | Out-Of-Plan Indicator | Member Covered At Time Of Service |
| 27 | **Primary Diagnosis Code** | Icd9 |
| 28 | **Secondary Diagnosis Code** | Icd9 |
| 29 | **Procedure Code** | Cpt |
| 30 | **Procedure Modifier** | Cpt Modifier |
| 31 | Inpatient/Outpatient | |
| 32 | Anesthesia–Units | |
| 33 | Admission Date | |
| 34 | Discharge Date | |
| 35 | Length Of Stay | In Days |

(*Continued*)

(*Continued*)

| Field # | Field Requested | Notes |
|---------|-----------------|-------|
| 36 | Attending Physician | |
| 37 | Covered Days | |
| 38 | Noncovered Days | |
| 39 | Drg Code | |
| 40 | Outlier–Days | |
| 41 | Member-Eligible Indicator | |
| 42 | Date Claim Received | |
| 60 | Fee Schedule | If Multiple |
| 61 | **Payment Status** | Paid, Pending, Rejected |
| 62 | **Payment Date** | Initial Payment |
| 63 | **Billed Amount** | Charge |
| 64 | **Allowed Amount** | Covered Amount |
| 65 | **Paid/Adjudicated Amount** | Amount Paid To Provider |
| 66 | **Coinsurance Amount** | Coinsurance Associated With Claim |
| 67 | Write-Off Amount | Savings |

If one cannot get this type of a claim set, a synopsis or summarization may suffice. In working with analysts, the manager should attempt to define (at least) the employee base and its historical utilization of primary care services.

# Appendix C

# Pro Forma Example

A pro forma, or financial projection, can take many forms. The most voluminous can be 50 pages of assumptions, details, derivations, and projections. The most complex and the most difficult are those that are required to summarize material into a one-page executive summary.

These sheets are examples from a typical pro forma, but not from a typical employer. There is no such thing as a typical employer. They are included for reflection, discussion, and to give readers a sense of proportion and detail. The basic inputs are the most important, and a few are listed here. Everything else is simply spreadsheet acrobatics, knowledge of healthcare service ratios, and guesswork.

Input? Firm-specific and historical inputs include the claims file (of course), the number of employees, the firm assignment of land or facility cost, a local construction estimate, the existing and proposed benefit structure, and estimates of future employee counts. There are some financial indicators that are necessary and sometimes unique to each business enterprise. These include depreciation schedules, overhead allocations, and utility cost assignment. If the firm defines cost of capital or an internal rate of return, these are useful. Everything else is derived from claims history or the local cost environment and indicators that are available in the healthcare literature for utilization, staffing, and resource deployment.

It is necessary to address accuracy because spreadsheets do have unlimited ability to provide decimal-place depth to numbers. The first time an assumption is made that there will be a level of utilization annually, the level of precision is open for question. See the text for detail.

Table C.1 "rolls up" the savings for a sample employee base of something in the range of 3,000 employees with modest estimates on clinic acceptance and utilization.

There are several things to note (and to wonder about). This example projects the capital need at $1.2 million. This is the level that might be found in a buildout of existing space. There is a pre-project cost that is often overlooked in an analysis in the rush to positive numbers; however, there has to be some amount assigned for preliminary architects' work and legal and anticipatory staffing.

Many assumptions, the most important of which is facility utilization, produce the net savings of $3.3 million over five years with a "payback" on the original investment of 27 months. The reader should note that this is a program that, in this case and in most others, relies heavily on "care management savings." This is also a program example that does not have any pharmaceutical or rehabilitation programming. Why? Just to keep it simple.

The spreadsheet in Table C.2 gives the detail on the savings and cost categories, on a department-by-department basis.

Note that the numbers will only tie on the next page to the $4.9 million in savings. In the summary above, we have added a cost-based management fee that will have to be recognized as part of the cost. This is our estimate based on a staff-cost-plus model of staffing and program management, but probably many of the vendors will quibble with our estimate.

An example of the material from which the previous cost and payback projections were derived. "External cost" is the estimate of the cost to buy the services from the market, on the basis of past claims experience.

Table C.3 is a sample of the type of input that is developed in searching through claims and employer records. The acronyms are intuitive (OV = office visit, OOP = out of pocket, etc.). The table goes on for many pages, applying historical rates and estimates to pharmacy, laboratory services, radiology, hospital inpatient use, etc. The key estimates are for utilization that is derived from the employee and dependent acceptance of the on-site program. Get what you can, use what you get, and estimate the rest. This is one page of a six-page summary of assumptions and derivations that are standard to most cost analyses.

Table C.4 represents the area where there is most dependence on educated projections (guesswork?) based on fundamental program features. The bolded lines reflect the projected estimate of total employee and beneficiary on-site acceptance. The visits are arrayed per quarter to allow seasonal adjustments in other tables that define staffing and other costs.

**Table C.1  Project Summary/Cost Savings over Time**

| | Pre-Project | Year 1 | Year 2 | Year 3 | Year 4 | Year 5 | Total |
|---|---|---|---|---|---|---|---|
| Projected External Cost | 0 | 2,266,678 | 2,633,841 | 3,041,990 | 3,495,206 | 3,997,952 | $15,435,666 |
| Projected On-Site Cost | 121,786 | 1,934,456 | 2,166,560 | 2,419,701 | 2,770,299 | 3,066,539 | $12,479,340 |
| Projected On-Site Savings | (121,786) | 332,222 | 467,281 | 622,289 | 724,907 | 931,413 | $2,956,326 |
| Care-Management Savings @ 3.0% | | 335,973 | 361,171 | 388,258 | 417,378 | 448,681 | $1,951,460 |
| Total Project Savings | (121,786) | 668,195 | 828,452 | 1,010,548 | 1,142,285 | 1,380,094 | $4,907,786 |
| Cost-Based Management Fee | (23,359) | (243,731) | (268,552) | (294,938) | (337,900) | (366,777) | $(1,535,258) |
| Net Savings | (145,146) | 424,464 | 559,899 | 715,610 | 804,385 | 1,013,317 | $3,372,528 |
| Projected Capital Need | $1,272,444 | | | | | | |
| Capital Recovery In Months | 27 | | | | | | |

**Table C.2  Make (On-Site Cost) Versus Buy (External Cost)**

|  | Pre-Project | Year 1 | Year 2 | Year 3 | Year 4 | Year 5 | 5 Year |
|---|---|---|---|---|---|---|---|
| **Projected External Cost** | | | | | | | |
| Primary Care Services | | 1,014,735 | 1,155,570 | 1,311,499 | 1,483,994 | 1,674,664 | 6,640,461 |
| Specialty Care Services | | – | – | – | – | – | – |
| Laboratory Services | | 970,772 | 1,154,041 | 1,358,436 | 1,586,093 | 1,839,349 | 6,908,690 |
| Rehabilitation Services | | 281,172 | 324,230 | 372,056 | 425,119 | 483,939 | 1,886,515 |
| Radiology | | – | – | – | – | – | – |
| Pharmacy | | – | – | – | – | – | – |
| Total External Cost | | 2,266,678 | 2,633,841 | 3,041,990 | 3,495,206 | 3,997,952 | 15,435,666 |
| **Projected On-Site Cost** | | | | | | | |
| Primary Care Services | 63,117 | 682,326 | 756,086 | 835,368 | 995,139 | 1,081,992 | 4,414,029 |
| Laboratory Services | 14,268 | 747,047 | 881,197 | 1,029,842 | 1,194,399 | 1,376,417 | 5,243,170 |
| Rehabilitation Services | 14,267 | 169,143 | 183,406 | 198,389 | 214,123 | 230,639 | 1,009,968 |
| Radiology | – | – | – | – | – | – | – |
| Pharmacy | – | – | – | – | – | – | – |
| Care Management/UR | 30,134 | 335,939 | 345,871 | 356,101 | 366,638 | 377,490 | 1,812,173 |
| Total On-site Cost | 121,786 | 1,934,456 | 2,166,560 | 2,419,701 | 2,770,299 | 3,066,538.99 | 12,479,340 |

*(Continued)*

**Table C.2** (*Continued*)

| | Pre-Project | Year 1 | Year 2 | Year 3 | Year 4 | Year 5 | 5 Year |
|---|---|---|---|---|---|---|---|
| **Projected Savings** | | | | | | | |
| Primary Care Services | (63,117) | 332,408 | 399,484 | 476,130 | 488,855 | 592,672 | 2,226,432 |
| Laboratory Services | (14,268) | 223,725 | 272,844 | 328,594 | 391,694 | 462,932 | 1,665,520 |
| Rehabilitation Services | (14,267) | 112,029 | 140,824 | 173,666 | 210,996 | 253,299 | 876,548 |
| Care Management/UR | (30,134) | (335,939) | (345,871) | (356,101) | (366,638) | (377,490) | (1,812,173) |
| Total On-Site Savings | (121,786) | 332,222 | 467,281 | 622,289 | 724,907 | 931,413 | 2,956,326 |
| Savings from Care Management | – | 335,973 | 361,171 | 388,258 | 417,378 | 448,681 | 1,951,460 |
| Total | (121,786) | 668,195 | 828,452 | 1,010,548 | 1,142,285 | 1,380,094 | 4,907,786 |

## Table C.3 Working Assumptions (from Claims)

| Enrollees | Total Employees | 3,000 | Rounded From Employer |
|---|---|---|---|
| | EE Capture | 1.00 | Estimate |
| | Covered Employees | 3,000 | Calculation |
| | Covered Lives Per Covered Employee | 2.00 | Calculation |
| | Covered Dependents | 3,000 | Estimate |
| | Covered Lives | 6,000 | Calculation |
| | % Within 30-Minute Drive Time | 80% | Estimate |
| | 2008 Projected Employees | 3,000 | Assumption |
| | 2008 Projected Dependents | 2,400 | Calculation |
| | 2008 Covered Lives | 5,400 | Calculation |
| | Annual Growth Estimate | 0.0% | Estimate |
| PCP OV | PC Office Visits | 11,340 | Calculation |
| | 2008 PC Office Visit Utilization Per Member | 2.1 | Tpa Hx Data |
| | Charge Amt Per Medical OV | N/A | |
| | Allowed Amt Per Medical OV | N/A | Adj Tpa Data |
| | Company Paid Amt Per PC Office Visit | $60 | Tpa Hx Data |
| | OOP Amt Per PC Office Visit | $20 | Estimate From Hr |
| PC Immunizations | PC Immunizations | 3,289 | Calculation |
| | Immunization Per PC OV | 0.29 | Regional Data Proxy |

*(Continued)*

**Table C.3** (*Continued*)

| | | | |
|---|---|---|---|
| | Charge Amt Per Immunization | N/A | |
| | Allowed Amt Per Immunization | N/A | |
| | Company Paid Amt Per Immunization | $40.67 | Adj Tpa Data |
| | OOP Amt Per PC Immunization | N/A | |
| | Ave Immunization Supply Cost | $25.00 | Estimate |
| Pc Injections | PC Injections | 1,667 | Calculation |
| | Injections Per PC OV | 0.15 | Regional Data Proxy |
| | Company Paid Amt Per PC Injection | $ 26.55 | Adj Tpa Data |

**Table C.4   On-Site Utilization Projections**

| Primary Care Visit Projection | | Hx | Pre | Year 1 | Year 2 | Year 3 | Year 4 | Year 5 |
|---|---|---|---|---|---|---|---|---|
| Total Visits/Yr (Historical) | | 12,600 | 12,600 | 12,600 | 12,600 | 12,600 | 12,600 | 12,600 |
| Total Visits/Qtr (Historical) | QTR 1 | 3,150 | 3,150 | 3,150 | 3,150 | 3,150 | 3,150 | 3,150 |
| | QTR 2 | 3,150 | 3,150 | 3,150 | 3,150 | 3,150 | 3,150 | 3,150 |
| | QTR 3 | 3,150 | 3,150 | 3,150 | 3,150 | 3,150 | 3,150 | 3,150 |
| | QTR 4 | 3,150 | 3,150 | 3,150 | 3,150 | 3,150 | 3,150 | 3,150 |
| *On-Site Utilization Projection* | *Estimate* | 0% | 0% | 40% | 45% | 50% | 55% | 60% |
| On-Site Visits/Qtr | QTR 1 | 0 | 0 | 1,260 | 1,418 | 1,575 | 1,733 | 1,890 |

(*Continued*)

**Table C.4** *(Continued)*

| Primary Care Visit Projection | | Hx | PRE | Year 1 | Year 2 | Year 3 | Year 4 | Year 5 |
|---|---|---|---|---|---|---|---|---|
| | QTR 2 | 0 | 0 | 1,260 | 1,418 | 1,575 | 1,733 | 1,890 |
| | QTR 3 | 0 | 0 | 1,260 | 1,418 | 1,575 | 1,733 | 1,890 |
| | QTR 4 | 0 | 0 | 1,260 | 1,418 | 1,575 | 1,733 | 1,890 |
| Total On-Site Visits/ Year | | 0 | 0 | 5,040 | 5,670 | 6,300 | 6,930 | 7,560 |
| Extra Visits From Increased Utilization | | – | – | 504 | 567 | 630 | 693 | 756 |
| *Total Medical Clinic Visits** | | – | – | 5,544 | 6,237 | 6,930 | 7,623 | 8,316 |

* This does not include projections for screenings, workers' compensations, occupational health, rehabilitation, pharmacy, laboratory, imaging, etc.

There is a key line here that anticipates "extra visits from increased utilization," which will occur because there is relatively easy access and a higher (more robust) level of primary care. In this model, there is more primary care, and more cost to each visit, generally, because of the nature of the service provided. This table reflects the concept of increased utilization.

Tables like this convert "visits" to providers needed to serve the program and project rooms necessary for providers to actually provide care. The result is square feet and the cost per square foot, and the equipment provided for each room is the source of the capital costs for the programming. Table C.5 shows the total and one area from which it is derived. Other areas, not shown, include rehabilitation and laboratory services and care management. This example does not involve pharmacy, imaging, or exercise and wellness components.

Table C.6 reflects the true scalability of the programming. It is a projection of staff needs, their cost, and the anticipated cost per year. Again, to conserve space in this appendix, it only reflects primary care and the basic staffing of the medical clinic. There are like sheets for each area. This table

**Table C.5 Development of Clinic/Facility Scope**

| Program Totals | | Primary Care | | | | | |
|---|---|---|---|---|---|---|---|
| AREA | SQ FT | Pc Providers | 2.2 | | | | |
| | | Rms/Prov | 2 | | | Size | Sq Ft |
| | | | # | | | | |
| Primary Care | 2,458 | Exam Rooms | 8 | 11 | X | 9 | 792 |
| Specialty Care | – | Treatment Room | 1 | 12 | X | 18 | 216 |
| Laboratory Services | 180 | Business Function | 1 | 10 | X | 15 | 150 |
| Radiology | – | Administrative Office | 1 | 9 | X | 10 | 90 |
| Rehabilitation Services | 1,750 | Provider's Office | 2 | 12 | X | 10 | 240 |
| Pharmacy | – | Nurse Station | 2 | 9 | X | 10 | 180 |
| Vision | – | Staff Room with Conference Area | 1 | 20 | X | 10 | 200 |
| Dental | – | Toilet | 2 | 5 | X | 5 | 50 |
| Wellness | – | Storage | 2 | 10 | X | 8 | 160 |
| Care Management | 300 | Reception Desk | 1 | 10 | X | 10 | 100 |
| | | Reception Area | 1 | 10 | X | 20 | 200 |
| | | Corridors | 2 | 8 | X | 5 | 80 |
| Projected Total | 4,688 | Projected Total | | | | | 2,458 |

*(Continued)*

**Table C.5** (*Continued*)

| Program Totals | | | | Primary Care | | | |
|---|---|---|---|---|---|---|---|
| Contingency | 10% | | 469 | Contingency | 10% | | 246 |
| Budgeted Total | | | 5,157 | Budgeted Total | | | 2,704 |
| Buildout per Sq Ft | | | $200 | Buildout per Sq Ft | | | $200 |
| Subtotal Construction Cost | | | 838,860 | Subtotal Construction Cost | | | 540,760 |
| Site Improvements @ | $5 | PSF | 25,784 | Site Improvements @ | $5 | PSF | 13,519 |
| A & E @ | 10% | | 86,464 | A & E @ | 10% | | 55,428 |
| Total Construction Cost | | | $951,108 | Construction Cost (Primary Care) | | | $609,707 |

**Table C.6   Basic Staffing Projections (Derived from Visits)**

| | PRE | YR 1 | YR 2 | YR 3 | YR 4 | YR 5 | Cost/FTE | YR 1 | YR 2 | YR 3 | YR 4 | YR 5 |
|---|---|---|---|---|---|---|---|---|---|---|---|---|
| Medical | | | | | | | | | | | | |
| Family Medicine | 0.1 | 0.74 | 0.83 | 0.91 | 0.99 | 1.08 | 194,670 | 148,784 | 170,533 | 193,453 | 217,594 | 243,010 |
| Physician Assistant/Nurse Practitioner | 0.1 | 0.74 | 0.83 | 0.91 | 0.99 | 1.08 | 110,313 | 84,311 | 96,635 | 109,623 | 123,304 | 137,706 |
| Total Providers | 0.15 | 1.48 | 1.65 | 1.82 | 1.99 | 2.15 | | | | | | |
| Management & Marketing | 0.0 | 0.0 | 0.0 | 0.0 | 0.0 | 0.0 | 109,551 | – | – | – | – | – |
| RNs | 0.1 | 1.0 | 1.0 | 1.0 | 2.0 | 2.0 | 69,383 | 71,464 | 73,608 | 75,816 | 156,181 | 160,867 |
| Medical Assistant | 0.1 | 1.5 | 1.7 | 1.8 | 2.0 | 2.2 | 43,821 | 66,983 | 76,775 | 87,093 | 97,962 | 109,404 |
| Receptionist | 0.0 | 1.5 | 1.7 | 1.8 | 2.0 | 2.2 | 36,517 | 55,819 | 63,979 | 72,578 | 81,635 | 91,170 |
| Transcriptionist | 0.0 | 0.0 | 0.0 | 0.0 | 0.0 | 0.0 | 47,472 | – | – | – | – | – |
| Billing | 0.0 | 0.0 | 0.0 | 0.0 | 0.0 | 0.0 | 40,169 | – | – | – | – | – |
| Medical Records | 0.0 | 0.0 | 0.0 | 0.0 | 0.0 | 0.0 | 36,517 | – | – | – | – | – |
| Total Support | 0.2 | 4.0 | 4.3 | 4.6 | 6.0 | 6.3 | | | | | | |
| Total Medical[a] | 0.4 | 5.5 | 6.0 | 6.5 | 8.0 | 8.5 | $1,802,271 | $427,362 | $481,530 | $538,563 | $676,676 | $742,157 |

[a] This is a representation of the basic clinic only and it does not reflect rehabilitation and laboratory services, pharmacy, or other units. The management and marketing line is left open (at no cost) because there is an assumption that there will be a contract with an outside provider to manage the operation.

has also been abbreviated in that it does not reflect the cost per category of employee per year and the ramp-up costs for the time when the clinic is under construction and in the planning, pre-opening phase.

This reflection of costs is also somewhat unrealistic because it uses FTEs in a decimal fashion when the hiring of a person is probably only possible in a threshold fashion. That is, there will never be 0.99 of a family medicine provider. This will be hired at 1.0 FTE. Scalability that is possible in a spreadsheet has to be converted to a real-life equivalent.

# *Appendix D*

# On-Site Provider Listing

This vendor listing is the best that can be done at the time of publication. Many firms will think they should have been included, and they might be right. In trying to provide a listing of the on-site care providers, there was no editorial bias to keep one firm in and another out. If someone was missed, it was because they were difficult to find through Internet searches and other reliable sources that track on-site care and on-site clinics. In addition to the Internet search engines that serve everyone and make us all look like researchers, our efforts tracked nationally posted conferences and referenced blogs and paid research services to qualify vendors. If there was an error, the oversight was unintentional.

We contacted most of the firms directly and, in some cases, visited their client sites to better understand the type of programming they are offering. This effort ignored agencies that seemed to focus on the following services—*urgent care and retail clinics* (except where they stated that they focused on worksite solutions), *staffing agencies* that merely provided nurse or physician staffing support rather than program organization and management, and *occupational medicine providers*. Many firms researched may have been in transformation or transition and our research did uncover a few that had "plans to provide" on-site workplace services. In most cases, our research focused only on those companies with some kind of track record. If a mistake was made or an error of omission committed, it was not through any attempt to arbitrarily omit any organization that has a major presence in this industry. Updates and corrections to this listing can be found at http://www.onsiteclinics.org.

## AllOne Health

70 North Main Street
Wilkes-Barre, PA 18711-0302
877-720-7770
http://www.allonehealth.com
Deb Talbot, Senior Vice President of AllOne Health
With a core business unit that has been around since the early 1970s providing on-site services HRC boasts more than 100 sites of service. It is now serving clients on a national basis and its focus has been on occupational medicine and on-site staffing. HRC (AllOne Health) prices services on a cost-plus basis, by the shift, or per assignment. HRC has now been incorporated within AllOne, which also advertises a wide range of services to employers including counseling services, employee assistance programs, prevention, wellness, and population health.

## Besiada Health Innovators, LLC

835 Potts Avenue
Green Bay, WI 54304
866-626-5758
http://www.besiada.com
Karen Besiada-Hansen, President
Besiada is a regional firm that has been in business for 10 years. Its clients are mostly in Wisconsin, and its experience is in moderately sized and smaller firms. It focuses on behavior change and healthy lifestyles as part of its basic business philosophy. The founder has a background as a physical therapist, and it uses traditional staff-pricing methodologies.

## Care ATC

9902-A EAST 43rd Street
Tulsa, OK 74146
918-779-7400
http://www.careatc.com
Ron Woods, President
This firm has been in business for 10 years and now has more than 40 clinics in 8 states. It has a presence in the Midwest and South but welcomes RFPs from all areas. It will do per-employee pricing (capitation), but generally the provision of services is on a per diem/per provider basis. It has a base of municipal and private industrial clients.

**CareHere, LLC**
205 Powell Place, Suite 108
Brentwood, TN 37027
615-221-5901
http://www.carehere.com
Ernie Clevenger, President
CareHere is a privately held company that has been in the on-site business
for 6 years. It has more than 80 clients, mostly in the Southeast, but its management will consider addressing RFPs from any region of the country. This
group has its own proprietary software and it provides support for other
health service operations in regions where it does not have a direct presence. It will do per-employee, per-month (capitated) pricing or cost-plus when
requested. Its analytics are at a high level of development and it has significant background in the modeling of best practices, population management,
and risk modeling.

**Cerner Corporation**
2800 Rockcreek Parkway
Kansas City, MO 64117
816-201-8912
http://www.cerner.com/public
Tami Hutcheson, Vice President of Cerner Health*e* Services
Cerner is best known as a major provider of healthcare IT services to hospitals and health systems. It has developed the concept of the Health*e* Clinic,
the mission of which is to "coordinate the resources, deliver the knowledge,
and connect the individual, family, and clinicians at the appropriate time
and location to achieve the optimal health outcomes." Cerner first initiated
services for its own employee base in Kansas City and then transferred
what it learned to other large employers. It is well capitalized and well posi-
tioned to expand, especially in healthcare institutions. As one might judge
from the base product, Cerner has a very robust medical record and IT
base. The clinic at its operation in Kansas City is a "best in class" facility by
any standard. It responds to RFPs on a selective basis and price services on
an individualized basis to client needs, always including its own ambulatory
EMR system.

## Cigna/Onsite Health

11001 North Black Canyon Highway, Suite 400
Phoenix, AZ 85029
800-806-2061
http://www.cigna.com
Kurt Weimer, President, Cigna Medical Group
Cigna is well known as an insurance provider that also has a tradition of taking an active role on the provider side. The company's on-site services are organized through a division that is closely allied with a multispecialty medical group practice it owns in Phoenix. The company considers itself to be a national contender in the on-site industry and it is anticipating that its management of medical processes and wide array of insurance and disease management products will distinguish it from other vendors.

## Clinical Resources Group, Inc.

6900 East Indian School Road, #106
Scottsdale, AZ 85151
866-606-6229
http://www.carecorpsclinics.com
Michael McGranahan, CFO
Operating out of Scottsdale, the Clinical Resources Group provides on-site programming through the trade name CareCorps®. The corporation is regional in scope and stresses the development of custom-tailored programs to employers and high patient service levels. It references evidence-based medical management in its promotional literature and has several well-established clients for whom it provides on-site services. CRG also clearly defines its services to be on-site and encourages employees to maintain their traditional healthcare relationships.

## Comprehensive Health Services, Inc. (CHS)

10701 Parkridge Blvd. 2nd Floor
Reston, VA 20191
703-760-0700
http://www.chsmedical.com
Mel Hall, Chairman and CEO
With the consolidation of CHD Meridian and Whole Health under the Walgreen Take Care Health organization, CHS is now the second largest vendor of on-site services. It has extensive experience in the field of industrial

hygiene and provides care in some truly unique sites and in various models. This is one of the only firms which can really claim to be not only national but also international in scope. CHS has recently invested a significant amount in IT and other program support functions to expand its scope of care and to foster true on-site integration. CHS responds to RFPs nationally and has a reputation for efficient and effective program implementation. It also has some sites that serve various businesses in a collaborative model that is unique in the industry. With government and industrial installations, it can deploy various outreach services on a direct-contract basis to address special needs (such as military and disaster response).

**Concentra**
5080 Spectrum Drive, Suite 1200
West Addison, TX 75001
972-364-8000
http://www.concentra.com
John diLorimier, Senior Vice President of Marketing
Concentra is a privately held company with urgent care centers, primary care workplace units, and occupational health programming. At more than 250 workplace locations nationwide, some sites are community-based and offer services to multiple employers where the public can access care, as well. Its staff will do training, provide preventive services and health promotion, and follow-up in various models. It provides service to firms using various pricing models and suits each program to the size and needs of the employer. Concentra has a national presence and over 30 years of experience in the provision of on-site services. Its experience with occupational medicine, employer workplace solutions, and the many community-based centers that it has developed are all distinguishing factors of the firm. It responds to RFPs and, depending on the location, may be able to fashion collaborative sites or sites that are supported by urgent care installations in the same region.

**CRAssociates**
8580 Cinderbed Road, Suite 2400
Newington, VA 22122
877-272-8960
http://www.crassoc.com
Paula Mullineaux, Vice President of Business Development
CRAssociates has taken the staffing agency to a level that delivers not only staff but also entire programs. It is well represented in government agencies

at the federal level and in a variety of workplaces. It runs primary care clinics and occupational health programs and tailors its responses to the needs of the workplace. Privately held, this firm has been in business for more than 10 years. The management team aggressively seeks out RFP opportunities, and it prices using various models including cost-plus and capitation. It has deployed an EMR and the Mayo personal health record.

**First Onsite, LLC**
One Maryland Farms, Suite 300
Brentwood, TN 37027
615-372-5340
http://www.FirstOnsite.com
Brian Jones, Vice President
First OnSite is notable in that it is a newly formed subsidiary of HCA. While it does not have a track record to speak of, HCA certainly does. This is an example of the dynamic nature of the industry and the changes that are occurring and that will occur. First OnSite will have both opportunities and challenges in this industry, and this is a group to watch as it becomes more visible and its programming more pronounced. One would think that the company could be formidable competition for other vendors in a marketplace in which HCA already has a presence with supportive and complementary healthcare services.

**Free First Healthcare Clinics (The Parker Group/HealthSmart) c/o HealthSmart Holdings, Inc.**
222 West Las Colinas, Suite 1600 North
Irving, TX 75039
806-473-3075
http://www.healthsmart.com
Brian Kersh, Vice President
This firm is a collection of businesses that now operates under the HealthSmart banner. It has on-site services primarily in Texas, but it will respond to inquiries from other areas of the country. It operates an on-site program and most of the functions that would support the workforce management effort. The pricing structure that it uses is flexible to each client, and it is now operating at five locations in the region. Its expanded services include data tracking, TPA functions, disease management, contract management, pharmacy solutions, etc.

## Healthstat, Inc.
4601 Charlotte Park Drive, Suite 390
Charlotte, NC 28217
704-529-6161
http://www.healthstatinc.com
J. Douglas Knoop, Executive Medical Director
Scalability is a key ingredient to what HealthStat offers employers. It will deliver an on-site solution at almost any level of employment or engagement. It has been in business for 8 years and has operations in 25 states. It makes extensive use of risk assessment tools and incorporates modern EMR technology at the sites where it offers a full range of medical services. It will respond to RFPs on a selective basis.

## IMC HealthCare
9143 Philips Highway, Suite 535
Jacksonville, FL 32256
800-878-1702
http://www.imchealthcare.com
Todd Keller, CEO
IMC is a large regional firm with national aspirations. It is well known and well regarded in the Southeast and it provides a full range of on-site services. The company is privately held, and it has a long history of providing occupational and industrial health services. It recently expanded into the full provision of primary care at the worksite and is in an investment and growth mode that includes an upgrade of data processing and electronic medical information systems. It responds to RFPs nationally and has a full complement of support functions for its on-site service. It employs several top-shelf partner-provided solutions, including the Mayo health access programming and claims modeling. It prices its services on a cost-plus basis but has the flexibility to conform to the needs of other models, if required.

## Interra Health, Inc.
5010 W Ashland Way
Franklin, WI 53132
414-755-4898
http://www.interrahealth.com
Derek Boyce, President
Interra is a Midwestern-based company that is privately held and has a dozen on-site operations and more in the planning stages. It focuses on employee

disease and injury prevention, and it has a primary care focus that would allow it to expand beyond the employee base and into dependent coverage if the employer required this service. It prices based on the creation of a flat fee and develops local relationships for laboratory and other ancillary support services. It primarily targets installations at mid-size firms but is willing to consider requests for any scale of programming.

**Marathon Health**

Tracey Moran
354 Mountainview Drive, Suite 300
Colchester, VT 05446
802-857-0400
http://www.marathon-health.com

Marathon is primarily in the East and Midwest, but it will respond to RFPs anywhere in the country. The firm has over thirty installations and is privately held. It has an occupational health background but has expanded into full on-site primary care. It prices its services using a traditional cost-plus approach, but is open to other methodologies including risk-sharing methods that are tied to contract objectives. The focus is on employee and patient engagement and on the management of the entire workforce population.

**Medcor, Inc.**

4805 West Prime Parkway
McHenry, IL 60050
815-363-9500
http://www.medcor.com
Curtis Smith, Executive Vice President

Medcor has more than 20 years in the on-site business and it is privately held (by the management team). It has installations throughout the country and it will size a clinic application to any need. Management ascribes its growth to referrals from customer to customer and to its emphasis on early intervention in the employee illness or injury process. It works with local medical resources and craft programs to fit the need of the employer and their employees. It has limited pharmacy coordination but a strong orientation to workers' compensation and occupational services.

## Novia CareClinics, LLC
503 East National Avenue, Suite A
Indianapolis, IN 46227
800-897-4093
http://www.noviacareclinics.com
Lanny Green, Vice President
Novia is primarily Midwest in scope and a more modest size than most of the other providers, but it has been around for more than 9 years. It is implementing on-site programming in a fashion that demonstrates that it has learned what is critical to program success as demonstrated by other providers. It is serving at least one school district and a couple of municipalities. It does respond to RFPs on a selective basis.

## QuadMed
555 South 108th Street
West Allis, WI 53214
414-566-3017
http://www.quad-med.com
John Neuberger, Vice President of Operations
This is one of the most mature and well thought out programs in the country. It is fully integrated and a solid regional player with high-quality service and great program depth. It is truly an original innovator in the field. QuadMed provides services to several local firms and responds very selectively to RFPs. This is one of the few programs that can chart progress on health savings, consumer satisfaction, network design and development, and quality scores over a time period measured by decades rather than just a year or so. It is interesting to note that this is a program based at a printing plant in Milwaukee, and it is on its second full-fledged EMR while local hospitals are still struggling with first. Furthermore, higher HEDIS scores for its programming than most HMOs and demonstrated consumer satisfaction.

## RepuCare
8900 Keystone Crossing, Suite 600
Indianapolis, IN 46240
317-578-2858
http://www.repucare.com
Billie Dragoo, President
This firm has been providing healthcare in various forms since 1995, but its entry into the worksite programming began in 2005. It is a regional firm

with experience in occupational health and wellness. It has governmental and industry contracts and its background is staffing. It is privately held.

## U.S. HealthWorks Medical Group
25124 Springfield Court, Suite 200
Valencia, CA 91355
661-678-2600
http://www.ushealthworks.com
Jeanne Osterlund, Regional Sales Director
This is a firm with 20 years of background and experience in the occupational health industry. Regional in scope, it operates over 100 sites with about one-third of them actually on a company campus. It is in an expansion mode and receives and responds to RFPs. At the time of this research it was not deploying electronic medical technology or engaging in pharmacy-related programming.

## Walgreens/Take Care Health Systems, Inc. (incorporating CHD I-trax and Whole Health)
4 Hillman Drive, Suite 130
Chadd's Ford, PA 19317
610-459-2405, ext. 100
http://takecareemployersolutions.com
Peter Hotz, President
This is the giant of the on-site provider industry. Take Care Health was a major retail provider before the acquisition of the two market leaders (CHD Meridian and Whole Health). They have it all— community outlets, pharmacy and PBMs, brand awareness, industry intelligence (through acquisition), critical mass, capital, etc. It is probably asked to respond to any, and every, RFP. Its opportunity will be to craft these pieces into something that is truly unique that employers will recognize as a different and far superior product.

## WeCare TLC
P.O. Box 952679
Lake Mary, FL 32795
800-941-0644, ext. 319 (Garber)
http://www.wecaretlc.com
Chuck Licata, Marketing Director

This is a modestly sized regional firm that is privately held and grew out of the insurance industry. It does full-scale clinics in about a dozen locations with disease management and on-site counseling, targeting small- to medium-sized firms. It maintains a close working relationship with the brokerage community, as one might imagine, given the background of its ownership.

**WorkCare, Inc.**
333 S. Anita Drive, Suite 630
Orange, CA 92868
800-455-6155
http://www.workcare.com
This is a physician-managed, multispecialty occupational health firm that appears to be regional, with corporate support offices in California, Utah, and North Carolina. It has a network that numbers in the hundreds of clinics that it has credentialed, some of which it directly staffs. WorkCare offers a variety of workplace services and solutions, including consulting, staffing, and prevention.

# Appendix E

# Workplace On-Site Program Consultants and Resources

These are all groups that can help you with your planning and programming and assist in keeping programs on track. This list, like any, is probably incomplete. However, it does include the resources that many of the firms deploying on-site programming are using. Also included are some of the groups that assisted with background material or references for this book. Updates and corrections to this listing can be found at http://www.onsiteclinics.org.

## Accreditation and Standards

Accreditation Association for Ambulatory Healthcare
5250 Old Orchard Road, Suite 200
Skokie, IL 60077
847-853-6060
http://www.aaahc.org

HEDIS
8834 Capital of Texas Highway, Suite 240
Austin, TX 78759
800-630-0972
http://www.hedis.com

The Joint Commission
One Renaissance
Oakbrook Terrace, IL 60181
630-792-5000
http://www.jointcommission.org

Medical Group Management Association
104 Inverness Terrace East
Englewood, CO 80112-5306
303-799-1111
http://www.mgma.com

The National Committee for Quality Assurance
1100 13th Street, NW, Suite 1000
Washington, DC 20005
202-955-3500
http://www.ncqa.org

## Benefits Consulting and Analytics

Aon Consulting (Joseph Marlowe)
Aon Center
200 East Randolph Street
Chicago, IL 60601
312-381-4844
http://www.aon.com

Hewitt Associates, LLC
100 Half Day Road
Lincolnshire, IL 60069-3342
847-295-5000
http://www.hewittassociates.com

Mercer LLC (Bruce Hochstadt, MD)
1166 Avenue of the Americas
New York, NY 10036
212-345-7000
http://www.mercer.com

Milliman, Inc. (David Mirkin, MD)
38th Floor, One Penn Plaza
New York, NY 10119
646-473-3212
http://www.milliman.com

Towers Perrin
1 Stamford Plaza
263 Tresser Boulevard
Stamford, CT 06901
203-326-5400
http://www.towersperrin.com

Watson Wyatt Worldwide
901 North Glebe Road
Arlington, VA 22203
703-258-8000
http://www.watsonwyatt.com

Towers Perrin and Watson Wyatt have announced that they are merging into one organization. However, each company is presently operating in its traditional form and individual listings are offered for each.

**Other Resources**
The Center for Health Value Innovation
12545 Olive Boulevard, Suite 232
St Louis, MO 63141
201-641-1911
http://www.vbhealth.org

The Forum for the Advancement of Workplace On-site Health Clinics
(A Web resource and information source)
http://www.onsiteclinics.org

HealthCare Strategies
9841 Broken Land Parkway
Columbia, MD 21046
800-582-1535
http://www.hcare.net

Ingenix
12125 Technology Drive
Eden Prairie, MN 55344
888-445-8745
http://www.ingenix.com

Mayo Clinic Health Solutions
Centerplace 9
200 First Street SW`
Rochester, MN 55905
800-430-9699
http://www.mayoclinichealthsolutions.com

MEDai, Inc.
Millenia Park One
4901 Vineland Road
Suite 450
Orlando, FL 32811
800-446-3324
http://www.medai.com

MyHealthGuide, LLC (Information for the self-funded firm)
567 Midway Circle
Brentwood, TN 37027-5178
615-221-5901
http://www.myhealthguide.com

Patient-Centered Primary Care Collaborative
The Homer Building
601 Thirteenth Street, NW, Suite 400 North
Washington, DC 20005
202-724-3331
http://www.pcpcc.net

PKC Corporation
One Mill Street, Box C13
Suite 355
Burlington, VT 05401-0530
802-658-5351
http://www.pkc.com

PlanIT Incorporated
W175 N11117 Stonewood Drive, Suite 209
Germantown, WI 53022
262-251-8970
http://www.planit.us.com

Verisk Health, Inc.
130 Turner Street, Seventh Floor
Waltham, MA 02453
866-292-6971
http://www.veriskhealth.com

**Facility Design**
Eckert Wordell
161 East Michigan Avenue, Suite 200
Kalamazoo, MI 49007
269-388-7313
http://www.eckert-wordell.com

Planetree, Inc.
130 Division Street
Derby, CT 06418, 203-732-1365
http://www.planetree.com

Rehler Vaughn and Koone, Inc. (RVK Architects)
745 East Mulberry Avenue, Suite 601
San Antonio, TX 78212
http://www.rvk-architects.com
210-733-3535

**Health Law (specific to on-site programming)**
Denise Webb Glass, Partner
Fulbright & Jaworski L.L.P.
2200 Ross Avenue, Suite 2800
Dallas, TX 75201-2784
214-855-8000
http://www.fulbright.com

Paul Seidenstricker
Hall, Render, Killian, Heath, & Lyman, PC
111 East Kilbourn Avenue, Suite 1300
Milwaukee, WI 53202
414-721-0442
http://www.hallrender.com

Michael J. Taubin, Esq.
Nixon Peabody, LLP
50 Jericho Quadrangle, Suite 300
Jericho, NY 11753
516-832-7521
http://www.nixonpeabody.com

## Associations and Organizations

Agency for Healthcare Research and Quality (government agency)
Office of Communications and Knowledge Transfer
540 Gaither Road, Suite 2000
Rockville, MD 20850
301-427-1364
http://www.ahrq.gov

America's Health Insurance Plans
601 Pennsylvania Avenue, NW
South Building, Suite 500
Washington, DC 20004
202-778-3200
http://www.ahip.org

Employee Benefit Research Institute
1100 13th Street, NW, Suite 878
Washington, DC 20005
202-659-0670
http://www.ebri.org

Health as Human Capital Foundation
1800 Carey Avenue, Suite 300
Cheyenne, WY 82001
307-433-9619
http://www.hhcfoundation.org/hhcf

Midwest Business Group on Health (Larry Boross, Executive Director)
35 East Wacker Drive, Suite #1500
Chicago, IL 60601
312-372-9090
http://www.mbgh.org

National Business Group on Health
50 F Street, NW, Suite 600
Washington, DC 20001
202-628-9320
http://www.businessgrouphealth.org

Wellness Council of America
9802 Nicholas Street, Suite 315
Omaha, NE 68114
402-827-3590
http://www.welcoa.org

Workforce Management
4 Executive Circle, Suite 185
Irvine, CA 92614
949-255-5340
http://www.workforce.com

# Index

# About the Author

Mike La Penna started his career in healthcare as an emergency medical technician when he was still in high school. He has worked in several support roles within the healthcare field during his college years while earning a BA in economics from Western University. After a stint as a faculty member at a community college in Michigan, he became Executive Director for the Southwest Michigan Emergency Medical Services Agency, which developed and coordinated pre-hospital care and emergency services for an eight-county region. He has been a hospital administrator and he has managed healthcare programs that range from ambulatory care and outreach services to healthcare cooperatives and shared service corporations. His volunteer work includes serving as the Board Chair of the American Red Cross Kalamazoo Chapter, the Chairman of the Kalamazoo County Overall Economic Development Council, and co-founding that region's American Heart Association chapter.

Mike holds a MBA with a specialty interest in Healthcare Administration from the University of Chicago. His healthcare consulting firm, The La Penna Group, was founded in 1986 and serves hospital and physician group clients across the country. The firm also has developed several ambulatory care sites and service models for health systems and industry and municipal clients that incorporate the ideas in this book.

Mike is regularly called upon to speak at national meetings regarding the healthcare industry and on financial issues affecting healthcare providers and their relationships with business and industry. He is a routine contributor to publications such as *Medical Economics* and *Crain's*, and he has been quoted in *Modern Healthcare*, *The Wall Street Journal*, and numerous other national publications.